SO-DJW-518

GENDER AND THE HOUSEHOLD DOMAIN
Social and Cultural Dimensions

Edited by

MAITHREYI KRISHNARAJ
KARUNA CHANANA

WOMEN AND THE HOUSEHOLD IN ASIA – VOL. 4

Series Editor:
LEELA DUBE

Sage Publications
New Delhi/Newbury Park/London

First published in 1989 by
Sage Publications India Pvt Ltd
32 M–Block Market, Greater Kailash I
New Delhi 110048

Sage Publications Inc	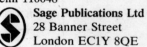	**Sage Publications Ltd**
2111 West Hillcrest Drive		28 Banner Street
Newbury Park, California 91320		London EC1Y 8QE

Published by Tejeshwar Singh for Sage Publications India Pvt Ltd., phototypeset at Mudra Typesetters, Pondicherry and printed at Chaman Offset Printers, Delhi.

Library of Congress Cataloging-in-Publication Data

Gender and the household domain: social and cultural dimensions / editors, Maithreyi Krishnaraj, Karuna Chanana.
    p. cm.—(Women and the household in Asia: vol. 4)
    1.Women—India—Social conditions—Congresses.   2. Sex role—India—Congresses.   3. Women—Health and Hygiene—India—Congresses.   4. Women—Bangladesh—Social conditions—Congresses.   5. Sex role—Bangladesh—Congresses.   6. Women—Health and Hygiene—Bangladesh—Congresses.   I. Krishnaraj, Maithreyi.   II. Chanana, Karuna.   III. Series.
HQ1742.G45 305.3'0954—dc20   1989   89–27840

ISBN 81–7036–175–3 (India–hbk)
    0–8039–9635–7 (US–hbk)

Contents

Preface

The Regional Conference for Asia on Women and the Household was held in New Delhi from January 27–31, 1985. Sponsored jointly by the Commission on Women of the International Union of Anthropological and Ethnological Sciences, Research Committee 32 ('Women in Society') of the International Sociological Association, and the Indian Association for Women's Studies, it brought together scholars and activists from the entire Asian region and gave them an opportunity to interact closely and share experiences with one another on five carefully selected sub-themes. Also present at the Conference were social scientists from other parts of the world—those who had a particular interest in the region and had carried out, or were currently involved in, research in Asia. The Conference thus proved to be an event in as much as it succeeded in bringing together scholars working on South Asia, Southeast Asia, East Asia, and West Asia for the exploration of various facets of a theme that has tremendous relevance for the Asian region as a whole.

The theme, 'women and the household', must be explained for it may give the impression of being narrow and limited, or worse, of reinforcing existing norms and values. In speaking of the household, we do not suggest that it is a woman's 'proper' place on account of biological determination: on the contrary, we assert that the household cannot be treated as a private entity separable from the context in which it is embedded. As the intimate experiences of life are structured by wider social relations, so in order to understand the position of women it is necessary to examine intra-household relationships, their dynamics and their historical, socio-economic and political contexts.

When we focus on the household in order to understand the predicament of women, we emphasise the necessity of seeing the various interlinkages between the individual household and the wider structures and processes of society. We deny, therefore, that any such thing as an isolated individual household exists. As we question the wisdom of treating women as individual entities, ignoring in the process the households of which they form a part, in research as well as in programmes of action and development, so also we question the assumptions that underline the treatment of a household as an undifferentiated unit in the study of social reality and in planning and action for bringing about social change.

The Asian region harbours a variety of production systems and diverse family and kinship systems and their variants. All the major religions of the world are represented here. There are significant differences between the various economies and polities. These constitute the contexts essential to an understanding of the lives of women and the role and significance of the household in shaping, sustaining and changing them. In any society the ideological bases for the formation, organisation and functioning of the household seem to be explained by these contexts and their interplay.

The theme also exposes the erroneous but very commonly held view that there exists an undifferentiated Asian model for the position of women and for gender relations. Perhaps the subtle differences in basic conceptions of gender differentiation, in the ways in which women are viewed and treated, and in women's entitlements and rights to resources across the region, can help us to evolve a better understanding of gender relations in human society. It can also enable us to understand the ways in which exploitative mechanisms at the national and international levels make use of what we might call less extreme systems of gender relations in Southeast Asia.

In order to understand the lives and predicaments of women, the centrality of the household as the entity in which the production and reproduction of social life in most societies is carried on, cannot be overemphasised. Women's experiences within the household vary by class, ethnic group, caste, culture and religion. We need to explore the differing principles and notions of family and kinship in different societies, because it is these that shape ideas about the normal composition of the household and its boundaries, about individual member's rights to the resource base of the household, and about intra-household and inter-household relationships. In the context of Asia, which contains diverse production, family and kinship systems, the relationship between the household, and the condition of women needs careful exploration in a cross-cultural perspective. This can help us to develop an understanding, in the context of their specific bases, of the similarities, variations, and differences in the position of women across the region.

Is the household the site of gender subordination and sexual discrimination? Upon what are these based? Do relatively egalitarian relationships between the sexes in the household and the kinship group (as they exist in some Southeast Asian countries) always help women or do they, on the contrary, make them more vulnerable as participants in the larger social processes? How do we assess the significance of class differences for a comparative understanding of the role of gender in intra-household relationships? What are the differences in the ideology of the household across cultures, groups and classes, and in what ways does ideology prove binding on women and limit their choices of action?

The household's relation to wider economic and political structures, and its use by them, raises a number of tangled issues for social scientists and activists. The policies of the state affect the household in diverse ways and require special consideration. Finally, we need to understand critically the manner in which the household is used as a unit of study in research and surveys and the possible implications of such treatment. The five collections of papers arising from the Conference deal with these various aspects.

Recent research has shown that by ignoring women as social actors who contribute to both continuity and change in society, the social sciences have seriously distorted their understanding of the total social reality. A balanced, bifocal kind of analysis has now begun to be undertaken—men are not to be ignored, but definite focus on women must be maintained so as to enable us to properly comprehend social and societal problems and processes. There is a new emphasis on the study of linkages, on the study of contexts. From this has emerged the consideration accorded to the household.

Gender and the Household Domain: Social and Cultural Dimensions is the fourth of five collection of papers selected from amongst those presented at the Conference. The first volume, *Invisible Hands: Women in Home-based Production*, edited by Andrea Menefee Singh and Anita Kelles-Viitanen, was brought out by Sage Publications in 1987. In 1988, Kali for Women published the second volume, *Structures of Patriarchy: State, Community and Household in Modernising Asia*, edited by Bina Agarwal. The third volume in the series, brought out by Sage Publications, is *Structures and Strategies: Women, Work and Family in Asia*, edited by Leela Dube and Rajni Palriwala. The collection of papers dealing with the efficacy and appropriateness of the household as the unit of data collection and analysis for understanding gender differentiation will be the fifth and the final volume in the series.

This volume brings together selected papers broadly dealing with structural and cultural dimensions of intra-household relationships. Besides those which were presented under the sub-theme of the same name, this volume also includes a few papers from the area of health which were originally presented under the sub-theme of the state, household and women, but are essentially concerned with the phenomenon of intra-household differentiation in resource allocation and its underlying assumptions. This volume is thus divided into two parts, each with a separate introduction.

All the papers in this volume are located in South Asia: seven in India and two in Bangladesh. The other papers presented at the Conference but not included in this volume—mainly because of the constraints of space and difficulties in obtaining properly revised versions—also brought in a wealth of information and ideals, raised questions, and stimulated discussions.

The two editors, Maithreyi Krishnaraj and Karuna Chanana, who were also the organisers of their respective sub-themes or a part of it, decided to divide the editorial responsibility for the two parts of this volume. Together, the two separate introductions (provided by them) bring into sharp focus important issues raised in the papers and place them in larger perspectives—regional, comparative as well as theoretical. Their styles and emphases are different but in the final analysis these differences have enriched the volume.

This volume is concerned mainly with relations within the household. The picture one gets of South Asian households, from the papers in this volume, reflects the diversity in their structure as well as in their reconstitution in new settings. The households in the urban slums in India have had to make adjustments which have definite consequences for women. The idea of a linear social development is untenable not only because of the persistence of patterns of gender disparity across cultures and across time but also due to variations within those patterns. 'Seclusion' is an overall ideology in South Asia, yet its manifestations vary—from purdah for women in Bangladesh, that deprives them of mobility and access to essential services, to a literal walling in of women within a fortress as in the case of a village in Tamil Nadu. Between these lie other variations, but whatever the particular manifestation, the ideological enforcement results in the confinement of women to only appointed locations and spheres of life. Seclusion is not only a physical veiling, but a broader principle of exclusion of women from economic, political and social power, authority and influence. Seclusion is also a corollary to the means required to uphold caste and class divisions, by vesting in women the duty of upholding caste purity or in treating women's work as a mechanism for maintaining class status or for class mobility. Socialisation tends to replicate both these principles even in a changing situation by modifying some externalities but retaining the core so as to keep the outcomes for women the same. These internal structures and accompanying ideologies define women's roles and entitlements within the household, but the so-called private sphere has ramifications beyond the household. These ideologies shape public policy. The impact of global and national level macro-changes have of late been the subject of considerable interest. When improvements come, women's initial inferior position gives them inferior access to these changes and thus disparities between men and women widen. This is poignantly illustrated in the way the health care system works. Exigencies of development priorities dictate policy options that cause special hardships to women, as in family planning programmes where what could have been liberating for women became the opposite. The papers drive home the point that any individual indicator such as earnings or owning property or having education by itself does not guarantee women equality or power. It is the special mix of structural and cultural factors in each situation, coupled with opportunities available, that determines the precise outcome. In the analysis of women and the household, the complex intermeshing of domination—nurturance and conflict—and supportiveness make any simple generalisation impossible. Nevertheless, the kind of detailed scrutiny attempted here brings to the surface the way in which different elements interact to influence the outcome.

The Conference was the result of collective endeavour. It is our hope that these volumes will carry forward the debates initiated at the Delhi Conference.

Nehru Memorial Museum & Library
New Delhi

Leela Dube
Series Editor

Acknowledgements

We are extremely grateful to Dr. Leela Dube for having given us the opportunity to organise separate panels at the Regional Conference on Women and Household in Asia, which has resulted in the present volume. Chanana would also like to express her gratitude to Dr. Dube for her constant moral and intellectual support and for drafting her into the organising committee of the same conference. Furthermore, this volume has come out largely due to her gentle persuasion and sustained interest in the series.

A written account or cold print cannot capture the lively exchanges that took place at the panel discussions. We regret that all the papers could not be included—some because the authors wished to publish them elsewhere, and some because they did not focus directly on the theme of the volume, while some others were incomplete in many ways. Nevertheless, we would like to take this opportunity to thank all the panel contributors. To the authors of the papers included herein, our gratitude for their patience and tolerance in waiting for the final appearance of their work in print. Chanana would like to thank Meera Chatterjee who was helpful in her search for information on health issues relating to women. We are also thankful to the Indian Association for Women's Studies for agreeing to meet the expenses incurred during the processing of the book. M. Krishnaraj would like to thank Ms. Usha Lalwani and Ms. A. Nair of the Research Centre for Women Studies, S.N.D.T. Women's University, for their able assistance in the secretarial work while Chanana would like to thank Mrs. K. Verghese and Mr. V.P. Tanwar for typing and secretarial assistance.

Although we have been responsible for the two sections of the book, the editing process has involved close cooperation between us. Therefore we wish to thank each other for the process of mutual support that made this book possible.

M. KRISHNARAJ
K. CHANANA

I
The Cultural Matrix

Introduction

MAITHREYI KRISHNARAJ

I

In Asia, women's lives are deeply embedded in the household and family. Their position cannot be analysed outside of this primary reference point. Understanding the structure and functions of this social matrix is an important first step in knowing where women are located in society; what the household or family is; how is it constituted; where its boundaries lie not only for the unit as a whole but for different members within it; when and how it changes and with what implications for its members—these are the kind of questions that arise in any examination of households.

The household and family have been perennial themes in sociological and anthropological studies. Yet, this perenniality has obscured the complexity of these social structures through their apparent ordinariness. Household and family overlap and intermesh in ways that defy analysis. We yield to this duality as we accept the wave and particle duality in the theory of light in Physics. Likewise, it is household one minute and the family at another depending on what you are looking for. In common parlance, these two terms are used interchangeably. What is objectionable is not so much this haziness in our definition but the assumption that the household is transhistoric, a genus that continued down the ages, and that empirical reality only deals with changes in its shape, size and composition over time. The variations brought in by state, class, ethnicity and economic conditions are not just numerical changes—these changes reconstitute the family in fundamental and qualitatively different ways. One cannot, therefore, see households in the present day Third World societies as mere remnants of a pre-capitalist era. While this volume is not concerned with changes in the household structure but much more with relations within the household, the picture one gets of South Asia from the papers in this volume reflect the diversity in structure as well as its reconstitution in new settings. The slum household (Usha Kanhere), the middleclass households (Hanna Papanek) are reconstituted units. To posit a linear progression from the unstructured primordial hordes of prehistory—giving way to matrilineal groups and then on to patriarchal families with their recognised marriage and inheritance through sons—to finally the modern day emergence of nuclear families with the rise of industrial capitalism is to ignore the enormous diversity of real life households and the coexistence in many periods of history of different types of households. By implication, women's lives cannot be traced as progressing from one stage to another. Linearity fails to explain the persistence of patterns of subordination of women across culture and across time as well as variations within these patterns. For instance, many papers in this volume highlight the role of seclusion of women as an ideology and yet their manifestations vary in pattern and degree (K.M.A. Aziz in Bangladesh and Kamala Ganesh in South India).

The criteria used for analysis of households need to be looked at more holistically in order to grasp the relationship of women to the household and family. What has prevented such an approach is the discipline dichotomy. To the economist, the household is primarily a unit of economic activity and in modern times basically a consumption unit. The sociologists and anthropologists are overwhelmingly preoccupied with the social composition of the family. It is like the four blind men describing the elephant.

What *is* a household? We can regard it as representing a multitude of roles and tasks encompassed within a relatively selective repertoire of shapes and sizes (Netting et al., 1984). The household and family are both culturally defined. The household may appear as a task oriented unit and the family as a kin-specified group but attitudes, location, function and kinship occur simultaneously and overlap in varying degrees.

A dichotomous view that uses household and family as mutually exclusive categories—the household being concerned with activities like production, consumption, reproduction directed to the satisfaction of human needs and the family as inhering symbols, values and meanings—misses the essential connection between the two. 'It is through their commitment to the concept of family that people are recruited to the material relations of the household' (Rapp, 1981). It is because people accept the notion of the family or family ideology that they enter into relations of production, reproduction, consumption with one another; they marry, beget children, work to support dependents, accumulate, transmit and inherit cultural and material resources. After all, it is a family (or parts of it) that lives in a household. It is not possible, in any case, to dissect the economic from the non-economic in Asian context, as is obvious from all the papers in this volume. Where we can see how much the economic is mediated through the non-economic institutions like kinship, ritual and religion, etc. What women can or cannot do; where and when they can work and at what tasks and what they receive in return are matters beyond the economic. The papers on health and health policy in the second section of this volume bring this out dramatically.

II

The household is a primary arena for age and sex roles, for forging kin solidarity, for socialisation and for economic cooperation. Decisions are not individual because the decisions of any member affect the morphology of the household. A male member's decision to migrate or a female member's marriage are actions that call for readjustments in the household. This is the fundamental dilemma for women. As their fate is linked to that of the household, they identify strongly with its welfare and, yet, the fear of losing its security generates special vulnerabilities. Episodes like widowhood, separation, divorce, abandonment are traumatic for women.

The household's choices are in turn circumscribed by the larger socio-economic order. In the highly stratified, densely settled, agricultural populations of Asia, differential access to productive resources and the systems of production and exchange involving transfers from client to patron, from worker to employer, tenant to landlord, producer to middleman, country-side to the city, from citizen to state are multiple determinants of household behaviour. They shape the types of productive activities available to the household and quantify what the household receives (White, 1984). Women's position within the household is subject to the additional influence of the placement of that household in the social hierarchy. As the following articles reveal, it makes a difference whether a woman is in an urban sector or a rural area household; it makes a difference of which caste she is, and class placement also has a bearing on her position in the household— whether she is landed or landless. It is important, therefore, to place the women in a household within this larger social order. Rural Bangladesh women in rice growing area (Aziz), urban slums (Kanhere) and marginal farmers of Kerala (Mencher) provide contrasts in the structure of opportunities available to the household.

Why are these conceptual problems of household and family structure—which we have discussed at length—significant? These are not merely matters of academic purism. Imprecise concepts are not innocent errors. They are by definition biased against women, by rendering them invisible, official policies, legislation and programmes avoid any definition of the family and use it as a substitute for the household. Public measures that seek to enhance the availability of different resources to the household assume that these will be automatically available to all members of the household. To understand the impact of socio-economic, cultural and political changes on women's situation we have to examine them not only within the context of the family but see them in relation to the qualitative and quantitative terms of the differential participation of men, women and children in the familial and household processes and the manner in which they may be reinforced or muted by the outside forces. Papers in section 2 are examples of this complex interaction.

The notions of the appropriateness of different kinds of work for women; the valuation accorded to women's work because it is women's work; the notions of male and female sexuality and above all the inbuilt imperative for the constraints on women to guard the purity and honour of the family or caste are running themes in many of the papers in this volume.

Women's right to property, inheritance and their entitlement to resources of daily living depends on their placement and recruitment to the family—the household, the location of their residence at marriage, nature of marriage alliances, conditions attached to them and so on. The role differentiation between men and women is determined by caste, religion and cultural norms. Caste rules limit individual freedom for men and women through marriage regulation, through restrictions on social and economic mobility and choice, and ritualistic norms prescribing purity and pollution. A striking case is that of women in a sealed fortress (Ganesh).

III

There have been family studies in India for several decades. This is not the place for a detailed review but a mention of some of the issues thrown up in some of the studies is in order, because they indicate the road hitherto travelled, and how the present set of papers in this volume show the change in direction. Earlier sociologists concentrated heavily on marriage and kinship patterns and on 'types' of family—joint, extended, nuclear, etc. (S.C. Dube, 1963; Desai, 1964; Kapadia, 1966). The emphasis was far too much on the form of the family and too little on the content of family life. A renowned family sociologist bemoans the fact that there is not a single respectable study on this (Shah, 1973). Much concern was expressed on the reasons for the disintegration of the joint family—was it property division, marriage of sons, or women's quarrels (Dube, 1961; Mandelbaum, 1972). The mother-in-law and daughter-in-law conflict is a refrain. None of these focused on the impact on women or the nature of intra-family relations and the value systems that governed day-to-day behaviour (L. Dube, 1974). The toll that poverty, illness, unemployment, drudgery of work, etc., took on different family members in poor households was not seen. At another level, a household or family's striving for social mobility had contradictory effects on women Marriage alliances have an immediate implication for women. The differential effect of brideprice and dowry have been examined by some (Kolenda, 1968). Kinship is a crucial dynamic of intra-household relations. In the South Asian context the position of daughters and daughters-in-law, old women and younger women, of natal kin and conjugal kin are differently structured (Karve, 1965). The role of gift giving, the asymmetrical relationship between the bridegivers and bridetakers has implications for a woman's powerlessness in the conjugal home (Vatuk, 1972; Sharma, 1980; Miller, 1981; Goody & Tambiah, 1978; Madan, 1975; and Das, 1975). These above studies reveal the material basis for a woman's oppression especially in North India. More reciprocal relations generally ensure a better status for a woman in her conjugal home. Religious values, myth and norms are often held to vest power in women (Srinivas, 1980; Thomson, 1981), but whatever this informal power could give to women, it gave them only limited access to wealth and authority and they could not mediate directly with the outside world (Jacobson, 1978). There is no reference to dowry or marriage alliances or kin as such in the above sense in the papers of this volume but they record some of the consequences including the limited access to the public sphere. The role of symbols in female subjugation can be seen in the metaphor of seed and soil (L. Dube, and Leacock, 1986). Different kinds of families provide different degrees of space and authority for women, according to some, but the existing typologies of joint, extended and nuclear families ignore class, ethnicity, caste and the role of the life cycle of the family-household. Despite severe limitations, certain broad features of the Indian (South Asian) family are now common knowledge and these provide a back-ground for interpreting the women's experiences described in this volume. Guided by traditional concepts of feminine behaviour and prodded by early socialisation, most women carry out their roles of chaste daughters and dutiful wives. Some exceptions to the dominant patrilineal family, where a woman's loyalties are divided between her conjugal and natal home, are perceived in tribal and matrilineal societies (Singh, 1972; and Sinha, 1977).

IV

Women's Studies has, while building on the insights of earlier research on family, taken a different turn in the last two decades. It has challenged, particularly, the assumption that the family is a homogenous group or that all the members of a household derive equal benefits, and has highlighted women's overwork, depri-vation and new forms of oppression. There has been a new focus on the urban and rural poor and their struggle for survival. There is a substantial body of literature on this theme and it is not possible to cite all of them here. Several bibliographies have been published that document this extensive research. This new research draws attention to the substantial contribution that women make to the sustenance of the household, their new burdens, and their relative powerlessness and inadequate returns in concrete, material forms like education, health, nutrition, etc. The assumption that a nuclear family gives more freedom to a woman may not be always valid because the strength of the ideology that confines women to restricted roles may still operate. For the urban middle class or in the event of male migration, an extended family can provide support from other female members.

Feminists contend 1) that a specific family arrangement is natural or biological in any timeless way is not true; 2) that sexual division of labour, male dominance and motherhood are subject to historical processes; and 3) that women experience the family differently than men and far from being a domestic haven, it is for them, the seat of oppression (Thorne, 1982).

The specific of daily living, such as, the allocation of tasks, experiences of work and leisure, rendering and receiving nurturance, conflicts, decisions regarding employment, migration, consumption, children are all subject to the underlying age-gender hierarchy. It is time, therefore, that we ask now, not what women do for the family but what the family does for the women.

We have today a greater appreciation of women's economic role. Economic theory has usually paid attention only to production, exchange, savings, investment and so on. The basis of reproduction of social formation is reproduction of human life. Reproduction is both primary and secondary—the first relates to reproduction of labour power, and the second to the reproduction of social and economic order to ensure its continuance as a definite social formation. A large part of primary reproduction in much of the world is outside the market economy and hence does not enter official statistics, planning or public concern. A large part of this subsistence production is done by women in the form of unpaid family labour. Subsistence production is not a relic of the past. It is a precondition for any society. All economies are a mix of subsistence production and market production. Whether people are proletarians, craftsmen, professionals, executives all are engaged in a complex mix of subsistence production and market production. The way production is organised and what proportion subsistence production forms depends on the nature of the economy (Dieter-Evers, 1984). The strategic importance of subsistence production continues even when Third World economies industrialise. The growth of the informal sector is evidence of this. Not only are women in the informal sector and thereby perform subsistence production, they also have to reproduce the labour in the subsistence production sector. These are done within structural-cultural parameters.

> The system of control over women, the original producers of human life and of labour power is reproduced within the household and kinship structure of a particular society. In order to ensure the supply of labour power, a definite family and household structure must be maintained. (Dieter-Evers, 1984)

Subsistence production (primary and secondary reproduction) is allotted to women, but as the Bangladesh papers show, reproduction of labour is culturally controlled. Socialisation, we see, in all the papers ensures secondary reproduction, i.e., the reproduction of the social formation. This explains the subordination of women despite the centrality of their role to the household economy. The functionalist thesis that the nuclear family and sex role division, of the bread-winner male and householding female, is ideally suited to industrial capitalism, is refuted by many who show that the nuclear family is *not* a child of industrial capitalism (Friedman, 1984).

In fact, the process far from being 'functional' is dysfunctional in as much as it has made female kin supports unavailable. This brings us to the issue of sexual division of labour. Does sexual division of labour by itself create subordination for women? Thomson argues that this happens only in the present context of a capitalist economy (1984). It is true that there are many societies where division of tasks by gender exist but areas of female autonomy are maintained. What has led to subordination is the relative valuation of commodity production to subsistence production and women by virtue of being in the latter, lose out.

The impact of global and national level macro-changes have been recently a subject of considerable interest. When improvements come, women's initial inferior position gives them inferior access to the improvements and thus disparities between men and women are widened. A most important case in point is that as men move to commodity production and urban jobs, women continue to remain in subsistence production. The household structure which gives preference to men in power authority, property rights and as bearers of lineage, gives also preferential access to development benefits. 'While reproduction is a central cooperative aspect of life, the differential roles of men and women have a profound effect on the bargaining position of women' (Sen, 1985). Women tend to select themselves out—we can see this in how girls are withdrawn from school (Kanhere). Sen has also demonstrated how conventional price theory which postulates an individual consumer exercising individual choice is at odds with reality. Men and women act as members of a group—the household and all members of the household do not have an equal voice; allocations within the household are not made through market transactions but the norms of the family. It is a model of simultaneous cooperation and conflict (Sen, 1983).

Our major problem in the analysis of women and the household is to, thus, understand adequately the mix of domination and nurturance, conflict and supportiveness that constitutes the household, taken in all the various formations. It is this contradictory formation that creates profound ambivalences for women.

V

This volume has been set out in two sections. Section I deals more with cultural modes. Section II relates cultural modes to issues of policy, particularly in the area of health.

The household can best be understood by looking at what it does. Both Usha Kanhere and K.M.A. Aziz describe the socialisation practices that groom girls and boys into adult roles. Kanhere also highlights the persistence of kin and caste ties even in a big city and she sees no evidence that urbanisation tends to loosen them. Urbanisation opens up new educational and employment opportunities but only for boys and men. Paradoxically, these aspirations for a better economic and social status are not realised in practice, despite efforts to do so. Schooling succeeds in alienating boys from traditional caste occupations but their lack of success in school takes away any possible alternative. They become 'problem' children and display delinquent behaviour. While son preference is marked, these lower classes and castes welcome girls too as assets: girls share in domestic work and also earn a livelihood or assist the mother in her economic activity. Notions of appropriate work for women vary between castes. What has been observed about poor households in so many other studies is corroborated here. Women are in traditional occupations or engage in various informal activities that are heavy on toil, low on returns, while men are in the formal sector. Women and girls sustain the household through subsistence production releasing time and opportunity for future mobility of the household. They are the basis for the family's stability as well as mobility. Girls do not only forego better jobs. Their lives are restricted. Gender roles are recreated and the structure of the household reproduced by confining their movements to the household or immediate neighbourhood and permitting social interaction only with females. Even when they go out to work, they can do so only if accompanied by elder female kin or other girls. They do not learn to interact with the outside world directly. The so-called 'freedom' of the lower castes is exaggerated.

Aziz employs an interesting methodology by capturing the actual statements of his respondents. The centrality of seclusion and modesty for women as virtues emerges clearly. The idea that female sexuality is dangerous to men and women have the onus of guarding their honour is reinforced through dress, attitudes of covering the body, restrictions on social interaction, etc. Even between parents and offspring, if they are of opposite sex, physical contact is discouraged. In the Ahmedabad lower class families, a woman's domestic role is emphasised but seclusion is not practised as severely. A silver lining is the changing attitude of women who have received some education. They value their daughters' education. In rural Bangladesh, Aziz notes the extra emphasis on the childbearing role of women and the marked son-preference in greeting a new born.

Seclusion pushed to bizzare limits is described by Kamala Ganesh. Generally it is believed that veiling and seclusion are absent in the South. She shows how more than anything else an ideology can cover a range of practices, from complete covering of the body and separate living quarters, to curtained spaces in public places or public transport and restrictions on movement within the household or neighbourhood, to prescriptions regarding who one can see, talk to, etc. The Pillaimar women in her case history live literally within a walled fortress. The purpose is to maintain caste status by retaining the purity of women. This seclusion, a mark of caste status becomes also a mark of self-esteem for women. Ironically, ritual status in caste hierarchy is determined solely by women's purity rather than men's. The power of chastity as both sacred and dangerous is a deeply ingrained Dravidian notion, glorified by folklore, legend, history and ritual. These secluded women inherit land, house and jewellery but enjoy little autonomy and cannot negotiate with the outside world except through male kin.

Joan Mencher also finds not much correlation between property owning and autonomy. While women may own land, they cannot use or dispose of it freely. Mencher addresses class differences primarily, taking examples from the land owning and the landless in Kerala. Laying down six indicators for measuring autonomy— right to one's earnings, right to buy things for oneself, decisions on household matters, ability to refuse money or jewellery to husband, control over her sexual relations with her spouse, and not being subject to beatings—she concludes that neither owning property nor earning by itself guarantees anything. A variety of social-cultural factors, individual good fortune in getting a good mother-in-law or husband, individual tenacity or confidence, all determine the outcome for a woman.

Hanna Papanek puts forward an interesting thesis that the withdrawal of women from paid work is not an end product of social mobility defined by status but is itself a strategy for further mobility. Women become engaged in status-producing activities, once the family resource base makes it possible for them to withdraw from paid work. She cautions however that this kind of status-production can occur only under very specific conditions of social and economic organisation.

REFERENCES

DAS, VEENA, 1975: 'Marriage Among the Hindus,' in Devaki Jain ed.,*Indian Women* (New Delhi, Min. of Info. Broadcasting).

DESAI, I.P., 1964: *Some Aspects of Family in Mahuva* (Bombay, Asia Publishers).

DIETER-EVERS, HANS, 1984: 'Subsistence Production—A Framework For Analysis,' in Joan Smith, Immaneul Wallerstein and Hans Dieter-Evers eds., *House-holds and the World Economy* (Beverley Hills, Sage Publications).

DUBE, LEELA, 1961: UNU Project, proposal for a background paper on Kinship as Family (Unpubd.).

————, 1974: *Sociology of Kinship—An Analytical Survey of Literature* (Bombay, Popular Prakashan).

————, 1986: 'Seed and Earth: The Symbolism of Biological Reproduction and Sexual Relations of Production,' in Leela Dube and Eleanor Leacock eds., *Visibility and Power* (Delhi, OUP).

DUBE, S.C., 1963: 'Men's and Women's Roles in India: A Sociological Review,' in Barbara Ward ed., *Women in New Asia* (Bangkok, Unesco).

FRIEDMAN, KATHE, 1984: 'Households as Income Pooling Units,' in Joan Smith et. al., eds., *Households and the World Economy* (Beverley Hills, Sage Publications).

GOODY, JACK and S.J. TAMBIAH, 1973: *Bride Wealth and Dowry* (Cambridge, Cambridge Univ. Press).

JACOBSON, DOREEN, 1978: 'The Chaste Wife,' in Sylvia Vatuk ed., *American Studies in the Anthropology of India* (Delhi, Manohar).

KAPADIA, K.M., 1966: *Marriage and Family in India* (Bombay, OUP).

KARVE, IRAWATI, 1965: *Kinship Organisation in India* (Bombay, Asia Publishers).

KOLENDA, PAULINE, 1968: 'Region, Caste and Family Structure,' in Milton Singer, and B.S. Cohen eds., *Structure and Change in Indian Society* (Chicago, Aldine).

MADAN, T., 1975: 'Structural Implications of Marriage in North India: Wife Givers and Wife Takers Among Pandits of Kashmir,' in *Contributions to Indian Sociology*, Vol. 9, No. 2.

MANDELBAUM, D., 1972: *Society in India* (Bombay, Popular Prakashan reprint).

MILLER, B.D., 1981: *The Endangered Sex: Neglect of Female Children in Rural North India* (Ithaca, Cornell Univ. Press).

NETTING, McROBERT and RICHARD WILK, 1984: 'Household, Changing Forms and Functions,' in McRobert Netting, Richard Wilk and Eric. J. Arnould, eds., *Comparative and Historical Studies of the Domestic Group* (Berkeley, Univ. of California Press).

RAPP, RAYNA, 1981: 'Examining Family History,' in *Feminist Studies*, Vol. 5.

SEN, AMARTYA, 1983: 'Economics and the Family,' in *Asian Development Review*, Vol. 1, No. 2.

————, 1985: 'Women, Technology and Sexual Division of Labour,' in *Unctad Review*, Vol. 6.

SHAH, A.M., 1973: *The Household Dimension of the Family in India* (Delhi, Orient Longman).

SHARMA, URSULA, 1980: *Women, Work and Property in North West India* (London, Tavistock).

SINGH, K.S., 1972: 'Tribal Situation in India,' *IIAS*, Simla, Vol. 3.

SINHA, SURAJIT and S.D. SHARMA, 1977: 'Primitive Tribes,' Government of India, Ministry of Home Affairs.

SRINIVAS, M.N., 1980: *Social Structure* (Delhi, Hindustan Pub).

————, 1981: *Position of Women in India* (Delhi, OUP).

THOMAS, C., 1983: 'Women, Fertility and the Worship of Gods in a Hindu Village,' in Pat Holden ed., *Women's Religious Experience* (London, Croom Helm).

THOMSON, VERONIKA BENHOLDT, 1984: 'Sexual Division of Labour,' in Joan Smith et. al., ed., *Household and World Economy* (Beverley Hills, Sage Publications).

THORNE, BARRIE, 1982: 'Feminist Rethinking of the Family,' in Barret Michelle, and Mary McIntosh eds., *The Anti Social Family* (London, Verso).

VATUK, S., 1975: 'Gifts and Affines in North India,' in *Contributions to Indian Sociology*, Vol. 9, No. 2.

WHITE, BENJAMIN, 1980: Rural Household Studies in Anthropological Perspective,' in Hans P. Binswanger, et. al., eds., *Rural Household Studies in Asia* (Singapore, Singapore Univ. Press).

Differential Socialisation of Boys and Girls: A Study of Lower Socio-economic Households among Gujarati Caste/Communities in Ahmedabad

USHA KANHERE

Gender is an important factor in the allocation of roles, status and power in all societies. In traditional societies, socialisation of boys and girls as well as child rearing beliefs and practices in general are organised on the basis of position-status, and roles of men and women in the family and in society. The traditional patrilineal joint family system confines women's roles mostly to the domestic sphere, allocating them to a subordinate status, authority and power compared to men. This is achieved through strict segregation of sexes so as to minimise social contact except among close kin, and through division of labour in day-to-day life. Men are perceived as the major providers and protectors of a family, while women are perceived as playing only a supportive role, attending to the hearth. Boys and girls are accordingly trained for different adult roles, statuses and authority.

In the patrilocal, patriarchal and patrilineal joint family system, boys assume adult status and roles within the same family where they are born and brought up. They are permanent members of their family. A girl, on the other hand, is looked upon as a transient member of the family in which she is born and brought up because on marriage a girl has to be transferred to her husband's family. It is in the latter family that she takes up her adult domestic roles. It is there that she gives birth to and takes care of her children, and of her husband's family. Whatever rights and duties she has, are in the family she marries into.

The development of appropriate personality characteristics and qualities for boys and girls during the socialisation process in the family emphasises this differential in their future adult roles. From the point of view of modern egalitarian values this practice heavily discriminates against girls and operates as a highly restrictive mechanism that thwarts the full flowering of girls and the development of their potential.

This paper examines the nature of differential socialisation of boys and girls in the family on the basis of data collected from a purposively selected sample of 130 families belonging to some Gujarati, Hindu, lower strata castes/communities settled in the city of Ahmedabad. While there is some knowledge of the upper caste Hindu family structure and family life, we have scant data on lower castes/classes. The three stages of infancy, childhood and adolescence were taken, and the indicators used for each stage were: 1) the differential treatment given to boys and girls by parents and elders in the family; 2) the prohibited and permitted activities for each sex; and 3) the differential expectations regarding personality traits.

SAMPLE AND DATA COLLECTION

In Ahmedabad the lower (socio-economic) strata castes and communities tended to reside in four types of residential areas, namely: (1) chawls (2) zoppadapattis (3) vas or mohallas of lower castes in the old city area and in (4) the old village area which became part of the expanding metropolis. While in all these four types of residential areas, the wider neighbourhoods were heterogeneous in terms of caste, religion, language and native place of the residents, the immediate neighbourhoods made up of thirty to fifty families were more homogenous. The majority of the families in such immediate neighbourhoods belonged to the same linguistic, religious group and/or caste-community. They were often also related to each other as members of a joint or extended family. Two such close neighbourhoods from each of the four types of wider residential areas were purposively selected. The criterion of selection being that the majority of families living in the neighbourhood should belong to Gujarati, Hindu, lower castes/communities (excluding scheduled castes and tribal communities).

The selection of families in these immediate neighbourhoods was done on the basis of the following criteria:

Table 1

Residential area of sample families

Community	Old City area	Old Village area	Chawls	Zoppada-pattis	Total p.c. in the sample
1. Vaghari	21.4	3.6	28.6	46.4	21.5
2. Thakarada	—	17.8	73.3	8.9	34.6
3. Rabari	—	50.0	16.7	33.3	9.2
4. Gola	100.0	—	—	—	5.4
5. Khalas	100.0	—	—	—	3.1
6. Bhisti	100.0	—	—	—	2.3
7. High Artisan Castes	53.8	23.1	23.1	—	10.0
8. Low Artisan Castes	—	70.0	30.0	—	7.7
9. Other	12.5	37.5	—	50.0	7.2
Total Sample	21.5	21.5	37.7	19.2	100.0 p.c.

* Residential area and caste community of the sample families in percentage P.C. total No. 130.

1. They should be staying in the area for more than ten years;
2. The male head of the family and his wife (if earning) should be engaged in blue collar jobs in organised or unorganised sector of urban economy and;
3. The total monthly income of the family should be Rs. 500 per month or above but not exceeding Rs. 700 per month.

The major part of the relevant data was collected in the year 1981 with the help of a structured interview guide. Interviews were held with both the male head of the family and his wife (N 130). Detailed interviews of members in one family from each major caste/community (N 10) were also conducted. This was supplemented by observation and informal talk with people in the neighbourhood during the field work visits.

SIGNIFICANT INFORMATION ABOUT NEIGHBOURHOODS AND CASTES/COMMUNITIES

All the sample families were settled urban families, the majority (85 per cent) being in the metropolis for generations. However, most of the families were earlier migrants from rural (72 per cent) or small towns (20 per cent) of Gujarat. Only a few families were born and grew up in Ahmedabad city.

The immediate neighbourhoods, in all the four types of residential areas (namely, chawls, zoppadapattis, vas or mohalla in the 'old' city or old 'village' area), were more homogeneous in terms of caste, language, religion and region, wherein the sample families lived an intimate social and family life. There was much mutual give and take. They spent time together and seemed to derive a sense of socio-economic security from this immediate neighbourhood. Socio-religious celebrations were organised in all these neighbourhoods by the Yuvak Mandals, Seva mandals, or some such organisation in the neighbourhood. So the sample families, even while residing in a cosmopolitan metropolis, lived and interacted with their own socio-cultural caste/community group. This strengthened both their adherence to traditional beliefs and practices of their caste, and their resistance to change. The melting effect of an anonymous urban set-up is over rated by our social commentators.

The sample families belonged to the castes of *Thakarda* (34.6 per cent), *Vaghari* (21.5 per cent), and *Rabari* (9.2 per cent). The higher status artisan castes formed 10 per cent of the total sample families, of whom *Panchals* and *Khalas* were 3.1 per cent, *Golas* were 5.4 per cent, and *Bhistis* were 2.4 per cent. The lower status artisan castes, such as, potters and barbers constituted 7.7 per cent of the families. Other lower castes comprised of 6.2 per cent. These castes form a fair representation of the main Hindu, non-scheduled-caste and non-scheduled-tribe lower strata caste/communities of urban Gujarat including the metropolitan area of Ahmedabad.

MAIN FEATURES OF SAMPLE FAMILIES

Most sample families (71 per cent) resided in nuclear households. After a couple of years following the marriage, the son or a brother of the head of the family usually sets up a separate household. Residential house-space being small, any opportunity to establish a separate household was availed of. Often quarrels between women folk led to the break up of the joint household. The house space was then partitioned into two household units. Though nuclear households were the most common, they existed in close proximity to the root family or different units of the joint family. About fifty-two per cent of the households had relatives in the neighbourhood and 33.1 per cent had their caste/community persons in proximity. The families maintained close familial relations with these other kin related households. This helped to retain traditional caste and joint family beliefs and practices.

Nearly 29 per cent of sample families were residentially joint families, having joint family relatives, consisting of usually parents, unmarried or married sons and brothers of the male head of the family. Only in one sample joint family, parents of the wife stayed with her.

More than half (54.8 per cent) of the sample families were medium sized having four to eight members in the household; 20.0 per cent were small with less than four members in the household; and 15.0 per cent were large with more than eight members in the household.

Earning a Living

Eighty-nine per cent of male respondents and 50 per cent female respondents were engaged in earning a livelihood. Nearly two thirds of the sample families had two or more earning members in the family, all of them being in blue collar jobs in the organised or unorganised sector of urban economy. Women and children were concentrated in the unorganised sector while more men were in the organised sector.

In nearly 11 per cent of the sample families, the wife's earnings were either the major or the only source of money for the family because the male respondent was old or ill. More than half (53 per cent) of the male respondents were employed in service jobs of various types, such as, peons, watchmen, or workers in shops, offices or in small factories; or as drivers or workers in a big textile mill. One third (34.6 per cent) of the male respondents were engaged in petty business or self-employment, such as, washing and cleaning auto-rickshaws, white washing buildings, working as a hand-cart puller, as carpenters, tailors, barbers, petty business of collecting and selling old clothes, used cans and plastic containers or old paper. Education appeared to have some influence on their occupations. More males (61 per cent) with some education were in blue collar level service jobs, whereas the illiterate males were more in self-employment or petty business (42 per cent). Blue collar service jobs were regarded as the most prestigious among these castes/communities as they were less strenuous; more secure with steady incomes; entailed wearing uniforms; had good working conditions where benefits, such as, provident fund, access to a credit society, casual, medical and earned leave, etc., were available. Self-employment, however, was perceived as more strenuous with uncertain incomes and lacking in any provision for old age. Most of the self-employed men wished that their sons would acquire some education so that they could get blue collar service jobs.

Among the female respondents who were earning an income, more than four-fifths were employed either in family business or a household based activity. Two-thirds were working in household based production; the other third went out of the house to earn. Of these third, one-fifth were found in blue collar work half of whom cleaned, washed floors or utensils in offices, shops or middle class households and the remaining worked as blue collar workers in a textile mill or a small factory.

It was observed that family and caste traditions played a major role in deciding whether the woman engaged at all in any earning activity and if so which economic activity she pursued. All *Khalas*, *Vagharis*, *Golas* and high status artisans engaged in some earning activity.

The choice of economic activity pursued by women in most cases was decided by their family or caste tradition. In the sample all the earning *Vaghari* women engaged in their family business— either of old clothes, used cans and plastic containers, or of selling vegetables. *Gola* women cleaned grain in grocery shops, in the nearby grain market or in upper middle class houses. *Rabari* women either kept milch cattle or worked as part time domestic servants in the upper middle class houses in the near-by areas. *Khalas* earning women carried on their traditional household industry of rope making at home. In the high status artisan castes women helped their husbands at home in their spare time or stitched beds, clothes, etc., at home. *Thakarda* women worked as *badli* or permanent workers in the mills and factories or else folded papers and made paper bags at home. A few *Thakarda* women could get mill jobs because of the contacts their parents or husbands had at the mills.

It was observed that husbands of many earning women worked at secure blue collar service jobs, while the wives carried on various types of informal activities, partly traditional, partly urban economy generated petty jobs, like, recycling waste. *Rabaris* and *Vagharis* were engaged in their traditional caste occupations like dairying and petty trade.

Economic Level

The sample families were all poor families as the total monthly income for nearly half of them (46.9 per cent) was between Rs. 300 to 500 p.m.; 36.3 per cent families had a total monthly income of between Rs. 500 to 700 p.m.; while for 25 per cent families it was less than Rs. 300 p.m.

The families barely managed to meet their survival needs and could hardly save anything. Only 24 per cent families could manage to save some money in the form of compulsory saving provident fund and contribution to credit societies. The families doing petty business invested their meagre savings (not more than a thousand rupees) in their family business. Some families used their savings to build or repair their houses or huts. It is significant to note that 71.5 per cent families incurred debts occasionally. The debts were for such social occasions as birth, marriage or death in the family; illness or religious observance in the family.

Age of Respondents

Forty-five per cent of the males in the sample families were in the 36-50 age group; 37.70 per cent were in the below 35 years group and 16.90 per cent were aged 51 and above. As for the females, 53.8 per cent were young (i.e., below 35 years); 36.28 per cent were in the 36-50 age group and 10 per cent were in the 51 and above age group. The average age of the male respondents was 29.90 years and the average age of the female respondents was 34.47 years.

Education of Sample Men/Women

Close on sixty-eight per cent of male heads of families had some education with 43 per cent of them having primary and 14.7 per cent having secondary education. The wives of the male heads (63.8 per cent) had more illiterates. Some 30 per cent had a couple of years of primary education and 6.2 per cent had some secondary education. None of the female respondents had any kind of certificate or diploma and were woefully devoid of any training or skill which could equip them for better jobs. Illiteracy also lessened the chances of their questioning old beliefs and practices. Compared to the females, the males were more educated. Even among the lower castes/classes we see the educational gap between males and females.

Acquiring an education also seemed to be associated with caste traditions. The majority of the female respondents in *Vaghari* (92.8 per cent), *Rabari* (75 per cent) and *Thakarda* (75 per cent) communities were illiterate; while majority of the females belonging to *Bhisti*, (100 per cent), *Gola* (87 per cent), *Khalas* (75 per cent), higher status artisan castes (75.0 per cent) and lower status artisan castes (73.8 per cent) had some education.

Among the males some castes received schooling—75 per cent among the *Thakardas* and *Bhistis*, 69 per cent among the *Golas*, and 100 per cent among artisans. The majority of illiterates, male or female came from the *Vagharis* and *Rabaris*. There was a big gap between male and female education in *all* castes but the greatest was among the *Thakardas*. There were only eight women in all who had received secondary education. Three were *Thakardas*. The others were one each from *Khalas, Bhisti* and artisan communities.

Number of Children

Children were found invariably within the household or in nearby joint family relatives' households. The average number of children per family was 3.8 of whom the ratio of boys to girls was 2.0 to 1.8. Four or more children were most typically followed by three or less. 3.8 per cent of the families did not have children at the time of the interview. The older women tended to have more children as compared to the younger. Fertility also varied between the castes. The *Vaghari* women had the highest number of living children, followed by the others. At the lowest end were the *Rabari* women. In a small sample this is not necessarily indicative of any causal connection. Most families had both sons and daughters; 6.2 per cent had only sons while 10 per cent had only daughters.

Practice of family planning was rare, being confined to a small section. The usual reasons cited were the desire for sons or for daughters (if they had only sons). They knew only about terminal methods, thanks to the emphasis on these in family planning camps and many were afraid of operations. Child mortality was high and this was another reason for avoiding terminal methods.

Avoidance of family planning was more frequent among the *Rabaris, Golas, Vagharis and Thakardas*, as compared to the average percentage for the total sample. It was also noticed among the sample couples that, where the wives were illiterate (71.1 per cent) more couples did not practise family planning as compared to the literate (46.80 per cent). Woman's education appeared to induce a more favourable response to family planning.

Those couples (37.7 per cent) who practised family planning did so only when (as they said) they had 'enough' children. 'Enough' for them in reality meant having at least two or more live sons and one or more live daughters. Only one couple mentioned the wife's health as an additional reason for acceptance of family planning. Miscarriages, infant and child mortality in these families were quite high. 91.6 per cent couples had experienced either miscarriage or had lost one or more of their children at infancy which discouraged them from implementing the 'small family' norm and encouraged them to have four or more children to ensure at least two live sons. Sons were needed for looking after them in old age.

All the families displayed beliefs and values relating to children common in the traditional Indian family and society. Children are never regarded as a burden. It was observed that all these men and women loved their children and were happy to live with them. They referred to their children as a source of joy and satisfaction. All of them *wanted* children. Childlessness was looked down upon and even regarded as inauspicious. They valued and wanted children for several reasons: a son was necessary because it was only on him that they could depend as a matter of right, particularly in their old age. However, compared to childlessness, even having a daughter was preferable, because they would then have a son-in-law to depend upon. Real satisfaction and happiness along with assurance of continuity of their family (*Vansha*) and socio-economic security, particularly in old age was felt only when they had many children. More than half of them wanted children—girls to help them in domestic work and boys for earning a living. Many couples also cited social prestige as an important reason for having children.

It is significant that all of them wanted 'enough' children of both sexes which meant four or more in all. Men and women in the lower strata communities did not have an excessive craving for sons alone. This is because both boys and girls assist in day-to-day household work, child care and also in the earning activity. Arranging a girl's marriage is not very difficult as no dowries are to be given, rather girls fetch bride prices. However, since the family is patriarchal, patrilineal and patrilocal, emphasis is on having at least one son.

INFANT AND CHILDCARE

Expectant mothers were usually given special attention. They took great care about their food and about various activities according to beliefs prevalent in their community. During pregnancy most of them continued their normal daily routine of domestic and earning activity. Deliveries took place in public hospitals except for 30.5 per cent women who had their deliveries at home with the help of a trained midwife traditionally employed in their community.

In these communities, during pregnancy and child birth, women stayed with their marital or conjugal family. Nearby joint family relatives often provided necessary assistance and ten days after delivery, women resumed their daily routine. This was true particularly for the *Rabari* women but applicable also to the others— the *Golas*, artisans, *Khalas*, *Thakardas* and *Vagharis*. They did not go to their mother's place for delivery.

There was some imitation of higher caste practices among some *Vagharis*, *Thakardas* and higher artisans, where the women went for their first delivery to the parental family. They went in the later stage of their pregnancy and came back after the birth of the child.

The women breastfed their babies. Particular kinds of food were eaten to stimulate lactation. Babies were always demand-fed. When the mother's milk was not available or was insufficient, buffalo milk or a semiliquid drink made up of flour, jaggery and water, or tea and milk was given. Alongwith the mother's milk when the infant was around the sixth month or so, it was given normal solid food, such as, rice, pulses and wheat preparations. Giving tea was very common.

The infant was kept clean, given a bath, clothed and protected from excessive heat, cold, wind, etc. Women remained in the home and did domestic work or a household-based economic activity as long as the baby was very small. In few cases the mother went to work, carrying the infant with her, as she had nobody to look after the baby at home. Standards of hygiene at their residences and neighbourhoods were very poor. With government dispensaries easily accessible, primary vaccinations were given to children. When ill, the children were taken to hospitals and dispensaries. They combined allopathic medicines with homemade traditional medicines and treatment.

The infant was mainly with the mother when very young. Other female members when available in the family (mostly daughter or mother-in-law) or the neighbourhood, assisted the mother. As the infant grew older, other women in the family looked after it. Only in a few families belonging to *Vaghari, Thakarda, Gola* and high and low artisan communities, younger sons (in eight families) and husbands or other older male members (in eleven families) rendered substantial assistance in the care of a small child, particularly when the mother was weak or sick or had to go out for earning an income. Neighbours and relatives lent a helping hand too. During the child's infancy, girls, grown up women and children fondled and played a lot with it. At a very early age the child began to grow in the neighbourhood and became a part of the community. The child was at no time exclusively tied or confined to its own family or parents.

It was fairly common for older daughters to help the mother with the baby when another baby was born or when the mother was busy in some paid work. On the eldest daughter fell the greatest responsibility, especially when no other adult female member was available in the household. The father also did baby sitting only when no female assistance was available. Among the *Vagharis*, not only did the father baby sit but also cleaned, clothed and fed the child. Among the *Rabaris, Golas* and *Thakardas* generally no male member ever offered such assistance.

In one area where an 'anganwadi' (day care centre) for pre-school children was available, most women sent their children to it. The women appreciated the free lunch made available to the child and the free time it gave them to attend to their work. Thus the pre-school child grew up in the immediate neighbourhood in the midst of other children and was looked after by sisters, grand parents and occasionally other relatives and neighbours.

During my field work in different neighbourhoods, I observed malnutrition in many infants and pre-school children of both the sexes. It was as much due to lack of awareness and information about nutritive food and hygienic practices, as their poor economic condition. For example, many men and women gave money (twenty-fifty paisa coins) to their children for buying eatables. The amount came, in many cases, to more than a rupee a day, and it was spent in buying cheap lemon drops and chocolates or fried snacks. The same amount could have been used in buying nutritive food, such as, milk, vegetables or fruits. Infant and child mortality was high. About ninety-two per cent of the women had, as we mentioned earlier, either a miscarriage or a death of the infant or child or both. Absence of any kind of non-formal education in childcare and hygienic living coupled with out-worn traditional child rearing practices appeared to account for most such avoidable deaths.

The birth of a boy as well as a girl was welcome in these communities and both were brought up with the same care. Only when the mother was nursing an infant or a son was born after a number of daughters or the child was an only daughter did it receive extra care and attention (four such instances were noticed). However, I did not come across a single instance of discrimination (or differential treatment injurious to girls) between a boy and a girl at the infant and pre-school age.

CHILDREN OF SCHOOLGOING (FIVE TO TWELVE YEARS) AGE

As children entered schoolgoing age the major concerns of almost all parents were 1) discipline, 2) education and 3) health. In disciplining the child, punishment rather than reward was routinely employed. Physical punishment, particularly beating was very common. Children were punished for not putting on clothes, or for demanding eatables or money to buy things frequently, for naughtiness, for disobeying parents and for creating hindrance in parent's work or rest. The child was rewarded far less often. The most frequent way of rewarding was to give the child ten or twenty paisa to buy some candy from a nearby petty shop.

When hungry, the children ate whatever was available in the house, leftovers or fresh wheat chappati, jaggary or hot chillies prepared for the day. Many women, particularly working women, grumbled that as soon as eatables were prepared or bought they were eaten up by the children; jaggary and sugar were also not spared. Parents frequently gave money to children to buy eatables from nearby petty shops. The amount so given to children came to a rupee a day. The practice of giving money to children was much more prevalent with earning women whether they were *Vagharis, Golas, Rabaris* or *Khalas.*

Children did not get any special nutritive food. They ate what adults ate. Only when the child was sick, care was taken to give him or her freshly prepared, soft, light food like *cunjee* (broth).

EDUCATION OF CHILDREN

All the boys and majority of the girls were enrolled in the public school. A metropolis had this benefit. In the sample interviewees, 57 per cent of the families had boys of school-going age and all the boys were enrolled in the school, not exactly at the end of the fifth year but around that age. In 43.8 per cent of families they were studying in a primary school, and in 5.3 per cent families they were in the secondary school. In 7.7 per cent families, in the 5–12 years age group, some of the boys had dropped out of school after just three to four years of schooling. Community-wise differences were considerable. Most boys of this age belonging to the *Rabari, Gola, Khalas,* high artisan and 'other' castes were in school, while those from some families belonging to the *Thakardas* (11.1 per cent), *Vagharis* (7.1 per cent) and low artisan castes (20.0 per cent) had dropped out. Boys who continued to study in the secondary school belonged to the *Thakarda, Khalas* and low artisan caste families.

At all levels, fewer number of girls than boys were enrolled in the school or continued their education. In the families having girls of school going age, more than one-third of them had never sent their girls to school. In slightly more than half the number of families, most girls had some primary education of two or three years or were studying in the primary school. Only in 7.1 per cent families did girls continue education upto the secondary school.

All the girls of schoolgoing age in the *Gola, Khalas,* high and low artisan caste families went to school, while among the *Rabaris* only half went to school; among the *Thakardas* it was about two-thirds. The *Vagharis* girls going to school accounted for less than one-fourth of the total number of girls in this caste. Girls in the

5–12 age group continued education in secondary school only among the *Thakardas, Khalas* and low artisan castes. The highest proportion was among *Khalas*, being cent per cent.

Mother's education appeared to influence the family's decision to send their daughters to school. The proportion of girls going to school from among those whose mothers went out to work were also higher. Girls enrolled in the school left it before completing primary education; they had only a couple of years of schooling. Of the 20 per cent girls studying in the secondary school, most were to drop out before completing secondary education. Only one woman of the lower artisan caste had determined to educate her daughter upto the secondary school level.

CONCERN FOR BOYS' EDUCATION

The families were acutely concerned about the education of their boys and wanted to give them as much education as the boys were ready for. Boys were not just enrolled, they were coaxed to go to school, to do school home work, rewarded with money when they went to school regularly or passed examinations and were severely punished when they played truant and did not go to school. The father would go to the school to enquire about his son's progress in school. Many parents told me during the interview that they told the teachers to teach the child and make him clever and to beat him if necessary to make him do his lessons. Some parents expressed indignation that even when their boys went to school for many years, they could not read and write, and that teachers in the public school did not teach well.

A few families belonging to the *Rabari, Vaghari*, high artisan and *Thakarda* castes sent their boys to private 'good' schools or to boarding schools run by teachers known to them. A few sent them to tuition classes, to help their boys do well in the examinations. One *Vaghari* family sent their boy to an English medium school with the hope that after completing secondary education, the boy could get a good job. The family had a tradition of education and both parents were literate.

Boys, not burdened with household duties or any earning activity, were forced to continue their education. School going boys were given a hero's treatment in the family and kept fully free for study. In spite of all this, 'drop out' was a serious problem which disturbed the parents. Most parents could not personally take interest in and assist their boys in their studies. All that they could do and did was to persistently tell them to 'study'. Perhaps this created a revulsion for school and studies among the boys particularly when there was no favourable environment, no concrete assistance in studies, but a lot of temptations and distraction in the neighbourhood. The school also could not motivate or sustain the interest of boys in their studies.

NO SUCH CONCERN FOR GIRLS' EDUCATION

Compared to boys, the families showed far less concern about the education of girls. For them, the goal of a girl's education was limited to functional literacy. They wanted them to be able to read and write. Being in the city they regarded literacy as useful—it enabled the girls to read numbers and routes off the public transport buses and read sign boards. It equipped them to read and write letters—a useful skill when girls went away to their in-laws' house after marriage. A girl's education was thus narrowly conceived. It did not include her personal development or social mobility or the acquisition of vocational skills. Only one family expected their girl to become a school teacher. Some women did not want to spend on girls' education, as the girl would not earn for them—she would leave the house after marriage and belong to the in-law's house. A boy earned for his parents.

Certain fears prevailed among the people about the consequences of a girl's education. Many men and women in the *Rabari* community said that their girls had to work with cowdung, look after cattle, etc; once educated these girls would not like to do this kind of work and they would become unfit members in the community. They cited the example of two educated girls in their community who had given up the community's special style of dress, ornaments, etc., and imitated upper castes in dress, behaviour and life style and, consequently, moved out of the neighbourhood. The families did not want their girls to 'go astray' like the girls in the example. The *Rabari* girls from an early age (around seven-eight) assisted their mothers in cattle care and began some earning activity. Most girls worked as domestic servants, either assisting their mothers or working on their own in other people's homes in the company of other girls in the neighbourhood. They spent the money earned in buying ornaments and dresses for themselves, in preparation for their marriage. During leisure hours the girls did embroidery work. Even if they went to school they invariably dropped out of school within a couple of years, hardly learning to read and write and whatever little was learnt was soon forgotten.

The *Vaghari* families did not believe in much education for girls. They believed that educated girls were not wanted in marriage. When parents and elders arranged the marriage of their sons, they preferred illiterate or a less educated daughter-in-law who would be obedient to them and serve the family. Often, for this reason, they preferred girls brought up in rural areas as brides.

The *Khalas, Golas*, higher and lower artisan caste families who sent girls to school did not want them to study beyond the primary or some secondary levels. They emphatically said that more education would make it difficult to arrange the marriage of their girls. Girls, after all, were to be given away in marriage and they were to work in the domestic sphere; this did not require any high level of education. So even when girls fared well at the school, they were forced to leave the school after a few years. In cases where girls did continue their education upto secondary school, the mothers turned out to be younger and educated at least to some level. Even when girls went to school they were burdened with domestic chores and childcare. Where the mother was in paid work, the girls—e.g., among the *Khalas* and *Rabaris*—had to assist their mothers in the household. They did not get enough time to do their school home-work and remained absent intermittently. Mothers, all the time hammered into the girls that they were to be good housewives and daughters-in-law, and discouraged them from giving more importance to education. The priorities were clearly differentiated between boys and girls. For a girl, work in the home became the main activity; she was allowed to continue in school only if she could combine her studies with her household duties. For girls, training in their double role started right from their childhood. The only concession was to study upto the primary or lower secondary education levels.

Girls in the *Vaghari, Gola, Khalas, Rabari* communities assisted in the economic activity of their mothers, hence they could not sustain interest in school and studies. Irregular attendance, undone school homework (because of demands of household duties), etc., resulted in lagging behind. The school also did not do anything to sustain the girls' motivation for continuing studies, and when they sometimes really did, parents did enough to discourage the girls. Eventually most girls dropped out from the school without learning to read and write or getting any skill that could help them in earning or starting 'new' types of economic activities. It is no wonder that their attitudes remained tradition bound.

DIFFERENTIAL TREATMENT

During pre-school age, both the boys as well as girls were given equal care and attention. However, the differential treatment began by about the age of six onwards. Occasions for reward were different for both of them. Girls were rewarded when they did more work in the household or looked after the younger siblings; while boys were rewarded when they fared well at school.

Boys and girls in the school going age group were treated differently for they were to be moulded differently as men and women. Girls were not allowed to roam about alone; they were supervised and kept under control. They played or sat and gossipped in the immediate neighbourhood and only in the company of other girls.

Boys roamed about, moved far and wide in the company of other boys and played outdoor games. They rarely assisted their parents in the home. They did an errand or two or brought something from the nearby market. In the family they ordered their sisters to serve them, which often the latter resented in the beginning but in the end accepted. Boys had to be brave men, to cultivate manly qualities, while girls had to cultivate feminine qualities of meekness, docility, servitude, obedience, and adaptability, and be efficient housewives and dutiful daughters-in-law. So when girls raised their voice or behaved adamantly, they were punished and by ten years of age they were strictly supervised.

Teenage Boys

About 40 per cent of the sample families had teenage boys in the family. In nearly half of these families teenage unmarried boys had some primary or secondary education and left the school; in the other half of the families, they continued studies in primary or secondary schools. It was observed that in nearly two-thirds of the families with teenage unmarried boys, the boys had studied upto the primary level, while in nearly a third of the families, they had studied upto the secondary level. Community-wise differences were significant. Nearly half of the *Rabari* boys, two-thirds of the high artisan caste boys, and one-third of *Thakarda* and *Gola* boys had studied upto the secondary level while only 15 per cent boys in the *Vaghari* families had done so. At the time of the study, teenage unmarried boys in 26.9 per cent families were studying in the school, another 12.4 per cent were also studying while earning side-by-side. In 60.2 per cent families, boys were in search of some earning activity, or intermittently doing petty paid work as and when available. On reaching teenage, only a minority of boys, who fared well at school and in passing examinations, continued their education confining themselves to school and studies. Most other boys were on the look out for some earning activity. However, it was not easy to find paid work. Boys whose parents were engaged in self-employment or petty business (such as, trade in used cans, plastic containers, waste paper, old clothes, or selling vegetables) did not want to be in that occupation, regarding these occupations as below the status of an educated person. They expected class IV jobs in the government or other institutions. On the one hand, many boys left school as they had lost interest in school and failed at the examinations. On the other hand, they did not find paid work. So they just wandered about. Many boys did not respect or obey their parents, frequently argued and quarreled with them. Parents felt frustrated in that the boys neither fared well at the school nor got any secure job in the organised sector. They were not ready either to take up the trades and occupations of their fathers. Some boys just roamed about, demanded money from parents and spent it on movies, hotels, cigarettes, *pan*, etc. Some resorted to gambling (for easy money), indulged in petty thefts and deviant behaviour which worried their families. Many parents were concerned about their sons, and were disappointed that they were not studying well enough to finish matriculation. Parents were worried when their sons did not assist their fathers or take up some earning activity. Parents were also anxious about the health of their grown up sons.

In the majority (80 per cent) of the families with grown up boys, parents complained that they had sharp differences with their sons. Differences arose on the need to study properly, selecting appropriate economic activities for them, extravagant spending, loitering, going to the movies, gambling or for their deviant behaviour, such as, theft. There was frustration among both boys and their parents as very few boys got 'good' education or secured jobs in the organised sector. This resulted in differences and conflicts between parents and sons. Adolescence to adulthood was full of disturbances, stresses and strains for the boys.

Nearly half of the sample families (47.8 per cent) expected that their boys should study well and get high status 'good' jobs. However, their expectation turned out to be unrealistic in most cases. 14.6 per cent parents had a realistic appraisal of their situations and expected their boys to earn well, at whatever occupation they chose; 22.6 per cent parents, in their expectations, referred to the personality characteristics of their boys. They expected them to develop into obedient sons, respectful of their parents, to be 'cultured' persons with 'sound' character.

More of the *Gola* (71.4 per cent), *Rabari* (58.3 per cent), *Bhisti* (66.7 per cent), higher artisan (53.8 per cent) and lower artisan (80 per cent) caste families expected their sons to acquire high status jobs. More of the *Vaghari* (25 per cent), *Rabari* (16.7 per cent), high (15.4 per cent), and low (35 per cent) artisan caste parents expected them to earn well in the family occupation.

Teenage Girls

Nearly one-fourth (26.2 per cent) of the sample families had unmarried teenage girls in the household (other sample families did not have any unmarried teenage girls). Married teenage girls behaved as grown up women, in the sense that for them education or training in any economic skill were considered out of question. They behaved as their mothers did—doing domestic work or paid work or they had already left for their in-laws' family on marriage.

In one-third (38.2 per cent) of the families the teenage girls were illiterate, and in another one-third families (35.3 per cent), the girls had studied for a few years in the primary school and then left their studies. Only in 23.4 per cent of such sample families girls had some secondary education. Communitywise differences were significant. All the unmarried teenage girls in the *Gola* and *Khalas* families, three-fourths of the girls in the high artisan castes, and two-thirds in the *Thakarda* castes had some education, while nearly half of the girls in the low artisan, *Vaghari* and *Rabari* communities had some education. Nearly half (55.00 per cent) of the girls with some secondary education continued their studies. In all but one (a low artisan caste) family, mothers were thinking of taking their daughters out of school, as they were planning to get them married. In the other 45 per cent families where girls had received some secondary education they had been already withdrawn from the school.

All the teenage unmarried girls were involved in a lot of domestic work in the household. In slightly more than half of these families (58 per cent) girls were confined to domestic duties only, while in slightly more than one-fourth families (29.4 per cent) girls were also engaged in some earning activity; mostly they either assisted or joined in the economic activity of their mothers.

These girls spent most of their time inside the household in the company of their mothers or with other girls in the immediate neighbourhood. They were never allowed to go out alone. They were constantly under the supervision and control of their mothers and elders. Whenever they went out (mostly for earning) they did so in the company of their mother or other girls from the neighbourhood.

Nearly half (47.5 per cent) of the sample women with unmarried grown up girls in the household, experienced minor conflicts with their grown up girls. All the *Khalas*, most *Thakardas*, half of the *Vaghari, Gola*, low artisan and nearly one-fourth of the high artisan caste families with teenage girls had differences of opinion with them. The women had differences on such issues as manner of doing domestic work of various types. Many girls grumbled about the domestic burden thrust upon them; a few girls resented leaving school or being made to do the economic activity indicated by the mother. However, most girls succumbed to parental pressures and accepted the traditional adult roles expected of them, namely to marry and be housewives and mothers; to confine themselves to domestic duties; or to take up an earning activity within their family and community. Future role expectations for them were clear and in line with traditional values. From early childhood they began to learn these roles by identifying themselves with their mothers. So most girls unwittingly passed from girlhood to womanhood. Right from early girlhood they took to domestic duties, were busy and confined to the household. There were no severe conflicts or teenage disturbances for the girls.

Most parents were anxious to get their grown up daughters married. They concentrated on training them for life, for the in-laws' family. Some mothers were worried about the quarrelsome or adamant nature of their girls. One mother was worried about the health of her daughter for these were perceived as difficulties in getting them married or in settling down in the in-law's family.

Nearly half (47.5 per cent) of the women having unmarried teenage girls in the family said that they tried to satisfy their girls by giving petty things they liked or by satisfying their hobbies (to do embroidery or fancy work). The women considered the opinion of their daughters, on their earning activity or marriage, with respect. However, their opinions were not considered on other important family matters.

Grown up girls (unlike grown up boys) were not consulted in arriving at other important family decisions. Rather, they were perceived as temporary or transient members in the family; the girl's permanent family which gave her a role and status was seen to be her in-law's family. In the sample, all *Khalas*, high and low artisan and other caste families, while most *Vaghari* (84 per cent), *Rabari* (71.5 per cent), and *Thakarda* (45.5 per cent) families did not involve their grown up girls in family decision-making.

The transplantation of women from their parental families to the in-law's family had its all pervasive influences on the nurturance of the girl. All the women expected their daughters to grow as cultured, docile, obedient women, efficient in household work, so that they would be well accepted and adjusted with their in-laws and enhance the prestige of the parents and parental family. Only 10 per cent women expected their daughters to get some education, and only 2.3 per cent expected that they take up a non-traditional job (mostly of a primary teacher) after completing the secondary education. Even these few women did not want to give more than a minimum education to their daughters as it would create difficulties in getting them married.

The families were asked whether they discriminated between their sons and daughters in their treatment to girls in relation to boys in different areas, such as, in giving food, clothing, medicine, education; in play, free movement outside and leisure activities; in entrusting domestic duties and outside household work; in earning activity; in supervision and control; in rewards and punishments; and in bestowing care and affection. Not a single family discriminated between a boy and a girl at the infant or pre-school ages.

Both were given the same type of food, clothing, medicine, care and affection. In a few cases, where there was an only girl or a girl after a number of sons, she was bestowed with more care and affection. In the case of a son after the birth of a number of daughters, he was given extra care and affection in many families.

With respect to children in the schoolgoing (5–19 years) age group, the majority (77.5 per cent) of the families admitted that their treatment of boys and girls was different. This led to discrimination against girls. Boys were given more choice things. It was observed in most families that boys could take or get as much food as they wanted, could more often take the choice food items they like. So no justice prevailed in actual distribution of goods and services in the family. Boys were given money to buy what they liked. In clothes also boys got preferred items more often than girls did. All the boys were enrolled and sent to school and their education was emphasised. They were given better facilities for studies. Even in bestowing love and affection discrimination took place in subtle ways. The extent of such discrimination differed in families belonging to different communities. All the *Gola, Vaghari, Khalas, Bhisti* and low artisan castes, the majority among *Thakardas, Rabaris* and high artisan caste families treated boys and girls in a differential and discriminatory manner, while more among the low artisan castes (50 per cent) and other castes (25 per cent) did not differentiate as much between a boy and a girl.

However, all the families differentiated between a boy and a girl in entrusting duties. Girls were to assist regularly in household chores and in looking after younger children; rarely were boys entrusted with work of this type. Boys were allowed to play freely in the wider neighbourhood, while girls were allowed to move only in the immediate neighbourhood. Girls being busy with household work had much less leisure time than boys. They were under more supervision and control compared to the boys; they were more frequently punished for disobedience, for not doing household work, or not looking after the younger siblings properly, or for running away from work. Boys were rewarded more frequently than girls with money to buy eatables and things they liked.

Teenage boys and girls were given markedly different treatment. Girls were confined to home and to household work. They were all the while with their mothers or other girls in the neighbourhood. They looked forward to marriage and were trained for life in the in-laws' family. Boys were coaxed to study well and failing that they were pressed to take up some earning activity or assist parents in the family economic activity, if any.

In this manner, differential (discriminatory towards girls) socialisation of boys and girls prevailed during childhood and adolescence in all the castes/communities of the sample families. Some differences, however, were noticed. Among *Vaghari* and *Rabari* a smaller proportion of girls were enrolled in the schools and those enrolled left the school within a couple of years. Girls among the *Vaghari, Rabari* and *Khalas* were engaged in the earning activity followed in the family. Girls continued schooling for a longer period among the *Gola, Khalas*, higher and lower artisan castes but they too dropped out when perceived as 'old' enough for marriage. *Thakarda* families not only gave much less education to their girls but confined them much more strictly to the homes. *Gola* and the high artisan caste families also confined their girls strictly to the homes in their concern for enhancing the social status of the family. 'Sanskritisation' or imitation of the life style of higher castes, adversely affected the girls, while paradoxically it opened up more avenues of education and jobs for boys, though they were not realised in practice.

The differential treatment given to girls and boys, springs from their different expected adult roles. Qualities and personality traits expected of a boy and a girl, traditional sex segregated roles, etc., result in harmful effects on the girls, restricting their development, in contravention to the egalitarian values professed by our Constitution.

Daughters and Sons in Rural Bangladesh: Gender Creation from Birth to Adolescence

K.M.A. AZIZ

Rural women in Bangladesh are largely confined to the household. They are mainly responsible for food processing and cooking, collection of fuel and water, child-rearing and house keeping. In performing these tasks their movements are confined to within the household and the closely surrounding area. There is, thus, a prescribed space and a clearly defined allocation of gender-based responsibilities resulting in the social powerlessness of women, even though the contribution of women through their economic activities, to the family resources is considerable. This subordinate position is reinforced through religious beliefs and cultural practices. The pattern of training imparted to a female child in Bangladesh emphasises her subordinate role within the household.

From birth, a female child is received in a different way than is a male child. The birth of a male child is usually celebrated by distribution of sweets, whereas the birth of a female child, by and large is not followed by any such celebrations. In Bangladeshi culture, the distribution of sweets symbolises the expression of happiness. The idea that women are inferior to men is stressed from the very moment a child is born, and is supported by the behaviour patterns prescribed for girls and women (Chaudhury

Acknowledgements: This research was supported by the International Centre for Diarrhoeal Disease Research, Bangladesh (ICDDR,B). ICDDR,B is supported by countries and agencies which share its concern about the impact of diarrhoeal diseases on the developing world. Current donors giving assistance to ICDDR,B include: Australia, Bangladesh, Belgium, Saudi Arabia, Sweden, Switzerland and the United Kingdom.

and Ahmed, 1980 p. 12). According to the Census of 1981, in Bangladesh there were 106.4 males per 100 females. Bangladesh and India follow Pakistan in having the highest male per female sex ratios. The reasons for this are still not clear. It is surmised that under reporting of females and higher female mortality could be plausible causes (Rabhani et. al., 1984). The purpose of this study is to investigate the role of gender in the determination of behaviour patterns for females from infancy to adolescence. In rural Bangladesh, from birth to adolescence the following life stages[1] are usually recognised (Aziz, 1980 p. 388):

LIFE STAGE	AGE IN YEARS
1. Infancy (*sisukal*)	0–5
2. Childhood (*balyakal*)	6–10
3. Pre-adolescence (*kaisorer prarambha*)	11–12
4. Transition to adolescence (*kaisor*)	13–15
5. Adolescence (*nabajauban*)	16–20

The first life stage is considered as a stage of non-reason (*abujh*). In this period children receive close parental attention. The children of this stage play with children of both sexes within the *bari* (homestead) or courtyard.

The second, third, and fourth life stages are considered periods of partial reason termed as the stage of *polapan*. In these stages casual physical contact or *cengrami* is likely to be a part of the behaviour with the opposite sex. This period marks the beginning of sex segregation and of task performance, which increases rapidly, and the continuation of the exclusive parental control of behaviour.

The fifth stage of life is considered as a stage of responsibility. In this period, casual physical contact with members of the opposite sex is considered inappropriate. There is imposition of parental pressure for full time task performance. In this stage attraction towards the opposite sex becomes apparent and social control on sexual behaviour is imposed.

[1] In this study references will be made to the above noted life stages whenever appropriate.

METHODS AND PROCEDURES

This study was conducted as part of a larger study for which the fieldwork was conducted between November 1977 to June 1978. Micro-level field work for this research, based on the in-depth data of an individual's life history, used the approaches of holism. Such detailed social anthropological studies are much needed to complement large scale KAP surveys because, although the latter frequently show statistically significant associations between variables, these surveys can rarely go further in explaining gender relationships. Nor can the KAP surveys suggest new types of data which should be collected to throw light on the central problem of gender differentiation in behavioural patterns.

A general purposive sampling was utilized, wherein thirty-two males and thirty-three females were selected so as to roughly represent the higher, middle and low income groups.

The respondents belonged to Muslim households and depended mainly on agricultural landholdings or agricultural labour without landownership. The respondents with specified characteristics came from 5 contiguous villages covering about 5 square miles of the Matlab *Upazilla*[2] in the Comilla district of Bangladesh In addition to having specific social and demographic backgrounds, each one of the respondents was required to be capable of articulation and willing to participate in the interview. During the interview mostly private and personal information was sought. As a result, only the willing respondents capable of expressing themselves were chosen for the interview.

In this study the use of open-ended inquiries ensured the accuracy and validity of the respondents' answers. The data gathered through such inquiries could not have been collected through any other pre-set alternative mode for replies. Notes were taken in the presence of the respondents about what they considered to be important in their lives. Potentially confounding variables, such as, the right ages at marriages, proportion of children living to those born alive, etc., are ignored in the selection of respondents. This interview was limited to women in the peak of childbearing age belonging to the age group of 20 to 29 years. The males interviewed were between 30 to 39 years of age.

[2] An *Upazilla* is an administrative unit of approximately 130 square miles.

I lived in the study area of Matlab and its neighbouring zones for over a decade, and had the opportunity to directly experience the everyday life style of the people I observed. During my frequent visits to the houses of the study population, I was viewed by many of them as one of their fictive kin. As a result, I had free entry into the homestead courtyards where I had the opportunity to make many observations on their daily activities. I interviewed the male respondents while a trained female assistant with a background in social sciences and experience of fieldwork interviewed the female respondents.

Privacy was essential in most parts of the in-depth individual interviews related to the topic of investigation—gender construction. The interviewer quietly suggested this need for privacy to the respondents of both sexes, and, in the case of female respondents, also to the husband and the household head.

The field data obtained from the respondents were compiled by assigning reference numbers to the forms of direct quotations and paraphrasings. At the end of every following quotation, the frequency of the response along with the respondent's sex and social class are recorded. For example, particular statements made by 4, 3, and 5 males always appears in the sequences of high, middle and low social classes while the absence of a respondent belonging to a particular class is indicated by a zero. The male respondents are indicated by the capital letter M and female respondents by the capital letter F. When there was no respondent of a particular sex then the capital letter signifying that sex did not appear at all.

RESPONSES AND COMMENTS

In this study, 'sex' (*linga*) refers to the biological aspects of a person, such as, his or her anatomical and physiological structure. In my discussion, the word 'gender' indicates the psychological orientation of the individual with respect to feelings of masculinity and femininity. Conceptions of masculine and feminine behaviour and emotions are imbued in individuals from their infancy. These conceptions are transmitted through the roles that people learn in their gender status as males or females.

Mothers in the study area clothed their female children earlier than the male children. Fifteen male respondents expressed the need to clothe a female child earlier than a male child and nineteen of the female respondents expressed the same need. The male-female differences in the perception of such a need were most prominent in the middle class, where six males and eight females felt likewise. In the words of the respondents, 'a female child has to be dressed earlier than a male child. The exposure of the sex organ of a female baby is more shameful than exposure of the sex organ of the male child' (M: 5, 6, 4; F: 6, 8, 5).

A father cannot show affection for his daughter by touching her body after she is 8 or 10 years old; then both the father and the daughter feel ashamed to come close to each other. The father can always caress his son. The mother cannot caress her son by touching his body or drawing him close to herself after he reaches 10 to 12 years of age for this causes both the mother and the son to feel ashamed. The mother can always caress her daughter. There is no similarity between the sex organ of the mother and her son, and of the father and his daughter. (M: 7, 6, 5; F: 6, 7, 8)

'Evil thoughts creep in the minds of sexually mature males,' the respondents said, 'when they see the uncovered female organ and they may imagine about the female organ of a sexually mature girl (F: 2, 1, 1). The mother will be criticised if she does not keep her daughter properly clothed' (M: 6, 5, 3; F: 7, 5, 8).
According to some of the interviewees;

A female matures several years earlier than a male. She should have a dress (*jama*) for the upper part of her body when she reaches the age of 5 to 7 years. When a girl becomes 8 or 10 years old, then she should wear a 'scarf' (*ornal*) to cover her breasts. The girls have to wear this scarf over dresses to keep their breasts covered from the male eyes. (M: 4, 6, 7; F: 5, 6, 8)

'If sexually mature males see developed breasts of a young girl, then they may say, "she has become a *mal*" (fit for sexual enjoyment)' (M: 1, 0, 0; F: 0, 1, 0). 'A girl develops rapidly after the attainment of menarche. During this time a girl even from a poor family wears a sari and a blouse' (M: 2, 0, 3; F: 4, 2, 1).
Girls, in the Matlab area, are categorised as *auisya* or *amuinya*

depending on the nature of the growth of their body. *Aus* and *aman* are two varieties of paddy which are sown at the same time but the *aus* is ready for harvest within three months, whereas the *aman* takes six. The *auisya* girl reaches the bud stage, marked by the rounding of the hips and the development of the breasts, earlier than the *amuinya* girl. Upon reaching this stage of maturation, however, both types of girls must wear saris to keep their bodies and heads covered. It is regarded as an act of sin if a young woman moves without having proper covering on her body. Such a sin is not to be pardoned.

If a female infant remains unclothed, the mother, the elder sister or any other female guardian might tell her that if she remains naked, her vagina might be taken away by a madman, or some insects or worms might enter it. These practices indicate the social concern for the protection of the vagina more than for the male sex organ. With the objective of 'protection' from sexual contact, females are often kept confined within the homestead. Symbolic of this confinement are the names of some females who were sometimes named after pet birds. On the other hand, males are often given names connoting qualities of courage and leadership.

As the female child's breasts and hips develop, the requirements of her dress gradually become more strict. Four male and six female respondents of the study area made statements on such requirements, which might have originated from both social and religious sources. Commentary on the Qur'an by Ali (Trans. 1938 p. 904) indicates:

> The rule of modesty applies to men as well as women. A brazen stare by a man at a woman (or even at a man) is a breach of refined manner. Where sex is concerned, modesty is not only 'good form', it is not only to guard the weaker sex, but also to guard the spiritual good of the stronger sex. The need for modesty is the same in both men and women. But on account of the differentiation of the sexes in nature, temperaments, and social life, a greater amount of privacy is required for women than for men, especially in the matter of dress and uncovering of the bosom.

It was observed that women were considered suitable for domestic duties only, whereas men were considered suitable mainly for duties outside the domestic circle. The males, in most cases, did not permit female participation in productive activities outside the homestead. Similarly, the females did not expect any assistance from males in most of the domestic activities. In some exceptional cases, and only on rare occasions, some males of particular kin categories, such as, the older sister's husband or his young brothers, the older brother's wife's brothers and the paternal or maternal grandfather are asked by the female kin members to cook. Cooking done by these males served as a lively topic for jokes.

While working in the field, men wear scanty clothing which is convenient for the performance of their duties; they work on dry land as well as in submerged areas. Women, therefore, cannot participate in such work as a result of the compulsory dress code, requiring them to cover most of their bodies.

Since they perform only household duties, which means mainly attending to the personal needs of their husbands and children, women in the study area earn nothing. However, the performance of these tasks helps her sons become earners, and keeps her husband fit for earning. But the wife is not usually allowed by her husband to take up assignments outside the homestead, particularly in the field and, thus, she does not have any opportunity to become an earning member of the community. She usually has no control over the earnings of her husband and son.

The bride performs all the domestic chores in her husband's house. In addition to cooking, child rearing, and housekeeping, she usually dries and stores various agricultural products, including paddy. Participation of the bride in these activities brings praise for her efficiency from her in-laws. Her contributions are recognised only through praise. She is not given any controlling authority over her husband's resources within and outside the household. (F: 3, 2, 5)

A female usually looks for power, authority and honour by bearing more children. However, it was observed that some women with few earning children were found to be leading a happy conjugal life. In a few cases, women who could draw resources from their parents to add to the family budget commanded authority within the household.

Following the attainment of sexual maturity, I thought I must take care of all family affairs. I decided that I would marry after I arranged the marriages of my younger sisters. (M: 1, 0, 0)

It becomes difficult for the parents to arrange the marriage of a daughter who remains unmarried for some years after the onset of menarche. After her marriage, a daughter goes to her husband's house and becomes a member of that family. (M: 2, 3, 4; F: 2, 4, 1)

'Following her marriage, a young girl should move with politeness. She should observe *purdah* and keep her head under the veil (*ghomta*)' (M: 6, 8, 9; F: 6, 5, 8). Following marriage, in the absence of her own mother, the bride receives her training about domestic duties and behaviour from her mother-in-law (M: 2, 0, 3; F: 3, 4, 3). While training the bride, the mother-in-law has to be cautious in her own behaviour (M: 6, 8, 5; F: 7, 6, 8). Soon after marriage, if any of the relatives of the groom comes to take the bride to their house for a visit, she can go in the company of her mother-in-law or any other reliable elderly woman when permitted to do so by her husband (M: 3, 2, 5; F: 2, 1, 3).

After the birth of a few children, the restrictions on a woman's movements are relaxed to a large extent and her visits to neighbouring houses are no longer criticised by members of the community (M: 6, 8, 5; F: 3, 5, 6). After obtaining permission from her parents-in-law or husband, a married daughter may visit her own parents, or take care of them temporarily during their illness (M: 5, 6, 4; F: 7, 4, 5). During her visit to any of the relative's houses, the bride must not joke or laugh with young men (F: 2, 1, 3).

All the respondents viewed males as the performers of tasks mainly outside the homestead. When males moved outside the homestead, there was no chance of their losing personal honour. On the other hand, females were viewed exclusively as performers of tasks inside the homestead. It was believed that if the movements of females were not restricted, they might be sexually abused by pleasure-seeking males. Compared to the male, the personal honour of a female was much more easily threatened. Fourteen males and seventeen females said that the female partner in an illicit coitus was subjected to more dishonour than the male partner. Consciousness about the loss of honour was found to be much greater among the high and middle social classes than in the low.

A young man does not risk conception. He may engage in coitus with several pubescent (*sabalika*) females. But a pubescent girl cannot behave this way (M: 6, 3, 4; F: 2, 5, 4). A pubescent girl, in spite of her greater sexual feelings in comparison with a 'sexually mature' (*sabalak*) male, does not engage in illicit coitus because she fears conception. Because a sexually mature male does not risk illicit conception, he does not wait to gratify his sexual desires. (M: 3, 2, 5; F: 5, 6, 4)

If a young man and a pubescent girl have illicit coitus and are detected on the spot, it brings more dishonour to the girl than to the man. Both partners are compelled to appear before the influential members of the community, who punish them. (M: 5, 6, 3; F: 8, 7, 2)

If a pubescent girl engages in illicit coitus and conceives, then she, as well as her parents, will be disgraced before the members of the community. (M: 1, 3, 2; F: 4, 3, 0)

In the study area I observed that sexual purity in a woman was considered to be a virtue. According to a traditional saying, 'chastity is a woman's best ornament,' but the task of defending female virtue lies with the males. A man's honour was related to the sexual purity of his mother, wife, daughter and sister but was not related to his own sexual purity. A virtuous woman, with a sense of shame, strove to avoid the human contacts which might expose her to dishonour. She could not be expected to succeed in protecting her honour without the guardianship of males. It was believed that the manliness of a father, brother or husband must be demonstrated in the defence of the honour of the daughter, sister or wife. Failure to do so resulted in disgrace for the person or persons concerned.

It was observed that the onset of menstruation in the female, irrespective of social class identification, typically produced reactions of anxiety in the minds of the study people. The menstruating female was usually viewed as sick (*sarir kharap*) and impure (*napak*). With its emphasis on the biological role of child bearing and the impurity associated with menstrual and postpartum bleeding, the society kept most females confined within the homestead (*bari*[3]), allowing a small number into the neighbour-hood, and only a few into the (*para*[4]). Twenty-two male res-pondents and seventeen female respondents commented on the need for *purdah* for pubescent girls; a lesser number of females indicated this need. Both sexes in the high and middle classes expressed the need for *purdah* much more frequently than their counterparts in the lower social classes.

A young girl is not allowed to speak loudly and is asked to talk softly and less, and to move politely (M: 4, 6, 3; F: 6, 7, 5). Marriage proposals do not come for a young girl who is not well behaved and polite. (F: 0, 1, 0)

A young girl is often restricted from talking and joking with the sons of her father's younger and elder brothers, with the sons of her father's sisters, and with the sons of her mother's brothers and sisters. (M: 6, 2, 5; F: 7, 5, 6)

A girl is taught compulsory prayers and fasting (F: 2, 3, 5). After menstruation, a girl is asked to observe *purdah* and is instructed to keep her head under a cover (*ghomta*) (M: 9, 8, 5; F: 7, 6, 4). She is kept engaged in domestic chores. She is not allowed to go outside the dwelling alone during the night and if it is necessary for her to go, then she is accompanied by an elderly woman (M: 6, 8, 3; F: 6, 2, 7). Some young men may lie in wait. If they find a girl alone, they may attempt illicit coitus by using force, which will bring disgrace (*Kalangka*) for the girl. (F: 2, 3, 1)

A young girl should keep her movements limited to within the homestead and should not go visiting the neighbouring houses. If she goes to visit neighbours, she may make jokes with young men and may develop an attachment. Members of the com-munity will criticise such intimate contacts. (M: 6, 7, 5; F: 5, 6, 4)

[3] *Bari* means a homestead accommodating one or more households around the same courtyard.
[4] Several *baris* make a neighbourhood or *ati*. Several *atis* make a *para*.

When a girl grows up, her parents should keep her movements under surveillance so that she may not talk with any young man. The parents of a grown-up girl should remain cautious so that any young man from a different family does not visit the homestead frequently. (M: 3, 2, 5; F: 6, 5, 4)

Sometimes restrictions on the movements of young girls impede their higher education. (M: 3, 2, 4; F: 2, 1, 0)

Nine male and seven female respondents said that problems arose if a pubescent girl remained unmarried for some years; delays in marriage sometimes lead to scandalous rumours on the sex life of such girls. The persons who circulated the rumours sometimes included close or distant relatives and neighbours. The spreading of rumours usually occurred as a result of jealousy for achievements in the field of earnings, leadership, etc., by the members of the daughter's family.

One low class and two middle class female respondents said that their husbands did not feel that they had anything to do with child rearing. However, it was observed that a father took care of his children to a certain extent. For example, sometimes he was seen helping the child to bathe, fondling the baby, feeding it or taking it on his lap. Eighty-five per cent of the child respondents in the study area reported that their mothers provided most of their care and only 8 per cent reported that their fathers provided it.

'A wife takes care of her parents-in-law; by offering personal services to them, she can earn her husband's favour. By bearing children, she satisfies both her husband and parents-in-law' (M: 4, 5, 3; F: 6, 2, 7). 'If a couple fails to have any offspring, then the wife is criticised for lacking the capacity to bear a child' (F: 2, 3, 2).

'The major responsibility of child rearing lies with the wife. The husband does not feel that he has anything to do with child rearing' (F: 0, 2, 1).

'A woman's health may deteriorate as a result of frequent childbirth. Consequently, the husband may develop an aversion to her and, as a result, may take a second wife' (M: 3, 2, 5; F: 5, 6, 8).

'A wife does not initiate divorce if she is childless because of her husband's infertility. If infertility is found in the wife, then the husband might take a second wife (M: 3, 2, 4; F: 5, 3, 2). If a couple remains childless because of the wife's infertility, the husband and other members of the family may, in some cases, initiate divorce' (M: 2, 3, 4; F: 4, 3, 5).

In the study area, significant differences were observed in the expression of parental affection. Avoidance of physical contact by the parent with a child of the opposite sex who had crossed the childhood (balyakal) period occurred much before the commencement of any physiological changes associated with sexual maturation. This practice might have developed as a result of the influence of religious instruction and social traditions.

Sleeping arrangements within the study area indicated that children over nine years of age were no longer considered suitable to share a bed with either of their parents. Forty-three per cent of the child respondents between six to nine years of age reported that they shared beds with both their parents. Neither boys nor girls over nine years old, however, slept with their parents.

While sex identification is determined at birth, the formation of gender identity is a much longer process. A male or female child is socialised or taught to think, feel and act in ways considered morally and socially appropriate and desirable for his or her sex.

In the study area, the male was generally viewed as an individual having a penis, and the female as an individual having a vagina. The vagina, however, was equated with the qualities of a bhodai (fool); the word bhodai is derived from the term bhoda (vagina). From this analogy, it was evident that females were usually viewed as foolish or lacking in common sense. When a fool was identified among males, he was sometimes referred to as a bhodai, or unfit to have a penis, if his foolish act was of a grave nature.

Women were frequently reluctant to make any statement on matters relating to property to anyone other than their husbands or fathers. This reluctance probably originated from the feeling that they 'lacked in common sense,' which they needed to retain property rights. This 'lack of common sense' among the women might have sprung from the immobility which accompanied an adherence to purdah and which resulted in widespread ignorance and inexperience in property matters.

Parker and Parker (1979 p. 298), quoting recent reviews by Money and Ehrhardt (1972), showed that the human infant was born with behavioural potentials or propensities which differed according to sex and which were, of course, subjected to the vicissitudes of the socialisation process as the infant grew up. Male-female differences based on biology, which were seen to prevail in the study area, might support Freud's theories of psychosexual development (1965–1966 pp. 248–258, 225–243, 112–135). Freud had noted that the female anatomy (the reproductive structures generally and the lack of a penis in particular) resulted in female penis envy, passivity, masochism, and a weaker superego. As a consequence of these reproductive structures, it was believed that women were characterised by other related traits, such as, lesser capacity for impartial judgement and weaker social interests. In the study area, it was commonly believed that the male was more intelligent than the female; the father always wielded power and authority in the family. It was his accepted responsibility to protect his family from physical danger, to provide food and at least minimal comforts. Against such a strong background of male authority in the study area, females generally viewed the male sex organ as a better possession than their own.

In fact it is not possible to prove one sex superior to the other if the categories of measurements are not listed. If superiority is measured by body size, phallic dimensions, skill in climbing trees or boat rowing or running, fatherliness, or production of sperm, females are unambiguously inferior and the differences can be measured. Likewise, if superiority is measured by the size of the bosom, gestational capacity, motherliness, capacity to ovulate, or protectiveness of children, women have the greater edge. In the middle lie innumerable skills in which neither men nor women inherently excel.

Possibly, with the increase in education and urbanisation, the sex stereotypes so prevalent in the society within as well as outside the study area will become less rigid.

PROCESS OF SOCIALISATION CORRESPONDING TO LIFE STAGE DURING BIRTH TO ADOLESCENCE

The people in the study area viewed the life of an individual from birth to adolescence in 5 stages. Infancy, or *sisukal*—which

Erikson (1977 pp. 222–245) divided into 3 separate stages—comprised of a single stage in which the baby remained dependent on its mother. A mother usually breastfed her infant for an average period of 30 months (Huffman *et al.*, 1980 p. 144), thus prolonging its period of dependency.

In order to survive and to develop, an infant must learn to distinguish between imagination and reality, and to interact with other people in the vicinity. If a mother remains overly close to her baby, such interaction might be delayed. Sosa *et al.*, (1976 pp. 179–180) observe:

> The safety, growth and health of the human infant largely depends on the strength of the attachment of the mother to her infant. Recently there has been intense interest in the processes by which the human mother forms a lasting bond with her newborn infant. Since it is possible that the duration of breast-feeding may depend on the quality of this attachment, these observations are of special interest. This possibility has stimulated investigations on possible relationships between the sensitive period and the initiation and duration of breastfeeding. Several studies strongly suggested that there is a period shortly after birth (the sensitive period) which may be optimal for the development of a mother's affectional bond to her infant.

In our study, it was observed that the strength of this bond was particularly related to the prolonged infancy of the child. As a result of the mother's over-protective attitude, an infant usually failed to discover reality by means of its own actions based on thought and reason. Appropriately enough the stage of infancy was known as the period of 'non-reason' (*abujh*).

In an interesting reversal of life-stage division, the people of Matlab broke down Erikson's (1977 pp. 222–245) single period of latency into 3 separate stages: childhood (*balyakal*); pre-adolescence (*kaisorer prarambha*) and transition to adolescence (*kaisor*). This emphasis on more stages between childhood and adolescence contrasts sharply with Erikson's perception that the stages are more sharply differentiated as between infancy and childhood, rather than between childhood and adolescence; the strict divisions aid their efforts to increase their control during this period of development, when a careless word or action by the child could damage both the parents' and his or her own social standing. From the child's point of view, the divisions signified marked decreases in the level of communication with his or her parents.

The people under study viewed these 3 life stages as a period of partial reason or a period of *polapan*, during which physical contact with members of the opposite sex in play was acceptable. Parental control over children of this age was formally recognised by the members of the community.

Roughly equivalent to Erikson's life stage, adolescence (*nabajauban*) was viewed as a period in which males or females would attain full reason and develop an interest in the opposite sex, and therefore the casual physical contact which was formerly acceptable was now considered inappropriate. Sons usually began to earn money during adolescence, but they were expected to hand over most of their income to their parents to be used at their discretion. According to the findings of Chowdhury *et al.*, (1977 p. 319) the average age for the onset of menarche among the females of the area was 15.8 years, after which time they were usually married off.

CHANGING ASPECTS OF FEMALE STATUS IN BANGLADESH

The aspects of life reflected in the qualitative analysis of this study are undergoing changes. These changes are indicated in the increasing literacy and higher marriage age over time amongst females as revealed through quantitative analyses of the population drawn from the study and its neighbouring and other areas.

Literacy is a useful index of the educational standard of a country. Education is both an indicator and a human factor in social progress. Literacy is the first essential requisite in education, which in turn, is the *sin qua non* to the process of progress. Table 1 presents the 1974 data on reported literacy rates of the study area and its neighbourhood at Matlab by age and sex. Total reported literacy rate is 41.5 per cent for males and 18.5 per cent for females (difference significant, $p < 0.001$). Males have reported a higher literacy rate (7.5 per cent) than females (5.1 per cent) in the age group of 5.9 years (difference significant, $p < 0.05$). Literacy rate among males (50.1 per cent) is more than one and half times higher than that of females (31.7 per cent) in the age group of 10–14 years (difference significant, $p < 0.01$). Male literacy rate

Table 1

Reported Literacy in Matlab by Age and Sex, 1974

Age	Population			Reported Literacy Rate		
	Both	Male	Female	Both	Male	Female
All	11304	5793	5511	30.3	41.5	18.5
5–9	1879	1093	786	6.5	7.5	5.1
10–14	2027	1014	1013	40.9	50.1	31.7
15–24	2448	1250	1198	43.8	57.1	29.9
25–44	2942	1386	1556	30.9	46.9	16.6
45 and above	2008	1050	958	24.6	42.9	4.6

SOURCE: M.S. Islam, G.T. Curlin and K.M.A. Aziz: 'An Estimation of Response Bias of Literacy in a Census of Rural Bangladesh,' (Dhaka, International Centre for Diarrhoeal Disease Research, Bangladesh), *Scientific Report*, No. 21, 1979.

(57.1 per cent) is about two times higher than that of females (29.0 per cent) in the age group of 15–24 years (difference significant, $p<0.001$). The literacy rate for males (46.9 per cent) is about three times higher than that of females (16.6 per cent) in the age group of 25–44 years (difference significant $p<0.001$). Males have reported a literacy rate more than nine times higher (42.9 per cent) than that of females (4.6 per cent) in the age group of 45 years and above (difference significant, $p<0.001$). In the age group of 5–24 years and 25 plus, the reported literacy rate is 38.8 per cent and 45.1 per cent respectively for males (difference significant, $p<0.01$) compared to 24.0 per cent and 12.0 per cent respectively for females (difference significant, $p<0.05$). Thus, it is clear that the discrepancy between male and female literacy rates increases with age. The narrowing of the gap between male and female literacy rates with the decline of age from 45 years and above could be viewed as an achievement towards social status of females. Given increased literacy, women are likely to have more effective participation in decision-making of households.

For Comilla district as a whole, the literacy rates for males were 36.2 per cent in 1961, 34.0 per cent in 1974 and 30.7 per cent in 1981 (Rabbani and Associates, 1984 p. 84). The comparable figures for females were 12.7 per cent in 1961, 14.8 per cent in 1974 and 16.6 per cent in 1981 resulting in a difference of 23.5, 19.2 and 14.1 percentage points for 1961, 1974 and 1981 respectively.

Thus, in 20 years there has been a major reduction in the

disparity between male and female literacy levels. For rural Bangladesh as a whole, the literacy rates for males aged 15 years and above were 34.6 per cent in 1974 and 35.4 per cent in 1981. The comparable figures for females were 12.1 per cent in 1974 and 15.3 per cent in 1981 resulting in a difference of 22.5 and 19.1 percentage points for 1974 and 1981 respectively. Thus in recent years, unlike Comilla district, there has been a small reduction in the disparity between male and female literacy levels. In spite of increased literacy rate amongst females compared to males at the national level since 1961, the former still lag behind. However, the difference in literacy rates has become increasingly narrower for males and females. It is hoped that the difference between male and female literacy rates will be gradually further narrowed with increased opportunities of employment for females outside the homestead and an increased female age at marriage.

Table 2

Mean and Median Age of Females at First Marriage in Matlab, Bangladesh

*(Categories A & B combined)**

Year	n	Mean	Median	Per cent of marriages occurred to women above 19 years old
1966	884	14.7	14.2	3.5
1970	907	15.2	15.0	4.6
1976	2238	16.7	16.5	6.2
1982	1799	17.7	17.0	20.3

* For the explanation of the categories of A and B combined, please refer to: H.A. Begum and A.K.M.A. Chowdhury: 'Recent Changes in the Age of Marriages of Females in Rural Bangladesh,' in paper presented in the 2nd National Population Conference of the Bangladesh Population Association (Dhaka), 1984.

In Table 2 mean and median ages for marriage in the study area and its neighbourhood at Matlab are presented, along with the proportion of first marriages occurring after the age of 19. It was observed that the mean and median age at first marriages in 1966 were 14.7 and 14.2 years respectively; the proportion getting married after the age of 20 in that year was only 3.5 per cent. The estimated mean age of first marriage was 15.2 in 1970, 16.7 in 1976 and 17.7 in 1982. The proportion married after age 20 was 0.20 in 1982 compared to 0.04 in 1966, 0.05 in 1970 and 0.06 in 1976). The data clearly indicates a pattern of a steady increase in age for marriage over time.

Two studies have shown that female education and literacy are greatly responsible for the postponement of marriage which causes reduction in birth rates.

The postponement of marriage to ages beyond 20 tends biologically to reduce births. Sociologically, it gives women time to get a better education, acquire interests unrelated to the family and develop a cautious attitude towards pregnancy (Blake, 1965 p. 132).

The average age at marriage for girls in Uttar Pradesh, Madhya Pradesh and Bihar ranges between 13 and 14. Literacy among women in these states is the lowest in the country, except for Jammu and Kashmir. In Kerala, where literacy is as high as 39.00 per cent, the average age at marriage is 21 years (Chandrasekar 1967).

In the study area we also noticed an increasing realisation that the daughters should be married towards the end of the period of adolescence. This allows for greater opportunity for education and an elaborate training of a daughter from her family of orientation before her marriage. The quantitative data collected clearly showed a raise in the age for marriage and an increasing rate of female literacy. These changes in marriage age and literacy amongst females indicate attainment of greater capability of women to undertake decisions of their own.

REFERENCES

ALI, A. YUSUF, 1938: *The Holy Quran: Text, Translation and Commentary* (Lahore, Shaikh Muhammad Ashraf).

BLAKE, J., 1965: 'World Population Conference, Belgrade,' *United Nations: 132* (New York).

CHANDRASEKAR, S., 1967: 'Should We Raise the Age of Consent?,' in *Illustrated Weekly*, August 13.

CHAUDHURY, R.H. and N.R. AHMED, 1980: *Female Status in Bangladesh* (Dhaka, Bangladesh Institute of Development Studies).

CHOWDHURY, A.K.M.A., L.H. SANDRA, and G.T. CURLIN, 1977: 'Malnutrition, Menarche and Marriage in Rural Bangladesh,' in *Social Biology* Vol. 24, pp. 316–325.

ERIKSON, E.H. 1977: *Childhood and Society* (Progmore, Triad/Paladin).

FREUD, S., 1965–66: 'Some Psychical Consequences of the Anatomical Distinction Between the Sexes,' in James Strachey, ed., *Complete Psychological Works of Sigmund Freud*, Standard Edition (London, Hogarth Press), Vol. XIX, pp. 248–258; 'Female Sexuality,' Vol. XXI, pp. 225–243; and 'Femininity,' Vol. XXII, pp. 112–135.

HUFFMAN, S.L., ET AL., 1980: 'Breast-feeding Patterns in Rural Bangladesh,' in *American Journal of Clinical Nutrition*, Vol. 33, pp. 144–54.

MONEY, J., and A.A. EHRHARDT, 1972: *Man and Woman, Boy and Girl* (Baltimore, Johns Hopkins University Press).

PARKER, S. and H. PARKER, 1979: 'The Myth of Male Superiority: Rise and Demise,' in *American Anthropologist*, Vol. 81, pp. 289–309.

RABBANI, A.K.M.G., ET AL., 1984: *Bangladesh Population Census 1981: Analytical Findings and National Tables* (Dhaka, Bangladesh Bureau of Statistics).

SOSA, R. and J.H. KENNELL, 1976: 'The Effect of Early Mother Infant Contact on Breast-Feeding, Infection and Growth,' in *Breast-feeding and the Mother, Ciba Foundation Symposium* (Amsterdam, Elsevier) Vol. 45, pp. 179–93.

Seclusion of Women and the Structure of Caste

KAMALA GANESH

Seclusion of women or *purdah* has familiar associations with Islam and is found in various forms in many traditional cultures of Asia, including parts of Hindu India. The spontaneous evincement of horror at the 'evils of *purdah*' need only be counterposed to the notion of the exotic East—and the role of *purdah* in compounding the Eastern mystique—to make evident that neither viewpoint has contributed to an understanding of the phenomenon of *purdah*. *Purdah* has many variations. The notions of separate living quarters for women (*zenana*), complete covering of the woman's face and body with an enveloping garment (*burkha/chador*), covering the face (*ghunghat*), separate, curtained seats in public transports, halls, theaters, etc., are perhaps not as common today as in the past. More enduring is the invisible *purdah* that restricts a woman's activities within and without the household and regulates who she can see, talk to, interact with, and what work she can do. These two manifestations of *purdah* are related.

In India, the usual assumption is that veiling is rare in South India. Many high castes in North India do practice *purdah*, but, again, the common assumption is that either this is a defence measure against Muslim rule or due to the demonstration effect of Islam. Both assumptions need modification. Historical and literary data of the pre-Muslim period indicate that among royal and noble families women were secluded. In a number of subcastes in South India, women are still (or till recently were) secluded to a greater or lesser extent. Moreover, the underlying idea has not to do with Islam, but with the structure of caste.

In this paper I present a concrete example from Tamil Nadu of a small subcaste called Kottai Pillaimar, among whom an extreme seclusion of women continues to exist as an accepted and respected institution.[1] The detailed data on the norms of seclusion and the extent of conformity among the Kottai Pillaimar is then juxtaposed with comparative data from other South Indian subcastes and also with the larger cultural context. My main argument is that the seclusion of women among the Kottai Pillaimar and other high castes is a device to control their sexuality, which, in turn, is considered to be crucial to the maintenance of the ritual purity of the caste. Thus the roots of seclusion are seen in the immediate cultural and social organisation rather than in the universals of female subordination. This does not preclude an appreciation of the need for cross-cultural categories in order to reach a fuller understanding of women's roles.

THE ETHNOGRAPHIC CONFLICT

A somewhat detailed ethnographic sketch of the Kottai Pillaimar (singular: Pillai), based on field work done in 1979–81, is necessary here in order to highlight the significance of the seclusion of women.

The Kottai Pillaimar (henceforth KP) are a small high ranking subcaste of Vellalas, the major agricultural caste in Tamil Nadu. They live in a fifteen acre mud-walled fort in the town of Srivaikuntam in the Tirunelveli district. The adjective 'kottai' (Tamil for 'Fort') is attributed to this distinctive mode of residence.

The women of this subcaste never come outside the gates of the fort. They are born within it; they live and die within it. Only after death are they taken out and that too for cremation. Males from outside the subcaste cannot enter the fort, except for specified families of specified subcastes who are permitted entrance on select occasions, for allotted tasks. With these families, the KP are linked in an intricate set of relations that closely resemble the *jajmani* system. The ban on outside males extends even to civic and judicial authorities. According to the senior citizens of the region this seclusion has been strictly adhered to as far as living

---

[1] The material for this paper is drawn from my unpublished Ph.D. thesis, 'The Kottai Pillaimar of Srivaikuntam: A Socio-historical Study,' Bombay University, 1982.

memory extends. The historical data indicates that the impenetrability of the fort is at least a few centuries old. Outside women can freely enter the fort. The KP men are of course free to leave and enter the fort at will.

The KP are endogamous. They strictly limit their marriage alliances to members living within the fort. For this too there is some historical evidence. Till recently, all members of the subcaste lived only in the fort. While subcaste endogamy is a cardinal principle of caste organisation, the very small endogamous circle among the KP (with a population of sixty-six)[2] is believed to have led to a steep decline in population.

However, a span of seventy years may not be sufficient to generalise, especially in view of theoretical developments in the field which indicate that under specific mating, fertility, and mortality patterns, an endogamous population of as low as 50–100 individuals can survive indefinitely (MacCluer & Dyke, 1976). However, endogamy combined with preferential cross-cousin and uncle-niece marriage has led to an exceptionally high rate of inbreeding among the KP.[3]

Descent is matrilineal through exogamous units called *kilais*. Residence is uxorilocal. Inheritance is partially matrilineal: most of the landed property is inherited by sons, but daughters are given some land as dowry in addition to substantial jewellery and other movables. KP descent, residence and inheritance are not typical of vegetarian *Vellalas* in Tirunelveli.

The KP do not have a complete and indigenous explanation for their unusual organisation, nor do they possess any historical records. Their own oral traditions say that they were ministers to the Pandyan kings and had the hereditary right of crowning them. They lived in a fort in Chelugai village (present day Melacheluvanur) in Mudukulattur Taluk, the district of Ramanathapuram. The KP fell out with a Pandyan king over the issue of his succession.

---

[2] In 1911 there were ninety-four persons, in 1932, sixty persons and in 1962, sixty-four persons. See respectively: *Census of India*, 1911, Vol. V, No. XII. Pt. I, Madras, 1912, p. 163; K.N. Krishnaswamy Iyer, *Statistical Appendix Together with a Supplement to the District Gazetteer (1917) for Tirunelvelly District*, Madras, 1934, p. 302; Uma Guha, 'The Fort Dwellers,' *Man in India*, Vol. 45, No. 3, 1965, pp. 228–32.

[3] I calculated the co-efficient of inbreeding for 55 KP for whom detailed data was available. The value was among the highest so far reported. Kamala Ganesh 1982, *op. cit.*, Ch. II.

The quarrel was compounded by the king's illegitimate son (through a low caste woman) who asked for the hand of a KP woman in marriage. The KP migrated to Srivaikuntam, where the local king Korkai Parakrama Pandyan gave them extensive lands to build a settlement and continue with their privileges.[4]

The fort of the KP is not really a fort in the conventional sense. It is a roughly rectangular enclosure about fifteen acres in area. The walls are of mud and are uneven, rising to an average height of six metres, with a thickness of five metres at the base and one metre at the top. Inside, the land is largely barren. Clustered at the centre are thirty-one houses and a seventeenth century temple dedicated to Vishnu. There is no electricity or running water, since the personnel for installing these facilities cannot enter the fort. On two streets just outside the fort, the KP have purchased a number of buildings each known locally as a *cer* (granary). These are used to store grain after harvest and also as offices of the KP men, from where they conduct their business transactions and meet friends. The fort is renovated and the walls replastered every twelve years. The government continues the tradition of an annual grant of Rs. 64/- for this, giving the official stamp of recognition to the fort. The grant is definitely pre-British in origin.

The fort is a prominent land mark in Srivaikuntam, located at its northwest end, a few hundred yards to the east of the Tambraparni river. It is flanked on the east by the Kailasanatha (Siva) temple, a major canonical temple of the region. Just beyond this is a *Saiva matham* (religious seminary) run by a Siva Brahmana group from Tirunelveli and with a recorded history of a few centuries. The local Vishnu temple, an *agamic* temple of the *pancaratra* school, and a major pilgrimage centre for Vaishnava sects, is situated just south of the fort. The four streets that once constituted the *agraharam* (*Brahmin* streets) flank the fort on three sides. On the fourth side lie paddy fields and the local irrigation tank fed by the Tambraparni. Srivaikuntam itself is a *brahmadeya*

---

[4] Based on original sources including temple inscriptions, palm leaf manuscripts of KP land mortgage deeds, archival records of the British period and oral traditions, I have traced the presence of the KP in Srivaikuntam to mid-fifteenth century. By implication, the fort, the jajmani system and the seclusion of women also date to that period. See Kamala Ganesh, 'Brief notes on the Kottai Pillaimar of Srivaikuntam' Paper read at the *Vth International Conference Seminar of Tamil Studies*, Madurai, 1981.

(Brahmin settlement) at least since the thirteenth century (Kaveri, 1979). The location of the fort at the virtual heart of the important Brahmanical institutions of the town, which moreover are/were major land holders, is significant in understanding the KP's social organisation.

Historically, and in the present day, the KP are mainly occupied with agriculture like most other Vellalas in the district and the state. Until recently, the KP were dominant, large-scale non-cultivating owners living solely on inherited land located in Srivaikuntam and five other villages of the *taluk*. These villages are at the tail end of the Tambraparni river valley with an efficient channel and tank irrigation network from the Marudur anicut, a fifteenth century construction. In this traditionally irrigated area, based on double crop paddy cultivation, historically, Brahmins and Vellalas were the land holders and villages were predominantly of the *mirasi* type.[5] Part of the KP's vast land holdings are held individually and the rest is held collectively in a trust. In the past, due to the ideological taboo on manual labour and even direct supervision of agriculture among upper castes, the KP had tenanted out all their lands either on *kattukuttahai* (conventional tenancy) or *peru* (which is, in my assessment, a special form of tenancy) (Ganesh, 1982) thus bringing the KP under the category of non-cultivating land holders. Though a few KP are now going into education-based occupations, land continues to be their main source of income. The organisation of their agriculture has changed only marginally and the relationship with groups who work on their land are still vital for the maintenance of the fort and its institutions.

The KP as a group have also been influential in all public affairs of the region. They were the hereditary custodians of the treasury of the local Siva temple. At the Vishnu and Siva temples they are entitled to temple honours. Some KP have been trustees in the pilgrimage shrines of Alwar Tirunagari and Srivaikuntam. In recent times, the KP have successfully associated themselves in leadership positions with secular and democratic institutions, thus keeping their traditional pre-eminence intact.

While considerable attention has been focused on the KP by

[5] A type of tenure, common in irrigated villages, in which land was held jointly by a lineage or caste.

the popular Press,[6] mainly on account of the unusual residence in a fort and the women's seclusion, beneath virtually all aspects of the visible social organisation lies the ideology of caste. In particular, both the *jajmani* system and the institution of seclusion of women are expressions of this core principle.[7] KP ethnography reveals a combination of the Brahmanical and *Kshatriya* models, giving them a unique position in the ritual hierarchy, simultaneously locking them into a rigid position with little leeway for change.

Nevertheless, the KP are in a process of transition due to a congruence of external circumstances and internal contradictions. It is likely that the fort and its associated institutions may in a few years time break up altogether.

KP WOMEN: DEGREES OF SECLUSION

The general rule of seclusion for all the KP women within the fort and exclusion of outside men from it is not the only restriction on the women's movements, though it is the most prominent one. KP women, on different occasions and at different stages of their lives are secluded to varying extents. So too, the families permitted entry (FPE) who come in are given differential access.

[6] The write-up titled, 'Women of Hindu Sect in India live out their lives behind walls of 20 acre compound,' in *New York Times*, Nov. 8, 1971, is typical. Others include *Femina*, July 2–15, 1976 and *Times of India*, Bombay, December 19, 1979. For more scholarly but brief accounts see:

1 Boyle, J.A., 1874: 'Notes on Castes in Southern India,' in *Indian Antiquary*, Vol. 3, pp. 287–289.
2 Pate, H.R., 1917: *Madras District Gazetteers: Tinnevelly*, Vol. I, Madras, pp. 438–440.
3 Thurston, Edgar, 1975: *Castes and Tribes of Southern India*, Vol. V, pp. 33, (first published 1909).
4 Ahmad, S.H., and I. Verghese, 1963: A Note on the Kottai Pillaimars—The Fort Dwellers of Srivaikuntam, Tirunelveli District,' in *Vanyajati*, Vol. 11, pp. 126–31.

[7] The KP have *jajmani* relations with specified families of sixteen subcastes (including carpenters, blacksmiths, stonesmiths, goldsmiths, Brahmin priests, non-Brahmin priests, potters, brick-layers, barbers, washermen, untouchable labourers and so on).

These FPE families (FPE: Families Permitted Entry) enter the fort for performing select ritual and secular tasks for the KP. The FPE also work as tenants and labourers on KP fields. They are generally paid during harvest and grain. The complex inter-relationship between the KP and FPE has the important function of making possible the survival of the fort and the seclusion of women.

See Kamala Ganesh, *op. cit.*, 1982, Chapters IV & V.

Birth to Puberty

Pre-pubertal girls are free to go anywhere within the fort. They may go to each other's house, the fort's Vishnu temple, or play in the vast grounds upto the gates. However, in practice, girls do not venture very far and are mostly at home or playing in the vacant plots adjoining their houses. For minor injuries, young girls are taken right upto the east doorway where treatment may be given by local (male) specialists with herbal remedies. In the past, young girls used to get their earlobes pierced and stretched to enable them to wear *pambadam* (heavy ear ring). This was done at the east doorway, by males of the Koravar subcaste, who were not permitted entry into the fort.

Puberty

The onset of menstruation marks a radical change in the rules of seclusion. Following her emergence from the period of ritual pollution and consequent seclusion, the girl is escorted by Kottaccis (Kottamar women. Kottamar are the bricklayers permitted entry into the fort) for a last visit to the fort's Vishnu temple and to the houses of the other KP, where she is blessed by the elders. From this time upto the time of marriage, the girl is completely confined to her house. Even standing on its threshold is not permitted. During the *cadangu* or ceremonies performed on the sixteenth day after puberty, the girl remains inside the house and the required rites are performed on her behalf by her father in the presence of the Brahmin priest. After puberty, the girl stops conversing with unmarried male relatives, except for classificatory brothers. If bachelor male relatives visit her house, she moves into an inner room out of their sight. The total conformity to these rules cannot be over-emphasised. Even in 1979, when some families had already left the fort, those living inside continued to observe the rules faithfully.

Marriage

On the day of the wedding, the bride steps out of the threshold of her house for the first time after puberty and enters the marriage *pandal.*

In the past, the bride would not walk to the *pandal* but would be carried by two Kotttaccis. She would sit through the ceremony with arms crossed across her breasts, with a betel leaf held in each palm to cover her eyes. This was feasible in the days of early marriage. But with brides getting older and heavier, this practice was given up. In the past, the officiating priest could not see the brides and would conduct the rites from behind a screen. Even upto a few years ago, in the invitation cards the KP sent to their numerous friends outside the fort, the bride was not mentioned by name but as somebody's daughter.[8]

Following marriage, some of the restrictions of puberty are removed. However, women still cannot visit the temple or any other area in the fort. They can see and talk to all the KP men. They can visit each other's houses, but in actual practice such visits are rare. The rule of uxorilocal residence means that on marriage a woman does not move into her husband's household. Her visits are confined to formal occasions. The only occasion when a woman moves out of her house for any length of time is when her younger sister gets married. She then shifts with her husband and children to a new house given by her father.

Widowhood

This marks a period of drastic change in a woman's life, where once again she withdraws into the threshold of her house, this time permanently. Following her husband's death, the widow is secluded for sixteen days in a dark room into which even her close male relatives including her sons will not enter. Her only companions during this period is the family Kottacci and occasional female relatives. The removal of the widow's *tali* and other symbols of auspiciousness is done by the family Kottaccis. Even after the sixteen days of formal mourning, the widow is expected to keep strict seclusion within one room of the house for a year. For the rest of her life she does not leave the threshold of her house. A widowed woman ceases to wear vermilion on her forehead, she removes all her jewellery and wears only white cotton saris. In the past, she would remove her blouse too; currently, this custom is observed only for the first year of widowhood. A widow ceases to

---

[8] No outside males can attend the marriage, but a big reception is held outside the next day at which the bride is not present.

oil and comb her hair. She gives up eating betel leaf and renounces the use of mattresses and pillows. She is expected to withdraw from participation in household activities, particularly those connected with auspicious events. Though there are no explicit dietary restrictions, she is expected to eat less, avoid passion-arousing food, observe elaborate fasts, and spend her time in quiet reflection.

These rules of widowhood are not uncommon among upper caste Hindus, though the severity of observance varies. Among the KP, the rules of seclusion of widows are exceptionally severe, and they are also meticulously followed in practice.[9]

The extreme seclusion of the widow is sometimes adopted by other women who have suffered tragedies. One woman whose married daughter died during childbirth was so affected with grief that she removed all her jewellery except her *tali*, exchanged her expensive clothing for rough cotton saris, and went into severe seclusion. She refused to participate in the normal household routine. An elderly widow who lost her son during the course of my field work was so affected that she retired to an inner room and withdrew from all household activities. For this reason, I was unable to see her, much less interview her.

Death

It is only after death that a KP woman can leave the fort. Even then, attempts are made to preserve her lifelong seclusion. The corpse of a woman is stitched into cloth sacks—white for a widow and red for others—by the family Kottacci and placed on a bier by her male relatives. The Kottamar carry the bier out via the north-east gate which is normally kept closed, and taken to a separate and secluded cremation ground adjoining the local irrigation tank. This way the funeral procession avoids going through the main streets. Appropriate rites are performed by the Kottamar after

---

[9] During my field work, I came across several startling results of such literal interpretation of the rules of seclusion. In one case, four widowed sisters and their widowed mother stayed in adjacent houses but had not seen each other for several years, since, as widows, they would not step out of their thresholds. In another case, a recently widowed woman withdrew from all household activity, participating neither in the ceremony nor in the preparatory activities of her daughter's wedding.

which they leave the place. The body is then cremated in the presence of a few close male relatives.

Seclusion on Other Occasions

Menstruation and child birth are occasions for strict seclusion of women. This is partly explained by the Hindu beliefs on the purity-pollution complex specially those characteristic of the higher castes, as is discussed later. For three days during the menstruation and nine days following childbirth, a KP woman does not take part in the normal household activity including cooking and worship. In addition, any kind of contact with the menstruating woman and with articles touched by her are considered to be polluting. She is required to withdraw into a five feet square portion of the front room where food is served separately to her. She may if necessary move out of this area, but only circumspectly and minimally. It is important to note that the restriction is not just negative in that women avoid contact with others, but is a positive restriction in which she shrinks from all interaction, eats less and carefully, talks less and so forth. She is integrated into the normal routine after a ritual bath. In the case of the new mother, the seclusion is for nine days but participation in worship is permitted only after forty days.

Restrictions on Interaction with the Families Permitted Entry(FPE)

The rules governing entrance of various FPE into the fort on specific occasions, for particular tasks and upto different points have been described elsewhere. The KP women may not see some FPE at all, while they may see but not talk to other FPE. With yet others, they may talk but not at length. The *Asaris* (artisans) who enter KP houses for repair work are always escorted by Kottamar. who announce their presence. The women then withdraw to an inner room. The Kottamar, who have free movement in the fort, will not see the KP women directly. Their conversation is limited to the functional, i.e., delivering messages or taking instructions. The *Vaittiyar* (healer) treats the women from behind a screen and the Brahmin priest officiates similarly. It is only the *Ulavar* (untouchable agricultural labourers) who are allowed free access with no restrictions.

ANALYSIS

With this data on the variations in the rules of seclusion of the KP women at different stages of their (reproductive) life, we are in a better position to grasp the underlying principle.

The present approach, as stated earlier, does not start with a generalised concept of women's status, but considers its different indicators separately, for these may not be correlated nor be based on the same principle.[10] Thus, in the context of the KP, the present approach is to look for the origins of a particular indicator like seclusion in the cultural and social organisation of the given society.

The KP data clearly shows an escalation of seclusion rules during the two stages of a woman's life: between puberty and marriage, and between widowhood and death. These are liminal periods when her sexuality is not harnessed, i.e., she is without a husband. Note that a married woman also has to observe certain rules of seclusion but these are relatively few, and the pre-pubertal girl, whose sexuality is still latent, is least restricted. Restrictions on a woman's conversing and interacting with men apply not so much to her own caste-fellows as to the families from different subcastes who enter the fort. Note also that all *Ulavar* are permitted entry; they can freely see and converse with the women, in contrast with the other FPE, among whom only certain families are permitted entry, and that too in a limited way. The implication is inescapable that *Ulavar*, as untouchables, rank so low in the hierarchy that conceptually they are not treated as males at all. In the migration myth of the KP, the tension between the ritually superior KP and the temporally powerful but lower-caste king/chieftain is symbolically expressed by the latter's aspiring for a KP woman's hand. The KP's flight to Srivaikuntam is, again, symbolically to guard their women's purity. The KP women's seclusion is seen both by themselves and by others as an explicit expression of

[10] To quote one study, Whyte's cluster analysis of fifty-two dependent variables of women's status in ninety-three pre-industrial cultures indicates that the pattern of association between the variables is weak. That is to say, the culture in which women's legal status is low may not be the one where their political or economic status is low, and so on. Martin King, Whyte, 1978: *The Status of Women in Pre-Industrial Societies*, (N.J., Princeton UP).

superior status. These facts, taken in conjunction with the general observation that seclusion is not common among lower castes, point to the strong possibility that it has something to do with (1) the sexuality of women; and (2) the ritual status in the traditional hierarchy.

In the light of earlier works it is specifically proposed here that the KP women's seclusion (and its variants all over South India) is an expression of the conceptual concern in a caste-based society with the group ritual status which in turn is seen as dependent on the (sexual) purity of women.

SECLUSION, PURITY AND RITUAL STATUS

The concept of the ritual status of a caste and the intricate rules of purity and pollution governing it have been discussed at length in many other studies. To summarise very briefly, the opposition between purity and impurity is seen to be at the heart of the ideology of caste. The pure is superior to the impure, it is also vulnerable to the latter and has to be kept separate from it. At the same time, it is dependent on the impure for the maintenance of its purity. A state of ritual purity is necessary to approach the supernatural. Any involvement in the biological aspects of life is a source of pollution. Therefore, all human emissions are impure: breath, spittle, nasal mucous, semen, blood, urine, faeces, sweat, etc. So is death as is meat eating. Alcohol is impure since it leads to lack of mental and bodily control. By extension, this logic can be applied even to parts of the body and to inanimate objects. All individuals go through periods of temporary impurity from which they emerge purified through suitable rites. But some groups, such as women and lower castes, are associated with a permanent and hereditary impurity[11] incontrovertible by cleansing actions. The purity level of each caste is transmitted from parent to offspring and is its prized attribute, to be carefully maintained by avoiding contact with impure castes. Two areas of intercaste interaction are

---

[11] Only with this assumption can one make sense of the maze of rules governing removal of pollution, as prescribed in the *dharmasastric* texts and their commentaries. For an analysis, see Orenstein, Henry, 1968: 'Toward a Grammar of Defilement in Hindu Sacred Law' in Milton Singer and Bernard S. Cohn, eds., *Structure and Change in Indian Society* (Chicago: Aldine Publishing Co), pp. 115–32.

considered to be especially sensitive to pollution: (1) the ingestion of food, an intimate biological act. Hence the complex rules regarding cooking, handling of food, and inter-dining, and (2) sexual relations, since the offspring carries the coded ritual status of *both* his parents. An offspring of an intercaste marriage endangers the ritual status of *all* the members of the superior caste. Hence appropriate sex and marriage are areas of great anxiety in the Hindu social order.

Somehow, and this is where existing explanations are not entirely satisfactory, the concern with ensuring pure offspring gets tied exclusively to the sexual purity of the women. This is why women's sexuality is hemmed by numerous rules, but men are not similarly restricted. Women are 'literally seen as points of entrance, as "gateways" to the caste system' (Das, 1976). Their inappropriate marriage choices threaten the purity of the entire caste. The Bhagavad Gita as a normative text *par excellence* captures this idea effectively.

> We know what fate falls
> on families broken:
> The rites are forgotten,
> Vice rots the remnant
> Defiling the women
> And from their corruption
> Comes mixing of castes:
> The Curse of confusion . . . .
> (Prabhuvananda & Isherwood, 1947).

The same idea is reflected in *dharmasastric* prescriptions for intercaste marriage, wherein *anuloma* marriage (hypergamy) is recognised, but *pratiloma* marriage (hypogamy) is looked upon as a heinous crime at par with incest. The ostensible reason is that children of an *anuloma* marriage can claim the status of their mother's (lower) caste, whose purity level can thereby only be improved, whereas in a *pratiloma* marriage, the children cannot claim their mother's higher status. By this logic, control over female sexuality becomes crucial, but mainly for upper castes. The higher the caste, the greater is the level of purity, the more vulnerable is it to pollution from lower castes and, hence, the more crucial is the need to ensure proper marriages for the women by controlling their sexuality. Conversely, the lower the caste, the lower its level of purity, the fewer are the possibilities of pollution from inter caste marriages and so the fewer are the restrictions on women's sexual behaviour.[12] Concomitantly, the upper caste male can only enrich the purity level of the group he marries into. Restrictions on his sexuality are therefore few. The fourth component of the paradigm is the lower caste male whose sexuality is a threat to upper caste purity and who has therefore to be institutionally prevented from having sexual access to women. Hence, upper castes resort to a variety of strategies to limit female sexuality. Seclusion is one of them.[13] In such an interpretation, Hindu seclusion would be seen as different in emphasis from say, *purdah* in Islamic societies, though some of the implications are remarkably similar.[14] The veracity of this line of reasoning by empirical data show that traditional disabilities of Indian women—*purdah*, child marriage, sati, taboo on divorce and widow remarriage, etc.—have applied predominantly to upper castes.

Limitations of the argument

Admittedly, the empirical situation governing marriage rules can make sense only by assuming that ritual status depends on

[12] Stereotypes about lower caste women usually portray them as sexually permissive.

[13] In a well-knit series of links, Yalman compares the puberty ceremony for females in some castes in South India and Srilanka with the well known pre-puberty rite (*tali-kettu-kalyanam*) among several sub-castes in Kerala, notably Nayyar and Tiyyar. He sees both as structurally similar. They reflect upper caste anxiety about the correct marriage of its women. The former is a symbolic marriage where the girl's potential spouse's family stake their claim on her sexuality, and the latter is a safeguard in view of the future polyandrous unions. Among Tamil Brahmins, this anxiety is assuaged through pre-puberty, i.e., (eventually infant) marriage. Nambudiri Brahmins whose preoccupation with ritual purity is well known, have neither pre-puberty marriages nor elaborate puberty rites, but the extraordinarily severe seclusion of their women serves the same function of controlling female sexuality. Yalman, Nur, 1963: 'On the Purity of Women in the Castes of Ceylon and Malabar,' in *Journal of the Royal Anthropological Institute of Great Britain and Ireland*, Vol. 93, pp. 25–58.

[14] Based on field work in India and Pakistan, Papanek demonstrates that Muslim *purdah* aims at providing women symbolic shelter from the hostile external world and from their own impulses whereas Hindu seclusion results from seeing women as temptresses whose sexuality poses a danger to ritual purity. This is why the former is far less class-based than the latter. Papanek, Hanna, 1973: 'Purdah: Separate Worlds and Symbolic Shelter,' in *Comparative Studies in Society and History*, Vol. 15, p. 311.

women's sexual purity, not men's. However, there is no satis-factory explanation on *why* this should be so. Caste being a bilateral membership group, there is no inherent reason in its structure as to why a *pratiloma* offspring should upset the purity level of the entire caste any more than an *anuloma* offspring. Yalman suggests that a man can repudiate his offspring while a woman cannot (Yalman, 1963). Another widely cited argument is that sexual relations lead to internal pollution of a woman, whereas a man can be purified by appropriate rites (Stevenson, 1954). These appear to be insufficient explanations, and the following additional factors operate in the creation of the sexual double standard.

Firstly, *pratiloma* is tabooed because it runs contrary to existing social arrangements based on patrilineal descent, patrilocality, and male authority. In a *pratiloma* marriage, the wife cannot live with her natal relatives since her children are of lower ritual status. She could move into her husband's patrilineage but as a member of a superior caste, she would upset the hierarchy of domestic relations based on male dominance and female subordination. Inter-sex relationships are as deeply hierarchised as inter-caste relationships and expressed in a similar language of subordination. A direct conflict between the two is avoided by banning *pratiloma*.

Secondly, by linking seclusion and related institutions solely to the structure of caste, their cross-cultural underpinnings are ignored. In many cultures across the world, a sexual double standard operates. So too, women's proper conduct is seen to reflect group status in many cultures. If *anuloma-pratiloma* was the sole factor governing sex and marriage, then a woman should not be barred from freely marrying, divorcing or remarrying within her own sub-caste. Clearly, there are other structural factors that have transformed the need to ensure group ritual status into a general rule of fidelity and chastity for one individual to the extent of mounting the funeral pyre or permanent seclusion within the threshold of one's home.Thus, an impasse appears to have been reached where one has to take recourse to the universals of female subordination. The caste factor goes far in explaining specific situations like that of the KP, but once the culture-specific rami-fications have been explored fully, it is obvious that cross-cultural categories are needed. Goody's broad contrast between areas of intensive plough agriculture and extensive hoe agriculture and the long chain of variables associated with each, culminating in dowry and positive value attached to women's virginity in the first case, and brideprice and relative sexual freedom for women in the second, furnishes a possible macro-canvas for such an analysis (Goody, 1973). The immediate referent for KP seclusion is the structure of the caste society. At the next level of analysis caste itself has to be linked with other forms of stratification thus, interweaving the universal and the culture-specific.

Cultural Context

The danger of female sexuality is a pervasive cultural theme in the Indian context. This sexuality, with its tremendous negative properties, can be transformed into a positive sacred power if harnessed appropriately through chastity and fidelity. The powers of unleashed female sexuality and its bounded form (chastity) are found as leitmotifs in varied spheres of Hindu thought like classical religious mythology, folklore, art forms, etc. (Wadley, 1974). Das shows how the portrayal of the female principle—Mother Goddess—captures this dichotomy. On the one hand, these goddesses are associated with terrible death, famine, disease, heat, anger and darkness. On the other hand, if propitiated with cooling measures, they are also capable of bestowing fertility and wealth (Das, 1976 p. 137). The supernatural power of a *pativrata*—the popular expression for a chaste woman—is visualised as akin to that of *Rishis* who practice severe austerities. Both epic and folk narratives abound with examples of women who could, through the power of their chastity, retrieve their spouse from the jaws of death (Savitri); curse to death men with evil designs (*Damayanti*); burn the world and stop the motions of the sun and moon (Gandhari); challenge a king's unjust decision and burn the city of Madurai (Kannaki); etc.[15] The belief that the spot where a woman burns herself on her husband's pyre is imbued with supernatural power is a still prevalent one.[16]

The concept of *pativrata* has its Tamil equivalent in the concept of *Karpu*, delineated in classical literature,[17] which continues as a

[15] The first three are heroines of episodes woven into the *Mahabharata*. Kannaki is the heroine of the Sangam period work *Cilappadhiharam*.

[16] For instance, see the report of a sati in Rajasthan in 1980 in *India Today*, October 1–15, 1980, pp. 16–17.

[17] By this we refer to the corpus of Tamil literary works datable roughly to the first to the third centuries A.D. and known as 'Sangam Literature.'

leitmotif even in modern literary works. Hart argues that this (Dravidian) concept of *karpu* is more vigorous and extensive than the Sanskritic counterpart as it connotes more than fidelity encompassing restraint in thought, speech, gestures, demeanour, deportment, and so forth. He also posits, based on examples from Sangam poetry, that the idea of a woman's sexuality harbouring sacred and dangerous power is an indigenous (Dravidian) one that worked its way later into Sanskritic culture.[18] This is of course somewhat speculative but provides a context for viewing the KP seclusion.

It must be stressed that the power of chastity is not just a literary motif. It is a deeply internalised role model for a large proportion of women in contemporary India. Seclusion—symbolic or actual— is one of the most popular attributes of the chaste woman, as summed up in the well-known Tamil phrase, '*padi tanda pattini*'; the chaste woman is one who (is chaste because she) does not step out of her threshold.

Seclusion in South India: Comparative Ethnographic Data

Secondary sources furnish many examples from South India of subcastes which practice seclusion, though not in the sense of veiling the face. Interestingly, these subcastes are recurringly associated with certain features. Within the scope of this paper, a few illustrations should suffice.

For Nambudiri Brahmins of Kerala,[19] traditionally priestly landlords of the highest status, the need to keep scarce land in a limited circle led to an arrangement where only the first son of each family married within the subcaste and inherited the land. The other sons formed hypergamous unions with the matrilineal *Nayar*, and the children would thus belong to the mother's matrilineage. Nambudiri women could not marry outside the subcaste

---

[18] Hart gives examples to show that during menstruation and following child-bi. ', women were believed to be dangerous for men. So too, a widow, especially if young and highborn, held dangerous powers which had to be suppressed by practising severe austerities in dress, diet and style of living. Hart, George L:, 1973: 'Women and the Sacred in Ancient Tamil Nad,' in *Journal of Asian Studies*, Vol. XXXII, pp. 233–50.

[19] For an account of Nambudiris, see Thurston, Edgar, 1909: *Castes and Tribes of Southern India*, Vol. V, pp. 152–220.

since that would amount to *pratiloma*; many of them remained spinsters. Nambudiris practised a very elaborate and strict code of seclusion for women, and meted out extraordinarily severe punishments for sexual transgressions.

In Andhra Pradesh,[20] *Velamas* and *Kammas*, both agricultural castes, claim to have been one endogamous unit. They split as the latter gave up seclusion of women on the grounds that it prevented them from working in the fields. However, one small group among the Kammas readopted seclusion and formed an endogamous unit (*Illuvellani Kammas*). Among the *Velamas*, one group gave up seclusion and again formed an endogamous unit (*Adi Velamas*). Many *Velama* subcastes had close ties with the Vijaynagar kings, as retainers, and military chiefs (e.g., Padma Velamas and Razus). They claim purity of blood, and a few instances of sati have been documented among them. Seclusion of women is, of course, a cherished institution.

Among Tamil castes, both *Karkattar Vellalas* (Arunachalam, 1975) and *Kondaikatti Vellalas* (Barnett, 1970) have much the same profile as the KP: both are non-cultivating land-holders, with a history of service to ruling dynasties. Both are of high status, laying great stress on ritual purity. Predictably, among both the castes the women are strictly secluded, particularly during puberty and widowhood. Even in relatively low ranking subcaste like the *Shanars* who were toddy-tappers in the last century, there appears to have been an internal differentiation: a small group who owned the palm trees, considered themselves superior and did not inter-marry with the others, and sure enough the women practiced strict seclusion (Hardgrave, 1969). Thurston's encyclopaedic 'Castes and Tribes' is strewn with references to old poligar families where women lived in strict seclusion.

The comparative data indicates that seclusion invariably occurs among very high ranking groups who claim it as an index of superiority, and are rigidly endogamous within a small circle. Within a subcaste, a group may practice seclusion, claim superiority, and eventually becomes endogamous. Seclusion is also associated with taboo on productive labour by women and stress on concepts

[20] The following description is based on Thurston, *Ibid*, Vol. 3, pp. 94–106; Vol. 6, p. 251; Vol. 7, pp. 336–342.
See also Chetty, Narahari Gopalakrishnamah, 1886: *Manual of the Kurnool District*, pp. 138–39.

of ritual purity and pollution. Common occupational factors include land ownership and services to kings, zamindars, poligars, etc. Migrant groups often resort to seclusion to retain a distinct identity in a new hostile environment.

POSTSCRIPT

The thrust of this paper has been an analysis of the basis for seclusion of women among the KP and, by extension, other high castes. The important questions of the effects of seclusion and the mechanism of its acceptance have been dealt with elsewhere and are outside the scope of this article. However, a brief note may not be out of place.

By any objective test, the seclusion of the KP women has serious implications for other aspects of their role and status.

For instance, inspite of inheriting considerable dowry in the form of land, house, jewellery, etc., KP women are unable to transact business or control their income and expenditure. Being fort-bound, the women have no part in productive activity, either directly or in a supervisory capacity. In the public domain, they are totally invisible. They are not members of the corporate organisation of the KP formed to deal with common issues and are completely excluded from group decision-making. They are not represented in any of the KP's religious and secular activities in the locality. The women are mainly occupied in supervision of domestic chores, child-rearing and religious activities. Even in the latter, the women play a part only in domestic worship and are not involved in the KP's considerable participation in public religious activities. Domestic authority and decision making are predominantly male, though uxorilocality and the small and organic nature of the community enable women to exert some informal influence.

The KP women are quite articulate about their seclusion, for they have been often asked about it by curious visitors. They have a variety of defensive responses about why they have voluntarily accepted it.

One obvious explanation is that they have no experience of the outside world. The fort encompasses all their kin and affines and the totality of their social relations. Moreover, they do not have effective control over their income and property. Economic coercion and a psychological lack of alternatives are undoubtedly factors of control. However, conformity is extracted in subtler ways.

The norms governing seclusion have been thoroughly internalised by the women, and elevated, along with associated definitions of femininity into a generalised value system. This process rests on two ideological planks. First, even though seclusion is recognised by the women as involving some hardship, it is essentially seen as a positive value associated with *kattuppadu* (discipline), *karpu* (chastity) and *tuymai* (purity). It is seen as a vital element in the KP's superior status and is an important component of the women's self-worth. It is seen both by the KP women and by the local public as conferring on them sacred power. Second, the women do not feel that the seclusion deprives them of anything that other women possess. In practical terms, seclusion means separation of the domestic and public domains, and a segregation of the spheres of activity of men and women. These are perceived as part of the natural order. In spite of the obvious disadvantages of their position, the KP women do not perceive any physical coercion on them. The security arrangements in the fort are minimal, and there is no real way of preventing a woman from leaving or outside males from entering. That this has not happened as far as can be ascertained, bears out the premise that ultimately it is an ideological fort.

REFERENCES

ARUNACHALAM, M., 1975: 'A Study of the Culture and History of the Karkattan, *Bulletin of the Institute of Traditional Cultures*, Jan–June, pp. 1–72.

BARNETT, STEPHEN A., 1970: *The Structural Position of a South Indian Caste—Kontaikatti Vellalars in Tamil Nadu*, Ph.D. dissertation, University of Chicago.

MACCLUER, JEANS WALTERS and BENNETT DYKE, 1976: 'On the Minimum Size of Endogamous Populations,' in *Social Biology*, Vol. 23, pp. 1–2.

DAS, VEENA, 1976: 'Indian Women: Work, Power and Status,' in B.R. Nanda, ed., *Indian Women: From Purdah to Modernity* (New Delhi: Vikas), pp. 129–45.

GANESH, KAMLA, 1982: 'The Kottai Pillaimar of Srivaikuntam: A Socio-Historical Study,' Ph.D. dissertation, Bombay University (unpublished) pp. 74–5.

GOODY, JACK, 1973: 'Bride, Wealth and Dowry in Africa and Eurasia,' in Jack Goody and S.J. Tambiah, eds., *Bridewealth and Dowry* (NY: Cambridge University Press).

HARDGRAVE, ROBERT, 1969: *The Nadars of Tamil Nad: The Political Culture of a Community in Change* (Bombay), pp. 29–30.

KAVERI, S., 1979: 'Srivaikuntam,' dissertation submitted to the Tamil Nadu State Department of Archaeology, Madras, unpublished, n.p.; also, 1895: *Annual Report on Epigraphy (ARE)*, No. 174.

PRABHUVANANDA, S. and C. ISHERWOOD, 1947: *Bhagavad Gita* (London: Vedanta Press), pp. 36.

STEVENSON, H.N.C., 1954: 'Status Evaluation in the Hindu Caste System,' in *Journal of Royal Anthropological Institute of Great Britain and Ireland*, Vol. 84, pp. 45–65.

WADLEY, SUSAN, 1977: 'Women in the Hindu Tradition,' in D. Jacobson and S. Wadley, eds., *Women in India* (Columbia, M., South Asia Books).

YALMAN, NUR, 1963: 'On the Purity of Women in the Castes of Ceylon and Malabar,' in *Journal of the Royal Anthropological Institute of Great Britain and Ireland*, Vol. 93, pp. 25–58.

Family Status-Production Work: Women's Contribution to Social Mobility and Class Differentiation

HANNA PAPANEK

One of the persistent puzzles in the analysis of women's work is the absence of women from the enumerated labour force in the middle ranges of occupational status, class background, household income, and educational attainment. At the upper and lower ends of the occupational scale, many nations show much higher rates of female labour force participation than in the middle. In other words, gainfully employed women are distributed very unevenly throughout the social structure and the labour force in many societies, both among those whose economies are highly industrialised and those largely dependent upon agriculture.

My purpose in the present analysis is to suggest some of the factors that may be involved in this uneven distribution and to relate women's participation in remunerated work to the social status of their families. The concept of 'family status-production work' discussed in this paper is specifically intended to highlight the role that women of middle and upper classes play in family strategies of social mobility. That is, family status-production work enables us to see 'families as actively utilising women's work in ways that are deemed more productive for the entire family and [to see] women's withdrawal from paid work as not so much the end-product of mobility as a strategy for further mobility' (Ganesh, 1985 p. 687). In my view, the deployment of women to status-production tasks is often also associated with increased control over women's labour and mobility. In other words, when women are engaged in status-production work that is considered more productive for the family as a whole, they often do so at the cost of a degree of autonomy that may be associated with earning an outside income.

The concept of status-production, in this analysis, can be applied to all levels of status or household income and is not restricted to any one particular social formation. Indeed, the present analysis is intended to focus specific attention on those activities by women that may increase the competitive advantage of households that own or control assets other than their own labour when compared with households that have no other resources.

Finally, the concept of status-production is not intended to take the place of other explanatory variables useful in understanding social mobility and class differentiation. It is intended to focus attention on a neglected area in the analysis of women's work by raising questions concerning the broader context in which this work is carried out. A critical issue in the application of the concept of status-production is the implicit purpose for which the work is carried out. That is, the focus of this inquiry is not so much the concrete activity, as such—whether it is educating children or helping a man with his job—rather the role that activity plays in the family strategy for survival and mobility. What is the work's purpose, in other words, rather than what is its content?

FAMILY STRATEGIES

Before turning to a more detailed discussion of the varieties of work included under status-production, I will try to clarify the concept of family strategies used in this paper. This requires a view of the family—or, rather, the household—as acting in terms of some perception of the collective interest of this group. This is not to say that the perception of collective interest is based on a consensus equally arrived at by all members of the household. Far from it. In fact, the formulation and implementation of what is seen as the collective interest is often largely a means of enforcing conformity to the goals of those most powerful within the household. Family strategies embody inequalities and reflect differences within the household, usually based on age, gender, and marital status, especially in those societies with strongly hierarchical family structures.

But family strategies also reflect the prevailing ideology of what families should be, how women and men should behave, and what kinds of social actions are desirable in persons of a given social status. In other words, those who make decisions within the household about the best interests of the primary group usually believe that they are acting acceptably; others, who lack power to shape decisions within the household, usually share this belief. If socialisation processes are effective, this is one of the lessons everyone learns at an early age—that one's parents act in the best interests of their children.

My use of the term family strategies does not imply that these decisions are consciously formulated, like a military strategy, in terms of a long-term plan of action to achieve certain goals. Most families and most individuals do not approach life so mechanically, although some undoubtedly do so. Many of the decisions that form the basis of a family strategy are simply a matter of following prevailing norms and practices; they are perhaps best thought of as 'non-decisions' and are a matter of conformity.

Empirically, family strategies are better *inferred from observable actions* than from answers to the deliberate questions some social researchers have asked about 'decision-making', although such questions may yield some interesting answers. The process by which a primary group—such as, a family or household—reaches decisions that are implemented in action is one of the most complex issues in all of social science and is far from being understood.

Of more immediate relevance to the conceptualisation of women's work is the process by which individual members of a society learn *conformity to norms*. This is particularly important to the study of women. For example, what is the process by which relatively powerless members of a group are induced to act in ways that are not necessarily good for them? How do persons (or groups) even learn to think of what is 'good for them'? For example, how is an elder son in an Indian family induced to leave school (which he enjoys) in order to earn wages that will pay for the schooling of a younger brother? How is the concept of 'duty' learnt and implemented? What is involved when a daughter agrees to a marriage that—she has been told—will benefit the family's social standing (a collective interest)? How are young women taught that the judgment of their parents is superior to their own in the selection of their life partners?

In short, an understanding of family strategies relating to the interests of a family or a household requires an understanding of how conformity is achieved—precisely because so-called 'collective interests' are not based on consensus but reflect power relations within the group. Those who lack power are expected to conform to the decisions made *on behalf of the group* by those who have power within it.

Allocating female labour to status-production work is a part of this general process. Understanding how the process of forming family strategies operates is, therefore, necessary to the analysis of family status-production work carried out by women.

FAMILY STATUS-PRODUCTION WORK: DEFINITION OF CATEGORIES

What kinds of work are included in family status-production? In one sense, of course, everything that members of a group do affects the standing of that group in the eyes of others. For purposes of analysing women's work empirically, however, I suggest four categories of status-production work as particularly relevant (Papanek, 1979):

Indirect Support Activities for the Paid Work of Other Members

Observation and empirical research provide many examples of women's activities that enhance the earning capacities of other members of the family or household through indirect support activities. In fact, the ideology of female 'self-sacrifice' is directly geared to assure such support.

These support activities are particularly clear in those instances where the same services could be provided by hired workers or by the institution or employer paying the earning person's wages. For example, the laundering of required work uniforms could be done by workers paid by an employer; this often happens. When the service is performed by the women of the worker's household without remuneration—but the workers are penalised when uniforms are dirty—then, women in the worker's household are providing unpaid support services for the worker's job. To give another example, the clerical work or library research carried out without pay by the wife of a professional man (whether employed or self-employed) enhances his competitive advantage over those colleagues whose wives either lack the requisite skills or spend their time in directly remunerated work. This situation is often referred to as 'team-work' by a married couple. I have also called it engagement in a 'two-person career'—that is, two persons working at one career with only one person getting directly paid (Papanek, 1973a).

Another example of indirect support services can be drawn from the observation of women in agricultural settings, where the wives of farm owners may work to provide meals for hired workers. The provision of meals is part of the contractual agreement between workers and employers but the women themselves are neither remunerated for their work nor considered to be 'working' in terms of census definitions or popular language if these are the only kinds of tasks they do. Their work tends to be relegated to the category of 'housework,' one of the most misunderstood and misused categories of women's work.

Indirect support work is generally one of the kinds of work that forms part of 'what a good wife in this society does.' That is, the work is assimilated to the role definition of 'wife' rather than being specifically considered in terms commonly used to describe work: (1) in terms of its outcomes, or (2) in terms of the time, energy, and learned skills required to carry it out. As I discuss below, status-production work must be seen from both of these aspects, in spite of the fact that this is empirically difficult even if conceptually more clear.

Support for the Future Paid Work and Status Aspirations of Children

This category is the direct counterpart of the first, with the addition of a time dimension. In other words, work in this category is geared to *delayed rewards* and represents an investment in the future. Many instances can be found of women devoting considerable time and energy to the schooling of their children. This is another instance of women's unpaid work supplementing or substituting for the paid work of others, namely teachers. The phenomenon of the 'examination mother' is familiar in the middle classes of many societies, that is, among those where women are sufficiently educated to provide this service to children.

This category of status-production work is a particularly clear example of women's contributions to increasing the competitive advantage of the household on the basis of greater access to resources in the present generation that are being passed on to the children. To take only one example, an analysis of women's education in Egypt shows that in spite of a great expansion of access to formal education, children whose parents can afford tutors, or who are fairly well educated themselves to tutor them at home have a better chance of success in school: 'Those able to take advantage of the educational system are from the middle and upper classes, largely in urban areas' (Howard-Merriam, 1979 p. 261; also Papanek, 1985). In the Egyptian case—and probably a good many others—these advantages are more important in the case of daughters than for sons whose educational aspirations and performance are more clearly supported by other social institutions.

More generally speaking, families that have achieved their present income and status partly through formal educational attainments and in 'education-dependent' employment are keenly aware of the importance of schooling for their children's future employment chances. Hence mothers work hard to enhance their own children's competitive advantage in school work through coaching, exempting children from household chores (especially during examination time) and special indulgence and emotional support in times of stress.

But even where mothers lack the necessary education to give their children specific training in school activities, many women devote time, effort and skill to the work of teaching children status-appropriate behaviour. Especially in families with aspirations for upward social mobility, children may be taught the norms of a somewhat higher status level into which the family hopes to move in the future. This is particularly clear in language acquisition, especially where language may be a crucial factor in making status distinctions.

Another aspect in which this type of status-production may be seen is in the process of teaching daughters the skills appropriate for 'making a good marriage,' especially in societies where hypergamy prevails (i.e., daughters marry men of higher or at least equal status). In this sense, the process of Sanskritisation described by M.N. Srinivas is closely related to this aspect of status-production work.

In both the foregoing categories of status-production work, the 'covert integration' of women into a labour relation outside the domestic unit has taken place. That is, women are covertly integrated into a relationship with an employer or the school system. But this relationship is asymmetrical: the women are expected to perform certain tasks *because of their relationship* to a worker or student but the women are not directly rewarded for their work. The reward, such as a wage or school certificate, goes to the person who is directly involved in the relationship with the employer or school. Women's 'rewards' are typically phrased in unselfish terms, when they are noted at all; they are supposed to be gratified when husbands and children do well in their tasks but to ask nothing for themselves. In short, women are covertly integrated into the contractual relationship between employer and worker or student and school system. Sometimes, the integration becomes overt—as when schools assign vacation assignments—but it remains asymmetrical in the sense that the rewards for work do not go to wives and mothers directly.

In both instances, institutions and employers assume that women will comply with these covert work assignments or work expectations, on the basis of their kinship ties to workers and the prevailing norms for appropriate behaviour. Because the relationship is covert, however, it is often harder to disengage from it than in the case of an overt contractual relationship. For example, a mother who refuses to help her children with a vacation school assignment is likely to be seen as a 'bad mother' rather than as an overburdened worker rejecting a particular assignment.

The Politics of Status Maintenance

This third category of status-production work is more problematic than the first two. It is less clearly a matter of women's work being covertly integrated into the task performance of others in the household or family. Rather, it is a question of activities that directly affect status in the community or reference group—and that are intended to do so.

The inclusion of this category, however, emphasises my point that women perform status-production work at all levels of class, income, or status, especially in hierarchical social orders where survival may be directly dependent on patronage relations.

In many societies, family strategies of survival and mobility are contingent on the relationships of a particular family (or household) with others in a political system or patronage network. This is as crucial for the weak and powerless as for anyone else. Activities directly related to achieving or maintaining a particular position in political or patronage systems clearly affect the ability of the household to carry out economic activities to any advantage. For example, the ability to receive credit usually depends on participation in a patronage network rather than on the operation of institutions immune to patronage or influence. Achieving a degree of political connectedness, or even power, is essential for gaining control over resources. This access to resources is both the tool for gaining power and authority and the motivation for seeking status or power. In this sense, therefore, women's participation in the politics of status represent a significant contribution to the outcomes of the household's economic actions.

The types of status-production work I have in mind here may appear to be very simple and involve nothing more than gift exchanges between households. Indeed, gift exchanges in many societies tend to be the special province of women (see Eglar, 1960) but this facet of economic life has often been neglected by ethnographers. Gift exchanges among women may also be very different from gift exchanges among men; this difference may be among the reasons why early ethnographers overlooked them so completely (see Weiner, 1976).

But there is nothing simple about gift exchanges, as they reflect complex patterns of relationships among individuals and groups. Equally complicated aspects of the politics of status maintenance are the gathering and dissemination of information. When women do it, it is usually called 'gossip' but its relevance to the judgements of a community or reference group about a particular individual or family is generally recognised. Both overtly and covertly, gossip is a critical feature of status assessment. But should it be considered 'work' in any sense of that word?

Studies of family businesses in Mexico indicate the important role that women play in the collection and dissemination of information directly related to business activities (Lomnitz, 1976). In such a case, women's contribution of specific information on the availability of resources or the need for loans and jobs can readily be considered as an important part of family business activities.

Research on this particular aspect of women's status-production is very scarce at this time, as much more attention has been focused on subsistence activities and market-oriented production. Future research on 'informal sector' activities may yield new insights, particularly if attention is focused on the network-building aspects of some informal sector activities, such as, trade in large urban areas or the development of a clientele for self-employment activities.

Performance of Religious Acts and Rituals

The same question must be asked about this fourth category of status-production: should it be considered 'work' in any sense of that term or is it something else? Here again, the question of intentions and outcomes enters the discussion, as noted below.

The performance of some religious acts and rituals is sometimes clearly identified and being 'for the good' of others, either an individual or a group. For example, the performance of rituals such as *bratas* (vows to fast and perform specific rituals) may be motivated among Indian Hindus by the wish that a woman's son will pass an examination and it is clearly done for that purpose. In this instance, the notions of self-sacrifice, concern for others, and other expressions of nurturance and motherliness are very important. These ideas are clearly consistent with cultural ideals of the role of wife and mother. One might, therefore, think of the performance of *bratas* as an extension of coaching a child to do well in school.

But women's appearance at church services, in religiously observant Christian communities, may be more directly related to the wish to be well regarded and respected in a community of fellow-believers. In that sense, appearance at church can be seen, at least in part, as an example of status-production work. Like all other examples I have given, however, these activities have multiple determinants, such as, religious devotion, love for one's children, care for one's family, and so on.

Taking these multiple determinants into account, however, there is little doubt in my opinion that religious performances do constitute part of the status assessment process in communities or reference groups in which religious conformity matters to people. It is a kind of status politics. Women work to anchor the family in relationship to God in much the same way as women are also responsible for anchoring the family in the community through developing a network of relationships with other women and their families.

Purdah observance among South Asian Muslims often gives a vivid illustration of these symbolic actions. *Parda-nashin* (women who observe seclusion) are always particularly careful to show conformity to local norms when in the immediate neighbourhood where they live. Once outside the boundaries of the neighbourhood, the face-veil may be thrown back from the face or the *burqa* (covering cloak) discarded altogether (see Papanek, 1971, 1973b; Jeffery, 1979). Strangers—whose status judgements have no immediate importance for the family status—need not witness conformity. Neighbours do.

YES, BUT IS IT WORK?

The last two categories of status-production present particularly difficult analytical problems. Do these activities constitute work or should they be considered something else? Moreover, even if they are considered work, in the broadest sense, how are ritual performances and status politics tasks to be quantified? One can, of course, measure the time spent on them and consider them as part of women's overall workloads—what a 'good woman' is supposed to do.

Like the first two categories of status-production, which I consider to be more clearly defined but still very difficult to quantify, these last two categories must be seen in terms of their *outcomes and intentions*. As already noted, these types of activities are 'overdetermined', that is, caused by a multiplicity of factors. Mothers who help their children at home are emotionally gratified by seeing children do well; they seek to prepare them for a happy life in the future because they have learned a skill that will enable them to find a 'good job.'

In my view, the real importance of status-production activities, *when considered as part of women's overall workloads*, lies in the ability of women to do them at all. As long as women must spend their time and energy on subsistence production, unpaid family labour, and meagrely remunerated wage work, there is little time and energy left for anything else.

Status-production activities become possible to a significant extent precisely at the point where they may also be most relevant to family strategies. That is, in households that have sufficient resources so that at least one adult female can be spared from subsistence, unpaid family labour or wage employment, at least one person can devote time to status-production.

The household's ability to deploy female labour to status-production depends on a number of critical features of its socio-economic position and is significant precisely because using women to carry out status-production may further increase the advantages such a household possesses. It is for this reason that I have stressed the importance of women's status-production for the process of class differentiation. Those households that have enough so they can spare an adult female from direct earning and that can use them in activities with a delayed or indirect or unpredictable outcome are already, to some extent, privileged. Deployment of female labour to status-production builds on this privilege to gain an additional advantage that is not expected to come from alternative activities.

But it is also at this point of relative privilege, in comparison with others, that considerations of status become particularly relevant—indeed, in the life cycle of an upwardly mobile family, they may for the first time be even slightly realistic. An example is the frequently observed tendency to 'withdraw' women from the labour force, or even from all social interactions through newly imposed seclusion, just at the point where household income has increased slightly. New family strategies come into play in order to increase this slight advantage even further.

Answers to the question 'is it work?' must be inferential, rather than direct. Inferences can best be drawn, at this point, from situations in which rapid change occurs at the boundaries between socio-economic levels or income groups.

WITHDRAWAL OF WOMEN OF THE MIDDLE RANGE

As has been noted in many nations, both industrialised and largely agricultural, the distribution of women in the measured labour force is often sharply bi-modal. This uneven distribution in the labour force needs more explanation than it usually receives.

Women of the 'middle range' tend to be absent from the enumerated labour force in countries where poor women represent the bulk of the female work force, and highly educated women form a small but highly visible group in modern-sector occupations. The women of the middle range share several characteristics: they belong to households with above-subsistence but modest incomes; they are usually only moderately educated (e.g., primary or middle school) or even completely unschooled (especially older generations). Especially where formal education to levels above primary school remains the privilege of the urban upper and middle classes, and where female illiteracy rates are very high (75 per cent or more), women of the middle range are usually members of the urban lower-middle class or the upper peasantry in rural areas.

There are several related factors that account for the absence of women of the middle range from the enumerated labour force. Some of these factors are inherent in the structure of households, a feature that varies among societies and depends heavily on the nature of kinship systems. For example, multi-generational patrilineal households, such as those common in many parts of South Asia tend to have a high 'internal' demand for the labour of women. For these households to function, certain categories of females are more closely bound than others to perform tasks within the domestic arena. Typically, daughters-in-law are pressed to remain at home to assist their mothers-in-law with domestic tasks, to be trained in taking on the responsibilities of servicing household needs, and eventually to become mothers-in-law themselves. (Obviously, to become mothers-in-law, they must also produce sons—a point neglected by those analysts who see son preference only as a reflection of the culture's attitude toward males. I suggest here that basic labour considerations also matter: if older women want help with household responsibilities, sons are needed to provide daughters-in-law in multi-generational patrilineal households.) Under these circumstances, daughters are more likely to be released into employment and formal schooling.

But since households and labour markets are also in reciprocal interaction over time, there is unlikely to be much demand for categories of workers who are unavailable. Amongst the most interesting changes in the South and Southeast Asian region in the past few decades has been a change in the nature of labour demand. Economies with small modern urban sectors have typically generated little effective demand for workers that are constrained by both structural and attitudinal features of their society, as is true for women of the middle range. Demand can equally well be met by male workers with similar characteristics but without the structural and attitudinal constraints and, in the past, such it has been. However, as demand has risen with the introduction of new employers, especially in light industry, these constraints have been offset by a major advantage that employers have come to see in the employment of women. This is the possibility of discriminatory wages: because of their weak social position vis-à-vis men, women workers can be offered lower wages and pressed to conform to social norms of obedience in the workplace as well as, more generally, in society. Jobs then become categorised as being particularly 'suited' for women and wage discrimination is continued through occupational segregation. At the same time, consumer demand is fueled by the introduction of new goods, requiring cash incomes, that appeal particularly to households above subsistence. Women of the middle range then come to be more readily motivated to enter the labour force in order to purchase newly available consumer goods (Karim, 1984).

'ROLE CONFLICT' AND STATUS-PRODUCTION

The term 'role conflict' has gained currency in social science to describe the conflicts women and their families experience when new types of activities are added to women's workloads. Typical studies note the conflict between motherhood and careers or 'family work' and 'outside work' but these terms tend to be used more for middle-class women for whom outside work is relatively new than for poor women who have always had to earn. In other words, there is a presumption, both in social science and in popular conceptions, that, for some reason, 'role conflict' is experienced more often by middle-class women. This is a curious contradiction but also accurately describes the feelings experienced by women caught up in role conflict.

In terms of the analysis I propose in this essay, descriptions of role conflict usually describe conflicts between *old* obligations and *new* demands. That is, women from class backgrounds where paid employment has not been typical in past generations, or where paid employment outside the home was considered demeaning and unthinkable, are now faced by various pressures to change their working lives. Women from classes where both men and women have needed to earn in order to survive, because they control no resources and must depend on their labour, are rarely reported to experience 'role conflict' of the sort reported in research. But in terms of their workloads, poor women usually work harder and for longer hours than middle-class career women with family obligations. Recent studies of poor working women show very clearly that they work and earn *in order to* meet family obligations (e.g., educate children, build houses, earn enough to feed the family) and that the concept of role conflict would, therefore, be quite alien (see, Gulati, 1981; 1984). Indeed, their family obligations are such that they can be met only by engaging in wage labour.

Yet, as Leela Gulati notes of poor working women in Kerala: 'In the neighbourhoods where these working women live, the households which can afford not to send their women to work, specially manual work, gain in social esteem' (1981 p. 167). That is, these women and their families would often like to be able to withdraw from wage labour—even if this is not necessarily always the case—if they could afford to live without women's wage contributions. This is usually difficult, for poor families are proportionately *more* dependent than middle-class families on women's earnings to meet survival needs. Where returns to labour are low, and where families have no other resources, everyone in the household must somehow earn in order to survive. In more affluent households, studies have shown that women's contributions to household income are a smaller proportion of the total than amongst the poor.

The term role conflict, therefore, describes a specific situation, namely the conflict experienced by women for whom new pressures for additional income conflict with older expectations of 'what a good woman does.' In the terms used in my analysis of status-production, these older expectations include a great many varieties of family status-production which are very time-consuming and labour-intensive but not directly remunerated.

But neither the tasks of status-production, nor the emotional context in which such work is done, prepare women for other work contexts. For example, when women without prior employment must take jobs because of the death or disability of earning members of the family, it becomes clear that their actual earnings as independent workers may be far lower than the *incremental value* of status-production work carried out in conjunction with earning members in the household. As a result, female-headed households in highly industrialised societies, such as, the United States, typically experience a traumatic decline in household income. This is not only because the main earner's income contributions are suddenly missing but also because the only jobs open to new entrants into the labour force are low-paid entry-level jobs. Women who enter the labour force without experience ('displaced homemakers') are usually much older, better educated, and of higher social status than their co-workers.

This analysis also suggests that women's entry into the paid labour force is affected by various factors closely connected with class and status. For example, in households where women perform a great deal of status-production work, the *opportunity cost* of their entry into paid employment is well above zero. It is under these circumstances that role conflict—between 'family work' and 'outside work'—is most likely to be experienced, as women may need to scale down their involvement with status-production in response to job pressures.

Both these propositions—concerning incremental value and opportunity cost—suggest that the nature of status-production is qualitatively different from other types of work activities because of the way it is embedded in the context of household and family functioning. The multiple motivations for tasks, and their implications for many different areas of daily life, further complicate the analysis of status-production.

STATUS-PRODUCTION IN SOCIAL MOBILITY AND CLASS DIFFERENTIATION

From my description, these four categories of status-production work appear more typical of some class or status levels than universally applicable. In very poor households, it is very unlikely that some workers can be spared for activities that have *deferred* or *indirect* rewards. Status-production apparently requires that the household is able to survive on the direct remuneration earned by *fewer than all* household members, so that some persons can devote their time, energy, and learned skills to activities that are not directly or immediately remunerated.

But it is also necessary that an improvement in status should be seen as being within the reach of the household and not as something impossible. The deployment of female labour to status-production tasks is, therefore, more likely to occur at class and income levels where further upward mobility is not only considered possible but where resources can also be spared from survival efforts in order to achieve it. The household may need to be able to assume some degree of risk, as when a woman's withdrawal from paid labour decreases household income, but this risk is considered worth the possible rewards. At this critical juncture, therefore, women's activities can become important in increasing the pace of class differentiation and upward mobility.

In other words, households with a small advantage that have achieved some degree of social differentiation withdraw women from paid employment not only because this is considered a mark of status attainment. They do so because status-production tasks are seen as effective methods for further social mobility.

This insight marks the analysis of status-production work by women as more than a description of what everyone knows or of the activities that only small sectors of a population engage in where the majority of the population is very poor. It is precisely because the shift of women's activities to status-production is so critical to social mobility in the middle range that there is often so much resistance to change in the *status quo*. Analyses that have characterized women's domestic activities as unproductive—'only housework'—tend to overlook the role that such activities play in the broader strategies of families and households. More than men's comfort is involved when women's labour is deployed to family status-production activities.

CHANGES IN THE MODE OF STATUS-PRODUCTION

Recent developments in both industrialised and less industrialised nations suggest that important changes are occurring in the relationship between female labour utilisation and social mobility processes.

To summarise this point briefly in the present paper, I suggest that some of the traditional status markers have lost importance in comparison with conspicuous consumption and changes in lifestyle. The four categories of status-production that I have described tend to emphasise women's roles in kinship and community networks, supportive activities that display values and attitudes of conformity to older styles of life. The introduction of widely available new consumer products in low-income nations has begun to change the process by which social status is judged and aspirations for a good life formulated. The acquisition of consumer durables has become extremely important in the mobility strategies of even the lower middle classes in many low-income Asian nations, as a few households try to differentiate themselves from others in the community. Foreign remittances from Gulf countries, sent home by migrant workers from South, Southeast, and East Asia, further accelerate this process. Returning workers often bring or send consumer durables not otherwise available in their home countries.

These changes may mark a very significant watershed in social and economic organisation in those Asian nations with mixed or market economies. At the same time that new consumer goods appear on markets, changes in the organisation of production and the introduction of new types of producers also change the demand for female labour. As noted, this demand is supported by continued wage discrimination which makes female workers more desirable to employers in light industry. But the availability of consumer goods also increases the aspirations of consumers for cash incomes—incomes that may be newly earned by women workers. As aspirations rise, men's incomes are often unable to meet them, especially if men are working in occupations where real incomes have not increased significantly or have declined. As a result, women of the middle range—who have not previously participated in paid employment in significant numbers—may be 'pushed' into the labour market by their family's needs and aspirations in addition to being 'pulled' by increased labour demand.

The introduction of new consumer goods also affects how status is judged in communities and reference groups—a point made obvious in countless observations of rural and urban life throughout South and Southeast Asia. These changes obviously raise some problems in the analysis of status-production. If labour force participation by new cohorts of women is prompted by status considerations, does this mean that paid employment should also be included in status-production?

I think not. My analysis of certain kinds of women's work as status-production work is intended to focus attention on the significance of some neglected types of activities as part of a more general analysis of changes in female labour utilisation and family strategies. Broadening the category of status-production to include just about everything that women do would make the concept meaningless.

In addition, women's entry into the labour force constitutes a major change, not only in the economy but also in the household and in the lives of individuals. These changes cannot be overlooked as distinctive and significant in ways that include the problem of labour control.

LABOUR CONTROL

An important aspect of women's work in status-production is the implication of subordination of both the worker and the task to the control of others. The four categories emphasise what women do for others—support activities for men and children, status politics for the family as a whole, religious ritual for reasons of status and the success of others, and so on.

Two aspects are most crucial here but can only be noted in this paper. First, I have argued elsewhere (Papanek, 1984; 1985) that it may be a crucial competitive advantage in some societies if households can demonstrate strict control over women, with respect not only to reproduction but also to labour. Status-production work clearly falls into the category of closely controlled labour and may be valued particularly for this reason, in addition to the other consequences already mentioned.

Second, status-production work, as I have described it, depends on a specific pattern of household structure and organisation within a particular kind of social order. Hierarchical relations within the household and the society favour the emergence of status-production work by women. Interdependence among household members for task performance and amongst social groups are also factors that maximise the likelihood of status-production work. Under these circumstances, women—and especially younger women—are the most likely candidates for strict labour control by older women and men.

Although I cannot explore these aspects further in the present article, these points suggest that women's involvement in status-production work occurs under very specific conditions of social and economic organisation. While this might restrict the utility of the concept in terms of universal generalisations, I hope that it increases the likelihood that the concept can be fruitfully used in specific situations to increase our understanding of the dynamics of female labour utilisation, social mobility, and family strategies for survival and mobility.

REFERENCES

EGLAR, ZEKIYE, 1960: *A Punjabi Village in Pakistan* (New York, Columbia Univ. Press).

GANESH, KAMALA, 1985: 'State-of-the-Art in Women's Studies,' in *Economic and Political Weekly*, April 20, pp. 683–689.

GULATI, LEELA, 1981: *Profiles in Female Poverty: A Study of Five Poor Working Women in Kerala* (New Delhi, Hindustan; Oxford, Pergamon Press).

————, 1984: *Fisherwomen on the Kerala Coast* (Geneva, International Labour Office) *Women, Work, and Development Series*, Number 8.

HOWARD-MERRIAM, KATHLEEN, 1979: 'Women, Education, and the Professions in Egypt,' in *Comparative Education Review*, Vol. 23, No. 2, June, pp. 256–270.

JEFFERY, PATRICIA, 1979: *Frogs in a Well: Indian Women in Purdah*, (London, Zed Press).

KARIM, WAZIR-JAHAN, 1984: 'Malay Workers and Implications on Family and Women's Status in Malaysia,' Research Proposal presented at the First Regional Workshop of the Comparative Study on Women's Work and Family Strategies, United Nations University, held at New Delhi, 10–15 December.

LOMNITZ, LARISSA, 1976: Paper presented at panel on Informal Associations Among Women, Wellesley Conference on Women and Development, 2–5 June.

PAPANEK, HANNA, 1971: 'Purdah in Pakistan: Seclusion and Modern Occupations for Women,' in *Journal of Marriage and Family*, Vol. 33, No. 3, April. Reprinted in Hanna Papanek and Gail Minault, eds., *Separate Worlds: Studies of Purdah in South Asia* (Delhi, Chanakya Publishers; Columbia, Mo., South Asia Books).

————, 1973a: 'Men, Women and Work: Reflections on the Two-Person Career,' in *American Journal of Sociology*, Vol. 78, No. 4, January, pp. 852–72. Reprinted in Joan Huber, ed., *Changing Women in Changing Society* (Chicago, U. Chicago Press).

————, 1973b: 'Purdah: Separate Worlds and Symbolic Shelter,' in *Comparative Studies in Society and History*, Vol. 15, No. 3, June, pp. 289–325. Reprinted in Papanek and Minault.

————, 1979: 'Family Status Production: The "Work" and "Non-Work" of Women,' in *Signs: Journal of Women in Culture and Society*, Vol. 4, No. 4, Summer, pp. 775–81.

Papanek, Hanna, 1984: 'False Specialization and the Purdah of Scholarship: A Review Article,' in *Journal of Asian Studies*, Vol. 24, No. 1, November, pp. 127–48.

————, 1985: 'Class and Gender in Education-Employment Linkages,' in *Comparative Education Review*, Vol. 29, No. 3, August, pp. 317–346.

Weiner, Annette, 1976: *Women of Value, Men of Renown* (Austin, Univ. Texas Press).

Women Agricultural Labourers and Land Owners in Kerala and Tamil Nadu: Some Questions about Gender and Autonomy in the Household

A recent Wenner-Gren conference on households stressed the importance of looking at 'what households do, what functions they perform, and how and why they alter through time' (Arnould and Netting, 1982 p. 571). In looking at women in agricultural households, whether landless or landed, it is clear that the first priority of most able-bodied adults is to secure the survival of the household by providing food and other essentials. The composition of the household, the individual members' contributions to the household in terms of work, income, nurturance, and the organisational-managerial activities, all affect women's lives and are affected, in turn, by the women's situations—their degree of autonomy, their rights to the resource base of the household, their class position, and the extent to which the household is the focus of gender subordination and sexual discrimination. This paper examines the work that women in these agricultural households do in relation to food production, and the degree of autonomy their earnings bring for them.

The materials to be discussed include data collected as part of a recent large-scale study of women and rice cultivation in 28 villages in three states of India, as well as more intensive studies carried out over the past 25 years, chiefly in Kerala and Tamil Nadu. In discussing the situation of agricultural women, I will use a categorisation that was found useful in our large-scale study, i.e., I will distinguish between landless households, marginal landowning households, and (simply) landowning households. The intermediate marginal category includes those households which own small plots of land but whose members are still dependent on wage labour for economic survival. Households in this category are like the landless in that their members work regularly in the fields of others (as well as their own), but are like the landowning households in that their members participate in decisions about land management.

FEMALE AUTONOMY IN THE HOUSEHOLD

The notion of *autonomy* is extremely complex and I can only partially address it here, hoping mainly to raise a number of issues for consideration rather than to resolve them. There are many different ways of looking at the question of autonomy. It has been defined by Leacock as the extent to which women hold 'decision making power over their own lives and activities' comparable to the power men hold over theirs (1978 p. 247). In the present context, the focus is on women's participation in the economic life of the household. Autonomy is a useful concept in that it does not equate uniformity with equality, i.e., it does not assume that men and women do (or should do) the same things.

In talking about autonomy in Indian villages, it is clear that one must at all times take into account the powerful economic constraints which affect *both males and females* because of social class inequities, which in effect sets limits on the people's possible autonomy—the most obvious being perhaps the limited amount of disposable income and the need to avoid offending landowners who are potential employers. Nonetheless, even for the landless there are arenas in which men—and, to some extent, women—can exercise autonomy, as the following discussion will show. However, whether we are talking about women who are totally dependent on their husbands or about those who provide income for their households, it must also be recognised that there is an overriding social constraint on women's autonomy, resulting from the fact that the wider society and wider social norms are all ones that tend to favour patriarchy—though the extent and form may vary from region to region as well as between social groups within regions. Thus, our present discussion of autonomy is set within the context of a class- and caste-ridden society with a strong emphasis on patriarchal cultural norms. (It should be noted that these patriarchal cultural norms have become important even in Kerala where, until fairly recently, matriliny was the norm among some castes and where aspects of it persist even today.)

Any discussion of autonomy in this context must also distinguish among the three different types of households mentioned above: landless labourers, marginal landowners, and small or medium landowners. (Female-headed or female-supported households also have their own special characteristics, which will be discussed separately below.) For the landless, some of the criteria for measuring autonomy include (1) whether a woman is able to hold on to her own earnings or hands them over to her husband (or other household member, e.g., mother or mother-in-law; (2) whether a woman is able to buy things for herself without getting permission from her husband; (3) the extent to which she participates in decisions about household matters (such as, whether to keep a child in school, whether to build a new house); (4) the extent to which she is free to refuse to give her husband her money or jewelry when he asks for it; (5) the extent to which a woman may be subject to beatings for displeasing her husband, or simply so that he can let off steam; and (6) the extent to which a woman has any decision power over the couple's sexual relations, i.e., whether she has the right to refuse a request for intercourse. (I neither have, nor know of, any field data which would illuminate this last point.) One might also add, for unmarried women, the right to refuse a marriage proposal, and, in the economic realm, the right to seek alternative employment (for married or single women).

The areas of possible autonomy increase when we turn to marginal and—even more so—land-owning households, because having assets means that an individual faces many more types of decisions and is required to exhibit more managerial skills. This includes the question of which crop to grow (usually, but not always, dependent on type of land owned), the variety of seeds to use, the range of inputs to use, how work is to be organised (if only family labour is to be used or other outside labour as well, and if outside labour how it is to be managed, etc.) as well as decisions affecting the processing and selling of produce, etc. In addition, for a woman who is an owner/tenant as well as a labourer, there is a regular need to decide whether to put in a day's work on her own land or to go out for 'coolie' work. Of course, with land-owning households a woman may have less autonomy if the land and other assets are completely in the name of her husband or others in the household. On the other hand, I have not found any striking difference in this regard between households where some of the land is in the woman's name and ones where it is all in that of her husband.

In our recent study, as well as in my earlier more intensive research, all three types of households show a wide range in terms of the degree of autonomy exercised by women. I will first look at female agricultural labourers, both landless and marginal, and then turn to the case of land-owning households. (For the female-headed/supported households, see later).

Table 1 indicates the percentage of women in each of the villages who hand over their earnings to their husbands, and the percentage who keep it for their own use. (The table includes only those women who are living with their husbands: it excludes women who hand over their earnings to any other household member as well as some cases where data is lacking.) In the Tamil Nadu and Kerala sample presented here, we find that in only two villages more than 50 per cent of the women hand over their earnings to their husbands. (In most of the villages the figure is well under 50 per cent.) One of these villages is in Kerala and the other in Tamil Nadu. At the moment, from the data at hand it is impossible to pinpoint the reasons for these two deviant cases, but it is interesting to note that both are relatively better-off villages where the husband is able to earn a substantial non-agricultural income. (However, there are other better-off villages where women still retain their own earnings.) It is possible that we might not ever be able to explain the reason for this anomaly. Unless we were to check in a nearby village, there is no way of knowing whether there is some chance factor working here.

In many of the households where the women retain their earnings, their husbands actually hand over their own earnings, less what they keep for personal expenses, to their wives for managing the household. But does that constitute autonomy? When one realises that we are talking about households living always at the edge of poverty even if they are not actually suffering from starvation, it is clear that there is very little that the women

Table 1

Number of Women Handing Over Their Earnings to Their Husband

| State | Village | Number Handing Over Their Earnings to Husband | | | |
| | | Yes | | No | |
		N	%	N	%
Kerala	Palghat (1)	1	8	11	92
	Palghat (2)	26	70	11	30
	Malappuram (1)	13	31	29	69
	Trichur (1)	11	40	18	60
	Trichur (2)	15	48	16	52
	Alleppey (1)	8	17	38	83
	Alleppey (2)	7	22	25	78
	Trivandrum (1)	6	23	20	77
	Trivandrum (2)	3	15	42	85
Tamil Nadu	Chingleput (1)	5	23	17	77
	Chingleput (2)	6	29	15	71
	South Arcot (1)	8	17	38	83
	South Arcot (2)	13	27	36	73
	Thanjavur (2)	6	21	22	79
	Kanya Kumari (2)	18	41	26	59
	Tirunelveli (1)	31	84	6	16
	Madurai (1)	1	3	36	97

NOTE: The number of cases varies considerably from village to village for two reasons: (a) Some cases were not included because they were irrelevant, for example households without a husband, and (b) in some villages the question was not asked of all the informants, thus the data is missing.

CREDIT: This Table appears first in **J. Mencher** 'Women's Work and Poverty: Women's Contribution to Household Maintenance in Two Regions of Southern India' in **Dwyer, D.** and **J. Bruce**, eds., *Women and Income Control*,forthcoming.

can do with their earnings apart from buying food and other essentials, such as, minimal clothing, and related items, such as, toothpaste or brushes, an occasional extra school book, or absolutely essential house repairs, and from time to time meeting family obligations (such as giving something for a marriage, or a death).

All of this leads to a general discussion of women as earners, and the extent to which this affects their status in the household. There is no question that in many of the households I have observed, the fact that a woman not only manages her husband's contribution to the household but is herself an essential economic contributor to it serves to improve her status and position within the household. But there are often some constraints. When she is living in her own home (with her mother and/or sisters, or else in a home inherited from her family) she is obviously in a better position than when she is living in her husband's home, even if she is a major wage earner and contributes more of her earnings to the household than he does. But, it is even more complex. Though I lack any concrete data, it is my strong impression that when a woman is free to return to her own family house (even if she is living with her husband in his), as in the case of some of the women I know in Kerala, she tends to get along better with her mother-in-law than otherwise. Perhaps this is because the mother-in-law treats her better but perhaps it is also because she feels herself under less pressure and can toss things off more easily. This kind of psychological point needs to be investigated much more fully.

Being married to a close relative can also affect the status of a woman in the household. This is extremely common in Tamil Nadu. In an earlier study in five villages in Chingleput District I found that among the large caste groups, such as, Paraiyan, Naicker, Gounder, and different subcastes of Mudaliars, cross-cousin and uncle-niece marriages accounted for more than half of all marriages. Under these conditions, after marriage a woman was under the control of her father's sister, mother's brother's wife, or her own maternal grandmother. While she could expect more understanding from these women, she was also socialised to accept their authority—and was more likely to be criticised if she walked out. If, on the other hand, a woman did not marry a relative, then she was more likely to marry someone living in the same village, often on the same or adjacent street. Under such circumstances also, she would be relatively freer than in those parts of India where women marry strangers or have to leave their natal village at marriage.

Following are brief descriptions of a number of actual cases, to indicate the range of variation found among the factors which have been discussed above.

Labouring Households

Case 1 (Tamil Nadu). Rajam is approximately 40 years old. She and her husband have five children between the ages of 18 and 3. She has been working as an agricultural labourer since she was married, about twenty-four years ago. Before marriage, she had only worked on the land owned by her natal family. Her husband was only very distantly related to her before marriage. She keeps her own earnings, and her husband hands over his earnings to her. She is in charge of all purchases. She spends close to Rs. 10 a day to feed her family, but she tries to save something. In her own words:

> Two measures of paddy are required for one time meal. Then I must buy other groceries like salt, red chillies, etc. All inclusive it comes to Rs. 10 so saving is very difficult. By curtailing this and that I manage to save a little, but when the savings swells to Rs. 50 or 60 then the whole amount is spent on clothes for the children. All these things I alone must look after. I do all the grocery shopping. He won't ask for money for drinking, but if he did I would not give. He only drinks if he gets something extra.

Case 2 (Tamil Nadu). Chinnamma (age about 40) is married to Bhiman (her mother's younger brother). They have three sons and a daughter. They also have about thirty-two cents of paddy land which her husband works on. He does not do any wage work, but she goes out for work as a day labourer, either alone or with relatives from the village. (When I first worked in the village in 1963, she only went out with relatives.) She worked up to her last day of each pregnancy but then took off for six months or so. She is by now a very experienced worker. She herself controls her earnings. She is a very hard-working woman who goes to other villages for weeding but not for any other work. She is responsible for all purchases of groceries, cloth, etc.

Case 3 (Tamil Nadu). Kantha lives with her husband and his mother, his two unmarried brothers and her own 9-year-old son. They own thirty-two cents of land and cultivate three acres as 50/50 sharecroppers. The 32 cents are in her mother-in-law's name. However, her husband is the one who manages the household finances. She gives him everything she earns, and he is in charge of all purchases including food.

Case 4 (Kerala). Kuttipennu and her husband have a son of 30, a daughter-in-law, two other children, and two grandchildren. While the house she is living in belongs to her, she gives all of her earnings to her husband and they jointly do the shopping for provisions. He drinks, but he does not ask or take her money for drinking. She started work when she was 15. When her first baby was three months old, she started going back to work leaving the baby with the grandfather and coming home often to feed the infant. In talking about freedom, she said that she is freer today because she has fixed hours of wage work and because she can work for whomever she pleases.

Case 5 (Kerala). Ambujakshi lives with her husband and three children aged 11–15. The two younger ones are studying. Eight years ago she lived with her husband's parents and brothers but then they separated. She handles all of the family's household money. Her husband gives her whatever he gets either in cash or in kind. But when he wants to drink he asks her for the money. Though she manages the accounts, she needs her husband's permission for buying clothes or anything that costs more than 10 or 15 rupees. She explains: 'Only when I purchase the provisions will the expenditure be within the limits. If he does it he doesn't know how to manage the money well.' When asked if she had any gold ornaments she replied that she has only small ear rings. Her child's chain was sold for buying provisions and for her husband's card playing. 'He will beat me if I don't give him. If I don't give him he will take them without telling me.' ·

Case 6 (Kerala). Kalyani lives with her husband, her mother, her brother and her brother's wife as well as her own child of 5½, and her brother's small child. Four of them work in the fields. Her mother used to manage the household expenses but nowadays Kalyani does this. She does not hand over her income to her husband. He gives her something for home expenses, but not very much because 'he cannot go without his drinks even one day. If he has no work he borrows and drinks. Even if he has work he gives only very little for home expenses.' Her brother and sister-in-law also hand over their earnings to her for the household expenses.

Land-owning Households

In my earlier fieldwork I collected numerous descriptions from informants telling how, even as far back as the late 19th century, their great-grandmothers managed their families' estates. Many of these women were exceptionally resourceful in making decisions about agriculture, while their husbands pursued other interests—ranging from scholarly or religious activities or professional careers in the law or medicine, to carousing and sexual orgies. In some cases these men died leaving young widows who, for a variety of reasons, came to assume significant agricultural managerial roles, even if there were other relatives around.

When we turn to the present, it appears that the most serious impediment faced by women in managing their own land is not lack of physical strength but special problems in dealing with the outside world. The data from my recent project show that the times these women need help seem to be (1) when they need to go to shops (usually outside the village) to buy essential agricultural inputs, and to bargain with people, or even to go to the government depot and deal with the male officials there, and (2) when selling their produce, if the merchant does not come to their house. (Where merchants come to the house the women are able to sell their produce, often driving fairly hard bargains.) Government offices and outside village markets are male domains and women do not feel welcome being there alone, though some women will go if they are accompanied by a male relative or a farm servant. Supervision of field workers, a task which some have considered to be a male domain, is a task which many women handle quite competently.

Among the land-owning households, as among the landless, one finds a range of situations—like the following case (Case 7)—from where the husband and wife manage their household economy as a partnership to those in which the women have virtually nothing to do with managing the land, and control only those resources which the husband considers not worth spending his own time on. This extreme type is found more commonly (but not exclusively) among the larger landowners and among the higher castes.

Case 7 (Tamil Nadu). Kanaka has a husband and two sons in their 20s. Her husband has not been well for some time. They own 2 acres of wet land and rent 1 acre in which they cultivate paddy. She supervises her cultivation daily. She does weeding along with her labourers, and if they leave any weeds behind she tells them to redo the area. She also supervises transplanting and harvesting. She does not go to shops for inputs or to sell produce; that is done by her husband or one of the sons. She has participated in an agricultural course for women that was given by the Farmers Training Centre run by the Agriculture Department at the nearby town. She said that both her mother and mother-in-law had also participated in agricultural supervision. Her husband discusses with her and their older son what kinds of seeds, fertilisers, and pesticides to use. They all listen to the radio and get information from the agriculture office.

Case 8 (Kerala). Eliamma lives with her husband, her husband's sister, who is a teacher, two of her three sons, and two young daughters. Her husband owns about 1½ acres, and he and his sister jointly own another two acres. Their fields are fortunately close to their household compound and can actually be seen from the verandah. Eliamma supervises from her own house but does not actually go to the fields, even if her husband is away. In her words:

> Only after deliberation are all decisions taken about fertilisers or pesticide, or seeds. We will decide jointly only after discussing; if either of us hears anything new, that will also be discussed. Both of us handle the money for household affairs or for buying things. . . We [women] have more freedom now than what we had earlier.

Case 9 (Tamil Nadu). Rajam is around 30 and lives with her husband and two small children. They own sixty-seven cents of paddy land. She is living near her mother's house, and her mother sometimes helps out with child care. She supervises a great deal of the field work, since her husband works as a coolie and is not always available. When the work in their fields is being done by women, she also works along with the labourers. An example from her diary shows that she did such things as irrigating the field, manually preparing the land for growing seedlings, engaging someone for ploughing and supervising that work. However, her husband buys all the fertilisers and he sells the paddy if they have any surplus. Her husband gives her what he earns every day, less Rs. 1.25 which he keeps for *pan* and tea. She manages the household finances, while he manages the rest (including buying the children's clothes and paying for medicines). If she wants a new *sari*, she asks him and they discuss it. Then they both go together to buy it.

It is clear that there is a wide range in the amount of autonomy that women in these agricultural houses enjoy. For example, I have seen men (both in land-owning and landless households) who took great pride in their wives' managerial and supervisory abilities, and even some who admitted to being less competent than their wives. But for every such man, there are others whose wives have very little scope to develop or demonstrate such skills.

Another set of factors that clearly affect female autonomy relates to the question of time. Throughout the world it has been noted that women work longer hours than men, and that a large part of that working time is spent in tasks that relate to the maintenance and reproduction of the household: house-cleaning, washing clothes, cooking, fetching fuel, fetching water, caring for domestic animals, and most essentially, child care. Whether we are talking about labouring or land-owning households, these tasks are primarily the job of women—though some are done by hired women in the better-off land-owning households.

Women have very little choice in how they spend their time. When I asked village women to name their most pressing needs, apart from direct economic benefits such as more employment or animals, the most common requests were for improvements in the water supply (to have piped water near their houses, or at least a decent well nearby that would provide water throughout the year), and for free or easily available cooking fuel. In Tamil Nadu, apart from child care in the home, one major reason for keeping girls of 10 or 12 out of school is to save the mother from having to go and collect cow dung. Problems such as these could be the focus of development programs that take women into account.

A final point which may be mentioned here is the matter of physical abuse of women (most commonly by the husband, but occasionally by sons or others). This is more common among the landless and marginal households than among the landowners—though it is possible that it is also more easily concealed from the neighbours when one lives in a house surrounded by fields, than among those who live in one-room shacks right on top of their neighbours. Or, perhaps, it is more common in communities where men tend to drink more heavily, for a variety of economic and psychosocial reasons. Thus, the situation of women is also affected by cultural norms and values, and by the 'personality' of the husband. I mention this matter in passing, though it is clearly beyond the scope of this paper to discuss it in detail.

To summarise the preceding discussion, we see that in all three groups of households there is a wide range in female participation in work and in decision-making, in who manages their earnings and even the earnings of their husbands, and also in general in how their household finances are managed. There is also a considerable variation between villages. It is not clear how all of this affects the autonomy of women, but it is clear that having control over the family purse strings, and especially the fact that some of the money comes from her own work, does seem to improve the status of women within the household. As one woman put it to me, 'I know that I can work and support myself and my children and that as long as I am able to work, I do not have to feel totally dependent on anyone.'

It is hard to quantify any of this, but it is clear that the women are speaking out of their experience. Some are more articulate than others, and it is hard to gauge the feelings of those who are less so, but there does not seem to be any reason to assume that they are totally different from their sisters.

In an article dealing with rural women in Spain, Susan Harding has pointed out the significant role that women play in household decision-making, and what they do to ensure the survival of the household. However, she strongly critiques those who would argue on this basis that the ideology of male dominance is a myth:

> The argument for women having the upper hand in peasant society runs something like this: the informal power that women have in the household and the village is effectively greater than the formal power that men have in either domain. . . . There are several general criticisms I have of this line of argument. First, it seriously underestimates the power in men's hands in the household economy and the village polity. Second, it isolates the village from the larger structural context from which men derive much of their economic, political and ideological power in the village . . . male dominance. . . is a structural fact. . . . The powers women have . . . are the kind accorded to the subordinate group in any enduring relationship of interdependence. (1975 p. 306–8)

This certainly applies to the families I have discussed above, especially the women in the marginal and land-owning households though perhaps to a lesser degree when the women themselves have land legally in their own names. Among the landless, another factor is partially responsible for the degree of women's autonomy: their degree of organisation. Especially in Kerala, women as well as men belong to political parties and labour unions. Indeed, as Tharamangalam noted (1981 p. 73) and I have discussed elsewhere, one of the first strikes in rural areas in Kerala was called by female agricultural labourers and such activities continue among Kerala women even today. Still, there is no reason to assume that taking an active role in politics will necessarily give a woman more autonomy in the home, though in some families I know well, it appears to have done so. This is because the women in question have come to have a very different self-image and relate to their husbands differently from those women who are not so involved. The whole question of women's organisation and its effect on the women is a fascinating area that needs much detailed investigation.

FEMALE HEADED/FEMALE SUPPORTED HOUSEHOLDS

In an earlier paper, I noted that there is a tendency in the literature on India to pay very little attention to the existence of female-headed households, both among agricultural labourers and among land-owning families. It was further noted that labouring houses lacking adult male earnings (especially those with only one female's earnings) tend to be among the poorest of the poor. Such households include: (1) widows with young children, or older widows without adult sons or sons-in-law in the home; (2) women whose husbands are unable to work either due to illness or old age and who lack other male workers; (3) women who have been deserted by their husbands; (4) an occasional woman whose husband, while residing in the house, refuses to give her anything; and (5) divorced women. (In one of our villages in the Muslim-dominated district of Malappuram in Kerala where many males are now obtaining work in the Middle East, we have noted a number of divorced Muslim women among our agricultural labourer sample.) The extent of widowhood is in part the result of marrying girls to men ten or more years older than themselves, and partially due to the hazardous conditions of work for the men.

It is important, however, in talking about female-headed households to distinguish between authority in the home and sources of income. Even if a woman's husband is elderly or incapacitated and she is the sole earner, he is still considered the family head. Such households, which could be called female-supported rather than female-headed, are often as poor or poorer than ones without males, since the women's earnings also have to feed the husband and pay for his medical expenses. Thus, in one of the Tamil Nadu villages that I am very familiar with, a marginal household that was much more prosperous when I first met them back in 1963, now owns two acres of land of which one is given to a tenant on a 50/50 share cropping, while the other is managed with a permanent family farm servant in charge of supervision and day-to-day work. However, the wife also helps to supervise the field. The husband works as a tailor when he can, which is very rare since he is quite ill, and the wife goes out as a day labourer for transplanting, weeding, and harvesting. She also works on her own one acre along with the farm servant family. She has an adult son who does little work and comes to her frequently for money. In addition, she has married off two daughters and has one more to marry. Basically, apart from the yield from their one acre and their share from the *varam* land, the family is today living on her earnings. Yet, it could not be called a female-headed household. Because, even though he is ill, her husband is still the family head.

In Kerala, where both males and females tend to live longer, we find numerous instances of such households, often ones with no land at all, solely dependent on the woman's earnings. Such households are as poor as female-headed ones without males. On the other hand, there are also female-headed households among the landless and marginal land-owning groups that are somewhat less poor, because they are not exclusively female-supported, or at least do not depend totally on the earnings of a single female. These are usually households headed by an older widow whose sons, daughters, sons-in-law or daughters-in-law also work and contribute to the household. Thus, as noted above, in some of these households the younger working females may be expected to hand over their earnings to their mothers or mothers-in-law rather than to their husbands. Indeed, the husband might also be handing over some of his earnings to the household head (though normally not as high a percentage as that given by the females).

In looking at the family in terms of household cycles, we find that many women live for at least part of their lives in such joint structures. They may live in them as single adults or as young wives during their pre-marital years and when first married, and again later as middle-aged adults. Following are a few illustrative cases.

Labouring Households

Case 1 (Kerala). Kochi's husband died seven years ago, and with the household income reduced to her own earnings she was not able to continue to keep her two elder children in school (even though she did not have to pay school fees). She now has three sons aged 24, 18 and 11, and a daughter of 13. The two youngest children are still in school. Earlier, her husband's brother and their wives and children were all staying together but they have now partitioned and have built their own houses. She manages all of the household affairs, though her sons help in buying the daily provisions. She is better-off now than she was when her husband died, since now she has two adult sons to help.

Case 2 (Kerala). Thanka is a widow with only one son still alive. She lost two sons and a daughter due to illness many years ago. Her son is married and has four small children. Thanka is a very powerful woman who was involved with labour union organising from the late 1960s on. She is famous in the village for having personally stood in front of a tractor during an anti-tractor agitation in 1970. She was in charge of the family funds when I first met her in 1975, and her son used to hand everything over to her. Her son's wife is her brother's daughter. She is very fond of her daughter-in-law, but they maintain separate kitchens because her son is not 'careful' with his money. She and her son jointly maintain the house. It is clear that she gives food and many things to her grandchildren. She complains that her son is 'very strong willed. He never obeys anyone. My daughter-in-law has to suffer much because of this. She is only 23. My son never works steadily.' Thus, it is Thanka's earnings that help to keep the children fed, though in spite of this they are clearly suffering from malnutrition.

Land-owning Households

Case 3 (Tamil Nadu). Selvasundaram (a widow with 2 sons, both employed outside the village): she owns 1.70 acres of paddy land and 50 cents of garden land. During the year prior to our study she had also taken 2 acres on lease from a relative but in the end he cheated her, so in the year of our study she was back to cultivating her 1.70 acres. During transplanting and weeding she goes to the field to supervise the workers. The sale of the produce and purchasing of inputs from the market or the cooperative society is handled by one of her sons with one of the workers. Selvasundaram works in the fields and also supervises agricultural work. If she wants any suggestions she consults her husband's brother. However, when asked about her use of fertilisers and pesticides she replied forcefully: 'I have a radio. I listen to the farm news and from that I will tell my son what sort of fertilisers we should use and what kind of pesticides to buy.' She says that if it is hot when the harvesting is going on, she will carry an umbrella and sit and supervise the workers.

Case 4 (Tamil Nadu). Kamalamma (a widow who lives alone except for a brother's daughter, aged 15, who is studying in the nearby high school): she owns 60 cents of paddy land and cultivates another fifty-seven cents on lease. She supervises her cultivation daily, but has to send one of her labourers to purchase fertilisers or pesticides. She supervises its application in the fields. She consults with her labourers about what to buy, but she too listens avidly to the radio farm news. She made a point in our interviews that she likes to stand on her own feet and support her family. She tries to avoid asking help either from relatives or from others.

Case 5 (Tamil Nadu). Saroja (a widow with four children, a son of 19 studying in Thanjavur, a daughter who helps with the housework, a son-in-law who works as a cleaner on a lorry, and 2 younger daughters): she cultivates three acres on lease (*kuthagai* land). She has been supervising agriculture for eight years intensively. She goes to the fields herself for all kinds of supervisory works though she does not go to shops to buy inputs or to sell produce. Her son-in-law, or her sister's son, or her labourers go to buy the inputs. She is fortunate in being able to sell the produce in front of her house. If she is sick, her son-in-law supervises the work. In her own words:

I discuss either with my son-in-law or with my labourers what kinds of seeds to use, the amount of fertiliser, pesticides, and related things. I get a lot of information from the radio. Also, I have vast experience in agriculture and with my experience I cultivate paddy

Case 6 (Tamil Nadu). Jayamani's husband works in Malaysia and has been working there since they were married. He comes from time to time to visit her in the village. She owns two acres of land in which she grows two crops of paddy each year. She has one servant couple who work for her permanently apart from the people hired on a daily basis. When her husband is out of India (which is most of the time), she looks after the land. 'I go for supervision when the work is going on in the field, because otherwise the workers don't do the work properly. I take my servant along with me and go to buy the fertilisers, seeds, pesticides, whatever we need.' As to the hiring of workers, she says:

> I tell my farm servant to bring workers and I will employ them. If we supervise them properly, they obey us. I learned about field work only after I was married. I also work along with the workers in the fields some of the time. They work better when I work with them . . . . The amount to be given to the workers is decided by me and then I write and tell my husband about it.

On getting information about new agricultural techniques, she says, 'Other landlords . . . give me information about it. Sometimes I learn through radio programs also.'
Case 7 (Kerala). Parvathy is a widow of 54. She has brought her younger brother and his wife and children to live with her since her mother died a few years back. She owns three and a half acres of paddy land, two and a half acres of garden land around her house for coconut and vegetables, and 10 acres of hilly land. Parvathy supervises cultivation. She also goes to the fields when her brother is not available, but he goes to the market and buys things for cultivation. She pays the labourers and keeps accounts. Until her mother's death she was not much involved in agriculture. She and her brother discuss what type of fertiliser or pesticides to use, and they jointly decide about the sale of paddy.
Case 8 (Kerala). Kartyayani is a widow with a son of 22, a daughter of 18 studying for pre-degree, two younger children, and her late

husband's widowed sister. She owns 4 acres of paddy land and 6 of dry land, for cashews and coconuts. She manages the land with the help of an older permanent labourer, who used to work for and advise her husband earlier. He brings the labourers when she needs them. She listens to the farm news and goes to supervise in the fields.

A few excerpts from the diaries of land-owning women will further illustrate the extent to which these women take responsibility for the day-to-day running of their households' agricultural holdings.

Diary 1 (Kerala). Sundari is a widow whose household includes her 40-year-old son, her daughter-in-law, her four grandchildren, and her 90-year-old mother. Her son is employed out of the village. They have two acres of land. She goes to the fields daily for one or more hours.

October 1, 1979: Went to the field by 7 AM. The land was ploughed. I supervised the work. Then women labourers pulled and put the seedlings in the field. Supervised that work also. Came home at 1 PM. Again by 5 PM went to the field and looked around the transplanted areas. Made the water position all right and came home by 6.30 PM.

October 9, 1979: By 7 AM went to the coconut grove. Engaged five persons in the job of cutting up the soil around the coconut saplings with a hoe in order to facilitate their survival and growth. Extracted good work from the labourers. Supervised the work. Came home at 3 PM.

Diary 2 (Tamil Nadu). Devaki has an adult son and husband and several younger children living in her household.

January 9, 1979: This morning went to the field and waited for the labourers to reach there for harvest. When they arrived, asked them to immediately start the work. I also joined them. After the operation, the stalks were bundled up and the bundles were brought to the threshing yard. Stayed there guarding the bundles till my husband arrived and then went home.

January 10, 1979: This morning reached the threshing yard early and waited for the labourers to arrive. When they came, the job of threshing began. I also participated in the work. Instructed them to be extra careful in the work so that the paddy grains did not get into the side by heaps of hay. After my husband came there from the field, I asked him to take care of the work and went for food. Then I inspected a different field to see if it had been irrigated sufficiently for ploughing. After doing that came home.

January 25, 1979: Went to the field in the morning as usual. Persons working in the adjacent field had thought that the water in their field was a hindrance to their job of transplanting and hence had cut the ridge of our field to make way for the water to flow into our field. Therefore, the water level in our field was in excess. That may cause a subterranean stream through which the dissolved phosphates would also be lost. Besides this the seedlings would also get rotten. I was sad that knowing fully well all these things, the neighbours had acted in an irresponsible way. Then I tried my level best to drain the extra water, and plugged the holes leading to the subterranean stream . . . I also asked my neighbours not to cause further damage to our field by their unfriendly act of diverting their field's extra water into our field.

The above case makes it clear that at least among some of the land-owning households, women can have considerable autonomy and exercise considerable managerial skills.

HOUSEHOLD COMPOSITION

The above discussion makes it clear that the subject of household composition, both among the landless and landed families, even within one state in southern India, is extremely complex. What is clear is that any individual woman is likely to spend at least some period of her life in households where, apart from their husbands, there is at least one other working adult, either of an older or a younger generation (parents or parents-in-law, children and/or their spouses). Table 2 shows this clearly for a few sample villages, with younger women tending to live either with their husbands and small children alone (or else with other kin from the older generation), and with older women more frequently living in households with their own adult working children. We do note some regional

Table 2

Household Composition by Village

State	Village	Type of Household*					
		(1)	*(2)*	*(3)*	*(4)*	*(5)*	*(6)*
Kerala	Palghat-1	21	8	1	8	7	2
	Palghat-2	12	10	8	7	3	0
	Malappuram-1	7	15	7	1	9	1
	Trichur-1	14	10	10	1	4	2
	Trichur-2	20	11	4	4	6	2
	Alleppey-1	20	12	9	0	6	2
	Alleppey-2	18	5	8	3	3	7
	Trivandrum-1	18	8	—	6	10	1
	Trivandrum-2	19	6	—	4	14	3
Tamil Nadu	Chingleput-1	19	17	3	1	4	1
	Chingleput-2	15	20	3	—	6	2
	South Arcot-1	14	13	14	2	5	0
	South Arcot-2	20	17	7	6	2	0
	Thanjavur-2	10	12	2	2	1	0
	Kanya Kumari-2	10	19	5	2	7	0
	Tirunelveli-1	14	20	5	2	2	1
	Madurai-1	13	23	—	2	9	1

* For the present purpose, household type is defined in terms of our main informant's marital status and her position in the household, as follows:

(1) two-earner households consisting of our informant and her husband (and possibly non-working children and/or elderly people);
(2) households with more than two earners including our informant and her husband and their child(ren) and/or children's spouse(s);
(3) households with more than two earners including our informant and her husband and other kin (parents or siblings of informant and/or husband);
(4) households supported by the wages of one woman (our informant);
(5) households supported by our informant plus her child(ren) and/or children's spouses;
(6) households supported by our informant and other kin (as in No. 3).

Note that types 1–3 and types 4–6 are parallel, differing only in that our informant has a working husband in types 1–3, but not in 4–6—i.e., she is not married (i.e., she is supporting her parents or other natal kin), is widowed/divorced, or has a non-working husband (ill or too old to work).

variation, with six cases in our Madurai sample of women under 29 who have grown working children. This is partly related to the fact of girls marrying when much younger in Tamil Nadu than in

Kerala, and possibly also to women having less accurate knowledge of their own ages.

There are, of course, some women who never experience this kind of joint living: their parents and their husbands' parents might have died young or living in a distant place; they might not have any married children during their lifetime; or their children (most commonly their daughters) might marry and move away. We have found in most villages at least one or two households with only old people, and in some villages there are many more. Among the labourers and, to some extent, among the small land-owning groups, even among patrilineal communities, there seems more flexibility in reality than the theoretical picture would lead us to believe. We find, for example, more men living in their wives' villages than one might have expected *a priori*. We also find numerous cases of people who have lived in more than one village during the course of their married lives. This is especially true of those who have no land and thus have less to tie themselves to. Whether it was as true previously in the days of attached labour is hard to say, though I would suspect that it occurred even then.

In looking at the data on household composition, we find considerable inter-village variation both in Tamil Nadu and in Kerala. One of the things this clearly indicates is the danger of making generalisations from single villages. Looking at these materials one thinks of many intriguing hypotheses, e.g., if we compare Alleppey-1 and Palghat-2 we find that in Alleppey-1, among the landless there seems to be a lower percentage of nuclear households with a weighted annual per capita income of more than Rs. 400 per year, i.e., most of the landless nuclear households seem to be poorer than those with more earners. However, when we look at Palghat-2, this generalisation does not hold up. There does not, in fact, seem to be any kind of generalisation relating to household composition and income that is not contradicted by comparing the two villages. If we look at the income of our main informant versus household composition, in Alleppey-1 it looks as if those main informants who live in households with only a husband and wife tend to be able to earn less than those who live in households with more kin, but that does not appear to hold in the case of Palghat-2. It might be argued that Alleppey-1 is much poorer than Palghat-2, which is certainly true.

However, at this stage, the points that seem to stand out are:

1. There does not seem to be any correlation between income and household composition:
2. There does not seem to be any correlation between income and the number of workers in a household (i.e., if there are more people working in a given household, there are also likely to be more mouths to feed, so that in effect they are not better off);
3. Most individuals spend some portion of their lives (usually at either end) in households that contain more than two generations.

It should also be noted that even when they do not actually live with extended kin there is a tendency (at least in nucleated villages) to live close to extended kin most of the time. The implications of this for agricultural labourer women are complex. On the one hand, having extended kin in the household can make it easier for a woman to work in the fields. But it can also mean that she is more subject to certain types of constraints. Women are aware of both of these factors: on the one hand, their emotional and practical need for extended kin, and, on the other hand, the problem which is often formulated in words such as 'what will mother (or mother-in-law) say if I . . . ?' On balance, I would argue that the emotional support from extended kin in most cases outweigh their disadvantages. Most of my informants over the years could not conceive of spending a night alone in a room, or being without others around all of the time. It is a matter of deep cultural attitudes which in this case tend to override the need for autonomy.

CONCLUSION

Women's control of the product of their labour depends on many factors. In the case of females who work on their own land, whether as labourers or supervisors, a great deal depends on whether they own or have some rights to the means of production. As Saunders has noted for one Egyptian village:

> unpaid work on the land of the husband or his father or tending their animals does not give control of the product. However, most or all of this will be allocated to domestic ends where

women have some say in management. On the other hand, when a woman owns land, or all or part of an animal she tends, it is understood that she should control the disposal of the product. (1984 p. 9)

It is certainly clear in the villages I know well that if a woman owns land or animals she has more say in the disposal of the product. Certainly they also have much more discretion in the use of funds derived either from their own land or animals, or (most of the time) from their own earnings. Thus, it is money they obtain from their own resources or work that is normally used by women to invest in chit funds, or to meet social obligations to their natal kin, or for their children, though fathers often pay school fees.

Nonetheless, in the last analysis a variety of cultural and socio-psychological factors also play a part in how much autonomy a woman has—not only in relation to her husband but also to sons and to elders. Some women early in life are able to earn a reputation for being able to handle people (including their husbands) and being able to manage things well. Such women often are able to gain considerable autonomy in their households, and even in the community at large. However, the personality of the husband and sometimes that of his mother and father can also affect this. For example, a quarrelsome and erratic man can make life very difficult for such a woman. On the other hand, a man who is very family-oriented and understanding can see to it that even a woman who is not exceptionally efficient or good at human relations has more autonomy. Thus, within the social, economic and cultural parameters mentioned above there is still room for significant individual variation among households.

If one listens to the voices of the women themselves—the messages that get repeated in village after village—one hears another set of pleas or longings apart from their obvious pleas for economic change discussed above. These are longings to be treated better or for more autonomy in their own home or village. These do not come from all the women. Those who are lucky enough to have 'a good husband', a man who gives them an equal say in their household, or one who cares for them well, usually have no pleas to make. On the whole, they are content with their lot on the interpersonal level. But those who have not been so fortunate, and there are many of them, are asking for very basic changes in the ideology of the household and the attitudes and expected behaviour of males and females. It is possible that improving their economic situation will help with this, but it is hard to predict at this point.

I have heard their pleas over the years, on the many occasions that I have lived in rural villages. At times women spoke of them more freely to me or my assistant because we were outsiders, and thus what they told us would not be repeated to others in the village. Often these pleas came out in the context of our collecting their life histories. One of the more recent occasions when it came out was in a Tamil Nadu village, at a meeting which had been called to try and get the village men and women to discuss some of their agricultural problems. During the meeting the women in the audience sat absolutely quiet. After the meeting was over the men all got up and walked out, talking animatedly. My female assistant and I were quite slow in getting our things together, and after the men had left we suddenly found ourselves surrounded by about fifteen or twenty women. All of them seemed to want to talk at once. At first we thought that they too wanted to talk about needing work, or about agricultural problems. But that was not the case. Each one of the women, in turn, started to talk about her personal grievances. What was striking was that most of the things they wanted to talk about were associated with their own menfolk. One spoke about how her son was beating her, another about how her husband would not let her do something, another about her husband's drinking. The list was endless. I asked them why they did not help one another. They listened, but then said, each separately, 'But we have no unity here. If I ask her for help, she will say that it is my problem and I have caused it to happen.' Finally one woman said, 'If someone comes and organises us, then maybe it would be different. Now we are all talking, but this would never have happened otherwise.'

REFERENCES

ARNOULD, E.J. and McC. NETTING, 1982: 'Households: Changing Form and Function,' in *Current Anthropology*, Vol. 23, pp. 571–575.

HARDING, SUSAN, 1975: 'Women and Words in a Spanish Village,' in R. Reiter, ed., *Toward an Anthropology of Women* (New York, Monthly Review Press) pp. 283–308.

LEACOCK, E., 1978: 'Women's Status in Egalitarian Society: Implications for Social Evolution,' in *Current Anthropology*, Vol. 19, No. 2, pp. 247–276.

MENCHER, JOAN P., 1962: 'Changing Familial Roles among South Malabar Nayars,' *Southwestern Journal of Anthropology*, Vol. 18, pp. 230–245.

———, 1978a: *Agriculture and Social Structure in Tamil Nadu: Past Origins, Present Transformation, and Future Prospects* (New Delhi: Allied, Durham, N.C.: Carolina Academic Press).

———, 1978b: 'Agrarian Relations in Two Rice Regions of Kerala,' *Economic and Political Weekly*, pp. 349–366.

———, with K. Saradamoni and J. Panicker, 1979: 'Women in Rice Cultivation: Some Research Tools,' *Studies in Family Planning*, Vol. 11, November 1979.

———, 1982a: 'Agricultural Labourers and Poverty,' *Economic and Political Weekly*, Vol. XVII, Nos. 1 & 2, Jan. 2–9, pp. 38–43.

———, with K. Saradamoni, 1982b: 'Muddy Feet, Dirty Hands: Rice Production and Female Agricultural Labour,' *Economic and Political Weekly* Vol. XVII, A149–A167.

———, with S. Guhan, 1983: 'Iruvelipattu Revisited,' *Economic and Political Weekly*, Vol. XVIII, Nos. 23, 24 pp. 1013–1022, 1063–1074.

———, 1984a: 'Landless Women Agricultural Labourers in India,' in L.J. Unnevehr, ed., *Women in Rice Farming Systems*, Gower Publishing Co., Ltd.

———, 1984b: 'Women and Agriculture,' in *Strengthening National Food Policy Capability*, ed. by C. Mann and B. Huddelstan (New York: Rockefeller Foundation).

———, with D. D'Amico, 1984c: 'Kerala Women as Labourers and Supervisors: Implications for Women and Development,' *Visibility and Power: Essays on Women in Society and Development* (New Delhi: Oxford University Press).

———, 1985a: 'Women's Work and Poverty: Their Contribution to Household Maintenance in Two South Indian Regions,' in D. Dwyer and J. Brues, eds., *Women and Income Control*.

———. 1985b: 'What Constitutes Hard Work? Women as Labourers and as Managers in the Traditional Rice Regions of Kerala and Tamilnadu,' presented at a symposium on Gender in South Asia and East Asia, in Denver at the American Anthropological Assn. Meeting, Nov. 14–18, 1984.

SAUNDERS, L.W. and MEHENNA SOHAIR, 1983: 'Unseen Hands: Women's Work in Egyptian Agriculture,' paper presented at the XI International Congress of Anthropological and Ethnological Sciences in Vancouver, Aug. 1983. Revised version submitted for publication.

THARAMANGALAM, JOSEPH, 1981: *Agrarian Class Conflict* (Vancouver, Univ. of British Columbia Press).

II

The Gender Dimension of Health

Introduction

KARUNA CHANANA

I

The papers presented here focus on the need to embed policies relating to nutrition and health of girls and women within the household. What these papers suggest is basically a change in the approach to reach out to women. It is a plea for a contextual focus to look at women as embedded within the household and to foresake the existing approach of formulating individual oriented policies. These papers voice a plea to the policy-makers not to formulate the policies on the mere documentation of 'what' are the problems but to incorporate the insights gained from the explanations of it. In addition, the emphasis on the causes should incorporate the economic as well as the social dimensions in order to understand the social reality of women. It is this understanding of women's social reality which will provide the perspective for the solution to health issues and problems.

The concern over the gender dimension of health was an outcome of trends reflected in statistical and other data collected through micro-studies conducted by researchers and activists working at the grassroots level during the last decade or so. As a result, various issues and problems relating to the health of women have been identified. Some of these were selected for discussion at the workshop. The following pages outline the issues discussed.

While the problem of survival is common to both men and women in poor households, there is a contradiction involved in the relationship between a household and a woman. While the survival of the household depends, on the one hand, on the woman's health it also depends, on the other, on more hands for agricultural labour. Therefore, a woman has to produce more children and also be the custodian of their health often at the cost of her own health. We should be able to see this paradox and resolve it while enunciating policies and formulating programmes.

Again, it should not be assumed that increased household income will improve a woman's health and nutrition because all members do not benefit equally from household resources. For instance, preference for male children results in the boys' preferential access to food, health care and education. Thus, internal inequalities among members of a household and factors like male preference which result in unequal distribution of literacy and food are crucial in any discussion on state policy.

The need for a disaggregated approach should be highlighted since the inter- and intra-regional and ethnic differences are significant. For instance, in 1981 the female literacy rate in the rural areas in India was 13.2 per cent (42.3 per cent in urban areas) and it was 6.44 per cent for the Scheduled Caste women and 4.85 per cent for women of the Scheduled Tribes. Statewise, it was the lowest in Rajasthan and the highest in Kerala. The same holds true for female mortality rates. For instance, in 1981 there were 870 and 879 women per 1000 men in Haryana and Punjab respectively and 1032 in Kerala. The question is: why this difference when Punjab is a relatively prosperous state and Kerala is not? If we cannot explain it in terms of wider socio-economic development indicators, then should we not link high female mortality to socio-cultural factors rooted within the household?

Again, while a lot of data is available at the micro-level through numerous studies undertaken by women's groups and organisations, can we integrate these with macro-data? For instance, the linkages between literacy and health indicators at the macro-level could be substantiated through micro-studies. This may be done to establish the linkages, if any, or to explode the myth, if there are none.

Professor D. Banerji, the Chairperson of the Session, introduced the sub-theme by pointing out that the issue of women's health could not be viewed in isolation of the total social context. He stressed the need for, what he called, an epidemiological approach. He also cautioned that the anxiety for dealing with issues related to women should not divert us from the power structure and from investigating the overall dynamics of the problem.

While the four papers included in this section do not answer issues posed above, they, however, present quite a comprehensive and analytical view of women's health and nutrition and the related state policies and programmes in India and Bangladesh. The papers by Shamima Islam and N. Mahtab focus on Bangladesh while those of Chatterjee and Miller discuss the Indian situation. Again, while Chatterjee and Mahtab focus on policies and are country-level analyses, Miller and Islam's articles are based on micro-level data. Miller, for instance, relates policy to its impact on the survival of girls in the son preference culture of Punjab in India. Islam presents case studies to demonstrate the effect of seclusion or *parda* on the health of pregnant women, the survival chances of their children and the contribution of the traditional mid-wives. Chatterjee and Islam highlight the fact that policies are neither receptive to the needs of women nor do they appreciate the importance of women's informal role as health care providers.

Meera Chatterjee's paper points out the paradox in the Indian situation where women are the chief providers of health care within the household but are the most neglected so far as their own health is concerned. They have little access to external health care facilities provided by the government, especially in the rural areas. In addition, they suffer from nutritional deficiencies due to poor literacy and traditional beliefs. Again, maternal education levels influence family health for several reasons since education provides awareness of illness and health processes and also generates further education. Therefore, access to external health care is closely related to the education and employment of women. Thus, individuals, communities and other target groups are less useful than the household wherein the mother is embedded as the key to health, hygiene and knowledge. Moreover, in India there is the extra dimension of seclusion which restricts access of women to health care facilities outside of the home. This is graphically brought out in Islam's paper.

Chatterjee points out that there are two aspects to the problem, viz., competence and care. While the policies focusing on literacy, education and employment of women increase her 'competence' they also improve her role and status within the household. This in turn affects the health and nutrition of the family, i.e., the 'care' of the family. However, the programmes aimed at 'competence' and 'care' are not integrated.

Barbara Miller's study is located in Punjab. She uses macro-

level data as well as data generated through a health care programme which was used as an intervention strategy to improve the
survival rate of daughters in what she called 'the son preference
culture.' The situation is similar in Bangladesh (Ahmed, 1981).
Her main argument is that gender and household are the two key
dimensions that might be incorporated in all health care programmes
and resource allocation related to it. She argues that preference
for sons affects resource allocation and is directly linked to the
birth and survival of daughters. In addition to sex, birth order is
also significant. Miller's contention is that health care programmes
must differentiate their targets by sex.

Barbara Miller's paper identifies the risk factors within the
household in general and those for boys and girls in particular. It
concludes by arguing that even if social change in attitudes is not in
the offing, the policies of the government should be so directed
(given the resources) so as to increase the chances of a girl to be
born, to survive, and to live a healthy life. Further, that health
care intervention programmes can alter the survival chances of
girls inspite of cultural prejudices and social values.

The negative contribution of traditional beliefs and values and
the role of *parda* or seclusion in Bangladesh is highlighted by
Shamima Islam when she relates the case of a woman whose child
could not be delivered in the house but she was not to be taken to
the hospital to save the 'honour' of the family. She describes the
process of dismembering the child to save the life of at least the
mother. The demand for 'barefoot obstetricians' is great in such a
society where issues of 'honour' far outweigh those of life. The
midwives, rather than the governmental health agencies are the
source of medical care, counsel and guidance to the rural women.
Thus, it highlights the need to look at the role of the midwife
within the socio-cultural context, improvement in her skill and
training as well as the integration of public health services within
the existing structures of values and needs. A concerted program-
matic action is, therefore, essential to deal with the demographic
and health goals to enable its percolation to the district and *taluk*
level.

The phenomenon of 'barefoot obstetricians' raises some important issues, viz., the inter-relationship between health and education because health training is not integrated with the education
system. While these midwives are a huge reservoir of knowledge,

there are gaps too, especially about birth complications due to lack of training. They also present the possibility of bridging the gap between formal and informal education by being adequately trained to perform the role of midwives (also Rahman and Ali, 1981).

Mahtab outlines the policies of Bangladeshi Government relating to health, nutrition as well as education. She mentions at the outset that it had been difficult to weave together the three aspects. Since 90 per cent of women live in the rural areas, she concentrates on the rural women. According to Mahtab, poverty, illiteracy and tradition are the main detractors in women's health and nutrition. The national statistics on health show that a majority of women suffered from malnutrition. Though the government had drawn up policies, there was a gap between policy and programme on the one hand, and programmes and their implementation on the other. The setting up of a separate ministry only complicated matters and delayed decision-making. She concludes by arguing that there is a need to change the attitudes towards women.

The discussion after the presentation of the papers centred on the following dimensions. First, that inspite of the global commitment to universal health care by 2000 A.D., Asia's problems continue. There seems no awareness of how statistics will be changed into reality. While policies have demographic goals, they do not incorporate ways of making women take advantage of available resources.

Second, statistics are ignored while formulating policies. For example, although about 65 per cent pregnant women and 55 per cent of non-pregnant women in Asia suffer from anaemia, hardly anything was being done to introduce programmes in order to improve the iron intake of women. A question was asked as to why there was no link between basic information on technology and nutrition with the situation that produced this poor health status. Again, while an Indian woman spent sixteen out of the thirty years of her reproductive life on pregnancy and lactation, yet no specific programme was focused on this group of women.

Women are forced into closely spaced multiple pregnancies because of the high value of motherhood especially geared to the birth of male children. It is ironic that even though they need more health care than men, they get far less. It was also pointed out that about 80 per cent of women in Bangladesh received health care from native healers who either lacked training or were improperly trained.

Bangladesh and India (and perhaps the other South Asian countries) share a common reality in so far as their women have a poorer health status than men. They suffer from protein and caloric deficiency apart from several diseases which are exclusive to them. Further, nutritional deficiency was culturally institutionalised in some regions of South Asia.

It was also pointed out that the phenomenal expansion in health infrastructure is not responsive to women's health needs as is evident from the morbidity figures. Also, the proportion of women dying in the age group of 15–35 years has remained constant over the past decades. Moreover, policies should incorporate insights gained from unreported data as well. For instance, for every two men only one woman was reported to be using public medical facilities. What were the reasons for this? Did women suffer from less diseases and illnesses or were they not provided medical care due to cultural prejudice and the constraining influence of seclusion?

Policies should identify health issues clearly. They should not be confused with family planning. Family planning programmes are female centred to the exclusion of other decision makers within the household. They put all the responsibility of the utilisation of family planning inputs on the women, who are not the decision-makers, and assume an automatic utilisation of facilities. This is yet another imposition on the overburdened woman who is treated as a passive receiver.

It was also argued that though poverty was an important factor to be taken into consideration in the analysis of gender based allocation of nutrition and medical care within the household, the fact remained that often the poor woman bears the double burden of lack of resources and cultural prejudice. Policies as well as programmes show insufficient appreciation of the informal role of women as household health care providers.

II

Numerous developments have taken place since this conference was held. Awareness about health issues and problems, especially those of women, has increased manifold. Information has been generated both at the macro- and micro-level on the various dimensions mentioned above. The information and data thus gathered has gone into the policy framing and programme formulation on health. However, while we have moved a little ahead, some of the problems and issues identified earlier continue and have attracted the attention of women's groups and development agencies. A survey of the scene does not seem to indicate a radical alteration in the health situation of women either in India or in Bangladesh.

'While India could boast of being the tenth industrial power, it was only three places from the bottom even among the Asian countries in the field of health.' This statement was made by Dr. C. Gopalan, President of the Nutrition Foundation of India, on December 19, 1988 while delivering the Seventh J.P. Naik Memorial Lecture in New Delhi.

> Out of 12 million girls who are born in India every year, only 9 million reach their fifteenth year. In fact one and a half million die within the first year and 85,000 within five years of their birth. (Chatterjee, 1988 p. 1)

Information on demographic indicators, such as, the declining sex ratio, high infant and female mortality, the unfavourable survival chances of girls and women up to the age of 35 years and the regional variations among them have been well documented. A woman in the sub-continent runs the risk of one in eighteen of dying from a pregnancy related cause (Chhabra, 1988 p. 9). 'Women face high risk of malnutrition, retardation in growth and development, disease, disability and even death at three critical stages in their lives, viz., infancy, early childhood and adolescence and the reproductive phases' (GOI, 1988 p. 97). However, some of these findings have been known since the publication of the report of the Committee on the Status of Women in 1974. This report highlighted the influence of social customs and attitudes on the health of women while the deterioration in the health status of women was brought into focus through demographic analysis.

The impetus received by women's studies and the data generated by the voluntary agencies working for the upliftment of women during the intervening fifteen years have generated further information to confirm the doubts raised and trends which were documented in 1974. Since then the Government of India has initiated various schemes focusing on the health dimensions of women. However, the most important programme to date which affects the health of women has been the family planning programme. The adverse effects of some contraceptives and the shift from vasectomy to tubectomy (and other female oriented techniques or contraceptives) have also been documented. Women's groups have been vaxing eloquent about the harmful effects and health hazards of this shift from men to women. They point out greater risks to women due to the insanitary conditions in which women live, and non-availability of post-operative care and follow up but also to the indifferent and callous attitudes of those involved in the implementation of these schemes. Therefore, even with the availability of advance medical techniques women suffer health hazards. However, the fact that the family planning programmes have pushed the health issue of women to the background is only one issue. Apart from that, it is also not conceived within the social context in which women are embedded, a point elaborated later.

Apart from the negative impact of health related and family planning policies and programmes on women, voluntary agencies have also compiled information on the development oriented policies and programmes. These agencies raise very pertinent and fundamental questions regarding the adverse impact of such programmes on women's health. To give just one example, the forest policy has not only denuded the forests it has also taken away major resources, namely, food, fodder and fuel from poor women. Their consequent shortage has affected the overall household resources as well as the health of women. Women have to travel longer distances to collect firewood and fodder and lift heavy weights for longer duration. It also means longer working hours for women. Therefore, several studies have emphasised the need to regulate policies on agriculture, employment, work, housing, etc., and also to take account of the health of the population in general but of poor women in particular while framing development policies.

Further, it has also been argued that research and development (R & D) in science and technology should focus on developing new and more efficient technology to safeguard women's health, for example, by improving the methods of cooking and by promoting better fuel which will be smokeless. However, whatever advances and innovations have been made so far have had very limited impact on the lives of poor women. Thus, most of these studies on the health dimension of development policies are in favour of identifying women as a specific target group and in regulating these policies.

Further, at the marco-level linkages have been established between several non-health indicators and the health of women. Of these, literacy emerges as a significant variable at the national and state levels. For example, in the lecture by C. Gopalan, referred to above, South Korea and Japan were mentioned as examples of countries which have done well on the health front and have achieved very high or full literacy. Education of women is linked to fertility reduction (Jain and Nag, 1985 p. 1). Again, educated mothers have a better command over medical knowledge and information about medical facilities (Flegg, 1982). Other micro-studies indicate reduction in infant mortality with increase in women's education (Mandelbaum, 1975). Therefore, it is being argued that the economic factors along with literacy and education are crucial in order to improve the health status of the poor in general and of women in particular. In fact, female literacy is assumed to be directly related to development. In other words, low literacy or illiteracy is negatively related to health indicators. Again, an inverse relationship is established between literacy and education, on the one hand, and fertility on the other (Chowdhury, 1976).

While the demographic trends and their linkages at the state level are significant, it is also important to outline the reality at the grassroots level. Studies undertaken by various groups and voluntary organisations in India and Bangladesh[1] have yielded rich data. Most of the findings are depressing since they highlight the continued neglect of the health of women. Some studies, for instance, have indicated that girls and women are not only the last to receive food but also receive less amount and food of lesser quality (Devadas and Kamalanathan, 1985; Mitra, 1983; Jorgensen, 1982 p. 11; Chen et al., 1981). In fact, discrimination in feeding begins very early. A boy, for example, is breastfed more often and for longer duration than a girl (Feldman et al., 1981 p. 7). Sen and Sen

[1] See Mahmuda Islam, 1984. It is an annotated bibliography of studies on women in Bangladesh and contains a separate section on health, nutrition and fertility.

Gupta have argued that development efforts and health programmes do not reach every family or its individual members
equally. Women and the girls benefit the least and the last (1983).
Moreover, there is a connection between the position of women
and under-nourishment since the relations between the sexes
determine the distribution of food within the family and the
household. Thus, there is a linkage between the power relations
between the sexes within the household and who gets how much
food. This unequal distribution is legitimated by food taboos
relating to meat, fish and eggs (Schrijvers, 1985 p. 6). Again, girls
and women suffer from malnutrition (Chen et al., 1981) and are
taken to consult doctors and hospitals less often than boys and
men, or they simply go without treatment (Mankekar, 1985).
Therefore, the health status of girls is poorer than of boys,
especially among the poor (Punjab, 1974; M.D. Oswal, 1986).

In addition, women suffer from many more chronic deficiencies
and diseases than men (Mankekar, 1985). The following quotes
from a study in Bangladesh refer to a situation which is applicable
to India as well, with minor variations in the percentages mentioned
therein.

> Expectant and lactating mothers also represent a large per-
> centage of malnourished Bangladeshis; 85 per cent of them
> suffer from low hemoglobin, 45 per cent from protein deficiency,
> 42 per cent from vitamin A deficiency and 42 per cent from
> clinic goitre. (Feldman, 1981 p. 7)

> Most women never get any compensation for their loss of blood
> at childbirth and during menstruation, and this in conjunction
> with malnourishment results in chronic anaemia. Almost all the
> women we talked to about their illnesses mentioned physical
> tiredness, headache and faintness as the most common physical
> troubles. . . . (Jorgensen, 1982 p. 12)

> An examination of 200 symptoms of women's diseases showed
> that, beside symptoms of anaemia, gynaecological problems
> were the most frequent. Those problems which were most
> common were prolapse, pain in the female organs, and irregular
> bleeding (Mahmuda Islam, 1980)

To summarise, it has been observed by several studies that some of the causes of female mortality are: poor health, recurring child-births, unhygienic conditions during delivery and lack of medical help, etc.

The above discussion leads to the main argument, namely, that while poverty or lack of resources continue to affect the health of a large number of women in South Asia, especially in India and Bangladesh, social practices and cultural norms also account for and explain some of the differences between the sexes. And that we have to focus on the household in order to understand the significance of the latter. In other words, gender and household, apart from class or poverty are two crucial variables that affect the health of women and therefore should be incorporated in the policies relating to health. Thus, there is need to undertake a two-level analysis while formulating policies on health. First, it is true that poverty and the resultant lack of resources affect the health of the poor, men as well as women, in India and Bangladesh. However, women are the worst sufferers on account of child-bearing and its direct effect on their health and health needs. For instance, they suffer from hunger and disease (not that poor men are exempt but they are less so) and sheer non-availability of clean water, sanitary living conditions, occupational hazards (so well documented in *Shramshakti*[2]) as well as from lack of information (e.g., tuberculosis being a preventable and curable disease). In this manner, the health problems of the poor women, who form a bulk of the population in these two countries are different from those who are not poor. However, at another level, women in general are separated from men of all strata. For instance, other things being equal, men get the best and more food and medical facilities than do women, a point we elaborate later. This difference can be explained with reference to the socialisation practices and cultural value placed on girls and women in a society.

III

Social customs and religious norms define the roles assigned to men and women within a particular society. It is within the house-

[2] Report of the National Commission on Self-Employed Women and Women in the Informal Sector, 1988.

hold that children grow up as boys and girls and imbibe the cultural values and behaviour patterns associated with appropriate male and female behaviour. Therefore, while poverty and incumbent scarcity of resources—or class, occupation and caste—may delimit the amount and quality of food, water, medical care and living conditions, cultural norms may further define or decide the distribution of these resources and facilities to each member of the household according to sex, status, age, etc.

> It is equally important to look at the way of life of the individual, or what D. Banerji calls the 'health culture'. This means, to put it briefly, to look at factors such as the food a person eats, his/her access to clean water and hygienic living conditions, the ecological environment, the meaning and significance given to sickness and disease in the community, the access to health facilities. These factors are determined for individuals by their status in the family and community, which in turn is a product largely of their age, sex, occupation, caste and class. That is to say, age and sex determine the individual's role status and so affect facts of his or her way of life, while caste, class and occupation determine the actual living conditions within which the individual has to operate. (Fazalbhoy, 1988 p. 16)

These variables are important and operate among all the sections of societies in India and Bangladesh with minor variations among the different religious groups, different regions (as in India), between the urban and the rural areas, among the rich and the poor, etc. While religion is crucial in defining cultural norms we are not going into the details except in so far as it enjoins seclusion for a majority of women in Bangladesh and also for women in those parts of India where seclusion is in practice. It affects the health status of women in these societies by depriving them of timely medical care in order to save their lives or those of their unborn or newly born children (refer to Islam's paper in this volume). Seclusion confines women to within the four walls of the household and also deprives them of opportunities for education and better health because they cannot be permitted to move outdoors to avail of schooling and medical facilities nor can they be allowed to be attended to by male doctors and taught by male teachers.

Added to the issue of poverty is the incidence of *purdah* or segregation between sexes and seclusion for women. The system of *purdah* affects women severely in terms of their mobility, schooling opportunities, access to communication, and their exposure to health care facilities. Beyond the issue of *purdah*, rural women are tremendously affected by their overall social status which considers women as a liability. (S. Islam, 1981 p. 3)

Apart from female seclusion, other notable socio-cultural practices and values that affect the health of women directly or indirectly are: the value placed on sons, the age at marriage, dowry, the expected role of the woman as daughter, as wife and as mother, etc. Papers by Miller and Shamima Islam in this volume highlight the role of socio-cultural values and practices and their impact on the health of women. While Miller focuses on the high value placed on boys in Punjab in India and its impact on the survival of female infants and girls, Islam highlights the constraints of seclusion and links it to the possibility of the unavailability of medical care outside the household for expectant mothers even at the risk of the life of the child and the mother. Sometimes, young married women, when hospitalised and needing extra blood, are not provided blood by their family members. Again, young married daughters-in-law may be sent home when they are ill.

Thus, the notion of 'proper' and 'improper', and the social value of the individual determine the access to health facilities outside as well as inside the household.

Power relations not only define what is health in the perceptions of women on their own health needs, but also determine access to health care (such as, food and medical attention) and the degree of control women have over body events that influence health, such as, pregnancy or child bearing and the amount of rest and recuperation available after sickness, after child birth and after work. (Krishnaraj, 1987 p. 219)

Thus, as mentioned earlier, the premise of the papers in this section is that the health of women, which includes birth and survival is rooted within the household. It is within the household that resources are allocated for food, medical care, etc., and are distributed according to the priority assigned to the different members of the household. It is one of the major assertions of these papers that cultural and economic factors overlap in denying girls and women their right to be born, to survive after birth and to live a healthy life in the countries of South Asia, especially India and Bangladesh on which these papers focus. Therefore, it is a plea to take the issue of the health of women out of their (women's) purview and to bring it within the household since all decisions affecting a woman's health are taken within the parameters of the household.

For instance, social norms prohibit women from eating with their husbands and the rest of the family. On the other hand, men are also socialised in a manner that they do not notice lack of food for their wives and children who eat after them. Nor are they aware of the health problems of their women.

> In terms of health care access, women's needs become sub-
> ordinate to women's status which is dictated by important
> family members and more often by husbands who, in many
> instances, consider public exposure, like clinic visit or confine-
> ment as a violation of *purdah* for the family (S. Islam, 1981 p. 3)

Women are also prohibited from discussing details of their health and medical problems with other members (especially the males) of the household. It is ironic that while women suffer chronically from iron deficiency and malnutrition, and while their body is constantly degenerated due to childbirth they are expected not to give too much importance to it (i.e., tell others about their ailments or expect medical treatment) in order to refurbish it. Women, therefore are expected to be an inexhaustible resource for men to draw from.[3]

In the patriarchal societies of India and Bangladesh a high value is placed on the sons for ritual and social reasons notwithstanding exceptions. This devalues the position of the daughters. The practice of virilocal residence, patriliny and dowry further augment this process of devaluation. As a result, girls are under threat right from conception. Thus, amniocentesis devised to detect deformities in unborn children has become a convenient tool to abort female

[3] G.P. Chattopadhyay, 1981: 'The Bovine Image of the Indian Woman,' in *Towards Continuing Education: Newsletter of the Public Enterprises Centre for Continuing Education*, New Delhi, Vol. 3, No. 5, pp. 231–32.

foetuses in our country. The fact that only a very small minority are affected by this practice or that the girls who hang themselves before marriage are few and far between is not important. What is at issue here is that even though people are receiving education, traditional customs and values are not getting eroded. It is symptomatic of the malaise affecting our societies which place low value on their daughters. This is inspite of the fact that international reports have highlighted the contribution of women to development.

IV

What is development if nearly half of the population of these countries is facing a threat at each step—a threat to their birth, survival and healthy living. Existing policies on the health of women fail to focus on the causes of poor female health except in a fragmented manner. The focus should be on the explanations and their incorporation in an integrated manner at the policy formulation stage. In addition to an integrated view of the women, an appraisal of the family planning programme is also required so that it does not push the health issues to the background.

The expenditure on family planning programme has increased from Rs. 409 crores in the Fifth Plan to Rs. 3256 crores in the Seventh Plan. The outlay on health in the Seventh Plan is also Rs. 3392 crores (NPP, 1988 p. 135). A cursory glance at the bibliography on the studies on health, nutrition and fertility of women in Bangladesh (M. Islam, 1984), referred to earlier, shows that a majority of the studies in this section are on fertility and population problems and therefore relate directly or indirectly to the family planning programme. During the last decade, studies on pregnant and lactating mothers have also assumed importance. Thus, the health issues of women seem to revolve around different dimensions of her reproductive role (Batliwala, 1983) whereas their health ought to be viewed in totality covering her whole life right after birth as well as in the context of the other variables, such as, education and work.

In fact, the latest UNICEF report on the state of world's children, 1989, suggests that national growth should be measured through economic as well as social indicators. It includes literacy levels, availability of food and water, sanitation and mortality rate of infants under five in the category of social indicators of development and growth. If one were to look at girls in India and Bangladesh and their access to these social indicators the future looks bleak and depressing indeed. Therefore, 'measures to improve the social and health situation would have to form part and parcel of a multi-sectoral package operationalised simultaneously, in complementary thrusts' (Chhabra, 1988 p. 2).

Several recommendations have been made in order to improve the health of women. Apart from the recommendations discussed below, there is also a felt need for building a data base. For instance, although several micro-studies have been undertaken yet we are nowhere near a systematic analysis of women's health status. More research should be undertaken on women's specific health needs within socio-cultural, economic and political contexts. Again, the linkages between female literacy on the one hand, and female mortality and infant mortality on the other, need to be substantiated and established at the micro-level. Further, as already mentioned, R & D in science and technology should focus on women's health.

As mentioned above, several recommendations have been made which are practical as well as theoretical. The first set of recommendations are practical and refer to a specific issue or some dimensions of women's health whereas the second set provides a framework within which to locate and understand issues of gender and health. In the first set one may include recommendations such as the need for community studies at the micro-level to identify areas of intervention. Or, for example, the impact of the policy relating to maternity leave on women. Or that the family planning programme should not be detrimental to women's health.

On the other hand, as a solution to the contradiction in the position of women, some voluntary organisations have begun to emphasize the need to change the position of women through the promotion of an awareness of and knowledge of their health, diseases, cleanliness, and body, etc. They prepare the women to demand the programmes that suit them and also organise protests against those which do not suit them.

Some have also argued that the solution to the problem of gender and health lies in viewing the latter as a part of general subordination of women in society (Krishnaraj, 1987 p. 251). Therefore, it is suggested that her capacity to take decisions and to earn income should be raised. Again, Islam's paper is a pointer in a direction that traditional midwives or barefoot doctors who are culturally acceptable may be retrained to fit the requirements of women's health even within the framework of modern medicine.

However, there is a limitation in that this awareness and knowledge has to be generated within the parameters of the family ideology since a direct questioning of family ideology is likely to be counter-productive. What can be done is to improve the quality of life of women and through them of the family members, to strengthen their position as individual members, to make them aware of themselves and their needs and what to expect from the society. Thus, in a way these may indirectly subvert family ideology but any consciousness on the part of the male members that the traditional role structure and relationships are being questioned or threatened may halt the process of change in the lives of women. However, what is crucial is to understand that health is a complex issue and is not a purely medical or an economic problem. Also, the distribution of resources within the household depends on the age, status and sex of each individual member. Therefore, 'household' should not be seen as a homogeneous group which satisfies the needs of all the members equally. 'The underlying assumption of harmonious relations hides the fact that households consist of individuals who have unequal power (men, women and children) (Schrijvers, 1985 p. 7). Therefore, it is misleading 'to use the concept of household as the smallest unit of analysis in the context of access to resources' (Schrijvers, 1985 p. 7). This is especially true in the context of women's health.

REFERENCES

AHMED, NILUFAR R., 1981: 'Family Size and Sex Preference Among Women in Rural Bangladesh,' in *Studies in Family Planning*, Vol. 12, No. 3, March.

BATLIWALA, S., 1983: 'Women in Poverty: The Energy, Health and Nutrition Syndrome,' The Foundation for Research in Community Health, Bombay, 18 February.

CHATTERJEE, MEERA, 1988: *Both Gender and Age Against Them: A Status Report on Indian Women from Birth to Twenty* (NIPCCD, mimeographed).

CHEN, L., E. HUQ and S. D'SOUZA, 1981: 'Sex Bias in the Family Allocation of Food and Health Care in Rural Bangladesh,' in *Population and Development Review*, Vol. 7, No. 1, March.

CHHABRA, RAMI, 1988: *Health and Family Welfare: Plan of Action for Women*, mimeographed.

CHOWDHURY, RAFIQUL HUDA, 1976: 'Education and Fertility in Bangladesh,' paper presented at the annual conference of Bangladesh Economic Association, March 15–18.

DEVADAS, R and G. KAMALANATHAN, 1985: 'A Woman's First Decade,' Presentation at Women's NGO Consultation, UNICEF (mimeographed).

FAZALBHOY, N., 1988: *The Health Status of Indian Women: A Reader* (Tata Institute of Social Sciences, Bombay, Unit for Women's Studies).

FELDMAN, S., F. AKHTAR, and F. BANU, 1981: *An Assessment of the Government's Health and Family Planning Programme—A Case Study of Daukandi Thana and North Mohammedpur and Charcharua Villages* (SIDA, Health Division), July.

FLEGG, A.T., 1982: 'Inequality of Income, Illiteracy, and Medical Care as Determinants of Infant Mortality in Underdeveloped Countries,' in *Population Studies*, Vol. 36, No. 3, pp. 441–58.

GOPALAN, C., 1988: 'New Health Order Proposed,' in *The Times of India*, December 20, Section 2, p. 1.

Govt. of India, 1988: *National Perspective Plan for Women: 1988–2000 A.D.*, Report of the Core Group set up by the Deptt. of Women and Child Welfare (New Delhi, Ministry of Human Resource Development).

ISLAM, MAHMUDA, 1984: *Bibliography on Bangladesh Women with Annotation*, second edn. (Dhaka, Women for Women).

ISLAM, SHAMIMA, 1981: *Indigeneous Abortion Practitioners in Rural Bangladesh: Women Abortionists, Their Perceptions and Practices* (Dhaka, Women for Women).

JAIN, ANRUDH, K. and MONI NAG, 1987: 'Importance of Female Primary Education for Fertility Reduction in India,' in Ratna Ghosh and M. Zachariah eds., *Education and the Process of Change* (New Delhi, Sage Publications), pp. 157–77.

JORGENSEN, VIBEKE, 1988: *Poor Rural Women in Bangladesh: Pregnancy and Health Status*, mimeographed.

KRISHNARAJ, M., 1987: 'Health—A Gender Issue in India,' in N. Desai and M. Krishnaraj eds., *Women and Society in India* (Delhi, Ajanta Publications), pp. 219–53.

MITRA, TARAES, 1983: 'Some Reflections on Women's Problems in India,' presented at the workshop on *Women and Poverty*, Calcutta, 17–19 March, mimeographed.

MANDELBAUM, DAVID, 1975: 'Some Effects of Population Growth in India on Social Interaction and Religion,' in Marcus F. Franda ed., *Responses to Population Growth in India* (New York, Praegar), pp. 62–116.

MANKEKAR, PURNIMA, 1985: 'The Girl Child in India—Data Sheet on Health,' (New Delhi, National Media Centre and UNICEF).

National Perspective Plan for Women, 1988–2000 AD: A Perspective from the Women's Movement, Report of a Debate, New Delhi, 22–3 August 1988.

OSWAL, MOHAN DAI, 1986: *Annual Report*, Ludhiana, Cancer Treatment and Research Foundation.

Punjab, Government of, and CARE, 1974: *Nutrition in Punjab* (Punjab Nutrition Development Project).

RAHMAN, ATIQUR and M. NAWAB ALI, 1981: *Indigeneous Birth Attendants in Bangladesh* (Dhaka, The Population Control and Family Planning Division).

SCHRIJVERS, JOKE, 1985: *Blue Print for Under Nourishment: The Example of the Mahaveli River Development Scheme*, Mimeographed.

SEN, A, and S. SEN GUPTA, 1983: 'Malnutrition of Rural Children and the Sex Bias,' in N. Fazalbhoy, *The Health Status of Indian Women: A Reader* (Tata Institute of Social Sciences, Bombay, Unit for Women's Studies), p. 24. p. 24.

Shramshakti: Report of the National Commission on Self-Employed Women and Women in the Informal Sector (New Delhi), 1988.

Competence and Care for Women: Health Policy Perspectives in the Household Context

MEERA CHATTERJEE

India's policies—their bases, their forms and their effects—can be examined in the framework of three propositions: (1) that health outcomes and household activities are intimately linked; (2) that within the household women are the main health care providers; and (3) yet, paradoxically, women's own health and the health of children who are most dependent on women's care is woefully poor. One can then proceed to examine whether state policies take into account the needs and circumstances facing women in the household, and, if so, how the relevant policies are translated into programme strategies, and what their impact is on the health of woman and the household.

A BASIS FOR POLICY

Proposition 1: 'Household' and Health are Intimately Linked.

How does the household impinge on health and nutrition outcomes? I am not a social scientist and so will refrain from discussing the merits and demerits of the choice of 'household' over 'family'. However, as a health and nutrition scientist and planner I find that the term 'household' has a particular significance.

Anthropologists describe the household variously as the unit of production, consumption, residence, reproduction, socialisation, or a combination of these. When considering health and nutrition outcomes one finds that all these facets of 'household' are germane.

As the unit within which people cooperate with one another to produce or acquire food, clothing, shelter, health care and other necessities of life, the household is in charge, as it were, of maintaining the health of all its members. Household production dictates health because the resources gathered determine the capacity of its members to acquire 'health goods and services'. Household consumption and, particularly, the intra-household distribution of 'consumables', such as, food, water and clothing determine the nutrition and health status of the individuals that comprise the household unit. Nutrition and health status are also the result of the balance between energy expended in production and that obtained through consumption, and so the aggregate household 'energy level' is an important determinant of the health of its members.

As a residential or dwelling group, the household is the immediate health environment of its members who 'share' (whether equitably or not) a common water source, sanitation facilities, breathing space, a hearth, and other facilities. This has important implications for the acquisition, transmission, prevention and treatment of disease.

As a reproductive unit, the household determines the number of children to be born within it. Child-bearing directly affects the health of reproductive women, and indirectly the health and survival of other children. Ultimately, the size of the household determines the *per capita* availability of resources, and, thereby, the health of all its members.

Finally, as a socialising unit, the household is responsible for other health 'inputs': the availability of health related knowledge through formal or informal education; the use of such knowledge through health care practices within the home or in interactions with external health institutions; the 'inheritance' or inter-generational transmission of such knowledge; the practice of health related rituals, and so on. Mental development and mental health are also important outcomes of the socialisation that takes place within the household.

From a methodological perspective, the understanding of health and nutrition outcomes necessitates attention both to the composition of the household (who resides within it, their ages and sexes as well as their relationships) and to its organisation function (who does what for whom, how much is consumed by whom, who makes the decisions and implements them, etc.). Whether or not related by blood or marriage, any inhabitant of a household has an effect on its health status and implications for its health care because (1) all individuals have a health profile themselves, (2) can be agents who transmit disease or prevent it; and (3) could (in theory, at least) be responsible for providing health care within the household or acquiring it from outside.

At this point, two caveats are in order. First, although the household is itself a complex system of cooperation, it is, in turn, linked to other households and institutions around it. It derives a livelihood from a variety of different external sources and activities. Certainly, any examination of its health status must pay heed to the environment—physical, social, economic, and political—in which it functions. Of particular concern are the agents and agencies from which it derives its food (nutrition), its water, its hygiene, and its knowledge, which are all important determinants of health, and the health care institutions with which it interacts. Second, even within the household unit there is 'differentiation'—by gender, by age, by role, and so on. This heterogeneity has important implications for health because it is usually associated with different sets of standards for different people. For example, there are often different rules on food and eating for different people within the household. 'Hot' foods may be considered appropriate for men but not for women and children. External health care may be sought more for males than for females, or for adults more than children.

Proposition 3: Women and Children Have the Worst Health.

It is this differentiation within the household that focuses attention on women—first in terms of their health problems and needs, and, second, in their roles and responsibilities in the sphere of health—bringing us to Propositions 2 and 3.

If one can discern shades of deterioration in India's overall poor health situation, women are amongst the worst victims of sickness, disease, malnutrition and premature death in the country. I have written on this in detail elsewhere (Chatterjee, 1983) and so will review it only briefly here. The situation can be clearly established by macro-level indicators such as age- and sex-specific mortality rates, life expectancy, and the sex ratio. In 1978, the countrywide death rate for females was significantly higher than that of males (14.5 per 1000 population compared with 13.8).[1] While in urban areas, males had a slightly higher death rate than females (9.6 and 9.1 respectively), in rural areas, where the bulk of the population is concentrated, the reverse was true (14.9 for males and 15.8 for females). Differences between males and females in rural and urban areas are greater in some states of the country.

A comparison of male and female death rates for the five-year age groups reveals that females have higher mortality than males upto the age of 35 years which includes female children, adolescents and most 'reproductive women'. Higher female mortality results in lower female life expectancy. For the period of 1970–1975 life expectancy at birth, at age 5 and at age 15 was about one and a half years less for women than for men. This gap has been increasing since 1921, prior to which women actually had a higher expectancy of life than men.

Another outcome of the higher mortality among females and the widening gap in life expectancy has been the country's declining sex ratio. Although the 1981 census seems to suggest a stabilisation of this trend, a level of 935 females per 1000 males is still markedly disproportionate.

The proximate causes of higher female mortality are higher rates of disease and malnutrition among them, which are inadequately documented in macro-level data but are usually clearly brought out by small-scale surveys and studies (e.g., Jesudason and Chatterjee, 1979). Perhaps the only proximate causes of death which are indisputably 'higher' among women are those connected with pregnancy and delivery, because, of course, there is no point of comparison with men! The aggregate maternal mortality rate of over 500 deaths per 100,000 live births is extremely high and reflects high rates of anaemia or general malnutrition, post-partum infections and inadequate obstetric care. Besides this there is evidence that women may suffer more from diseases, such as, tuberculosis, though morbidity data in the aggregate are woefully inadequate. Data on female morbidity are incomplete largely because they are collected at health centres to which women venture only infrequently. However, Kynch and Sen (1983) have cited a couple of hospital-based data sets which show greater illness among females than males.

[1] See GOI (1983) for these and other relevant statistics.

There are a few studies comparing the health of women and men in the same household. One such study followed 110 families over a period of almost two years and found a significant difference in the number of illnesses per year suffered by 'mothers' compared with 'fathers' (10.8 compared with 6.0) (Kamath *et al.*, 1969). Unfortunately, data on children under 10 and other members of the household were not disaggregated by sex, but had this been done the difference between males and females would undoubtedly have been greater.

That women do have a worse health status than men is widely believed. However, one recent note of dissent must be acknowledged. Kamala Jaya Rao (1984) has challenged the common assumption that women are more undernourished than men, and used data from annual surveys of the National Nutrition Monitoring Bureau (NNMB) to uphold her contention. The NNMB data shows that the per cent of females who consume adequate calories has been consistently greater than that of males in ten states surveyed over seven years of data collection. The greater shortfall among male intakes is reflected in their greater deficit of body weight for height. In the aggregate, women surveyed were 5–10 per cent closer to their 'expected' weights for height than men. Further, Jaya Rao has questioned the assertion that rural women expend more energy than men (made by Batliwala in 1983) by pointing out that their body weight deficits should then be greater than men's, which is disproved by the NNMB data.

These findings conflict somewhat with the 'conventional wisdom' that women eat far less than men (relative to their individual requirements) which has arisen out of the ubiquitous anthropological observation that food in Indian households is served first to men and male children, and last to female children and adult women. Although it is difficult to accept Jaya Rao's conclusion that because cooking and serving of foods are entirely in the hands of women, they are able 'to ward off any possible discrimination against them(selves),' the reasons for the apparent contradiction between anthropologic observation and scientific measurement must be explored. There are some plausible explanations. First, the NNMB data may contain a 'sex bias' because the women respondents do not 'admit' (realise) that they consume less than their share of the household pot or that men consume more. The parallel for this is the often reported finding that women do not admit to discriminating against their female children. (Although this time the evidence, as Jaya Rao herself says—e.g., higher levels of malnutrition among pre-school females than males—is indisputable. Indeed, Jaya Rao somewhat contradicts herself when she accepts that female pre-school children are more malnourished than males in the same age group *even though the NNMB data does not show sex difference* in caloric adequacy 'and only a marginal disadvantage to females in body weights.) Second, there may be 'investigator' bias in the data. This may be exacerbated by the inaccuracy of methods to measure calorie consumption at the household level, let alone for individuals within the household. The problems of accurately assessing nutritional status from diet surveys, which use the household as the unit of observation even if the data are collected separately for different age and sex groups, within the household have been pointed out (Gopalan, 1983). Third, there is the possibility that the weight-height standards are less appropriate for women than for men. The appropriateness of nutritional standards is an ongoing debate, though less attention has been paid to gender differences than to socio-economic differences. Fourth, if the data and interpretations are in fact unbiased, it is still possible that the findings hold only when a cross-section of economic groups (such as, those included in the NNMB sample) is considered. As socio-economic level rises and women's activity is restricted, the balance of consumption over expenditure is likely to favour women more than men. On the other hand, among the poor whose consumption is low, men may save energy through unemployment or under-employment while women become more malnourished because their domestic drudgery remains intense and unavoidable. Although Jaya Rao has stated . her purpose as 'not to minimise the magnitude of undernutrition among women but to show that men are equally malnourished,' one might conclude that the NNMB data do not, in fact, answer the question of comparative male and female nutritional status within individual households and that such cross-sectional data particularly obscure the adverse 'differentiation' that occurs in the face of extreme poverty.

Although the relative health of adult men and women may be a subject of dispute, the differences in the. health and nutritional status of male and female children are well documented. Sex differences in anthropometric measures of nutritional status such as height and weight among young children, and differences in child mortality between boys and girls provide clear evidence of the inequality of consumption and sex discrimination. Furthermore, that children as a group—particularly those under five years of age—have the poorest health is clearly established by mortality and morbidity data for this age group which need not be reiterated here (see Chatterjee, 1983).

The sociological reasons underlying the poor health of women and children are widely appreciated. In 'primitive' or poor societies, they appear to derive mainly from the importance accorded to adult male wage earners and to male children as potential wage earners within the 'unit of survival'—the family (*sic*). Unless the physical needs of the wage earner are satisfied, dependents have no entitlements, and, then, only in order of their potential economic value. Thus, a male child is treated preferentially compared with a female child, or even with his mother. A ten-year old boy will receive a food ration quite out of proportion to his requirements even when compared with his lactating mother. The same concern for the economic survival of the family is manifest in the greater utilisation of health services by males compared with females. Besides the lack of appreciation this situation spells for women's unpaid work, it is also somewhat paradoxical, when one considers proposition 2, that women are the main health care-takers within the (family and) household.

Proposition 2: Women are the Guardians of Household Health.

Within the household, women assume a number of responsibilities beyond their family roles. Besides being daughters, wives, mothers or mothers-in-law—with all the responsibilities these entail—they are also labourers, producers, cooks, cleaners, child-minders, nurses, and so on. This variety of roles makes them the 'guardians of health', and, traditionally, intra-household tasks related to health and nutrition have been almost exclusively the preserve of women. The provision of nourishment (preparation of food, cooking and feeding) and maintenance of hygiene (washing of clothes, cleaning of utensils, sweeping and swabbing household space, bathing of children, disposal of rubbish, treatment and storage of water, etc.) are women's responsibilities. Women also undertake the personal care of family members, care and supervision of young children, and of the sick, whatever their age or gender.

Because of these multiple responsibilities, one might assume that women make the health related decisions within the household. However, little is known about the processes of decision-making on the subject of health care within the poor rural Indian household (in contrast with the vast literature on family planning decision-making). As alleged for other spheres of social activity, decisions on child or personal care which affect the 'prevention' of disease or its cure—how to treat an illness, in whom, when and where—may be 'unspoken understandings' rather than actively reached stances. The oft-made assumption that household decision-making takes place as an apparent and concensual process (Anker, 1978) is not easily acceptable in the Indian context. Instead, processes of decision-making vis-à-vis health and nutrition are likely to be largely tradition- or rule-bound rather than 'active' or 'informed.' Thus, the nature of health decisions made by women in the household are probably a function of their status within the household and society. We know that this, in turn, is related to women's education levels and employment.

Women's Education and Household Health

There is substantial evidence that women's education plays a major role in determining health, particularly that of children. At the macro-level, cross-national studies show high correlations between female literacy and life expectancy at birth, higher than any other factor (UN, 1983). However, the possibility that education merely acts as a proxy for living standards has necessitated closer examination. Accordingly, Caldwell and others have carried out analyses of micro-level data on education and child mortality in Nigeria, Ghana, Upper Volta and elsewhere (Caldwell, 1975). These early studies estimated the net effect of education, without specifically being concerned with the mechanism through which it acted on health. They proposed that maternal education was an independent, and perhaps the most significant, determinant of infant and child survival. In Nigeria, Caldwell (1979) found that a mother's education influenced child mortality regardless of age, socio-economic background, or current status. For example, within each age group, mothers with more education had a smaller proportion of dying children. Caldwell showed that the mortality differentials by maternal education could not be ascribed to the better socio-economic situation of educated mothers. Further-more, place of residence, access to health facilities, and father's education did not have much significance, and Caldwell concluded that 'in terms of child mortality, a woman's education is a good deal more important than even her most immediate environment' (p. 405).

Similarly, data from Bangladesh have shown that, although all household educational levels (whether the highest, that of the head of household, or of the mother) bear an inverse relationship with child mortality, the effect of the mother's education is the strongest (D'Souza and Bhuiya, 1982).

The mechanisms whereby women's education results in lower child mortality are still the subject of speculation. Child health and survival are enhanced by better hygiene, improved nutrition and feeding practices, and timely medical intervention, whether in the home or at a health centre. There is, unfortunately, little empirical research to show that mothers' education improves these practices but the assumption is made widely that an educated woman is more likely to adopt strategies that favour the child health and survival (LeVine, 1980). Educated women may be more aware of how to treat children during illness and more knowledgeable about health facilities. Their tendency to treat rather than ignore a child's illness, or approach and get treatment from a health personnel is likely to be greater and this enhances a child's health status and chances of survival.

Another way in which education improves child health is through its impact on fertility. Decisions to delay child bearing, space children further apart, or bear fewer children enhance child health and survival. There is ample evidence that education changes women's child-bearing behaviour. Cochrane (1979) reviewed several studies in developing countries and found that women with more education had fewer children. The relationship between the husband's education and fertility was weak, and even weaker when the husband's education was controlled for income. On the other hand, when controlled for income, the relation between maternal education and number of children became stronger, implying that the effect of women's education on fertility is independent—and perhaps stronger than that—of income. Another important channel through which education may affect fertility behaviour—and child mortality—is by increasing the age at marriage. In Bangladesh, D'Souza and Bhuiya (1982) reported that educated women married later, thus postponing child birth until their 20s, when the risk of infant loss is less than in the teens. These social and biological factors obviously exert favourable influence on child mortality.

Other explanations for the effect of women's education on child mortality relate directly to the nature of decision-making on health and illness within the household or family unit. While the assumption that mothers are the main decision-makers and 'managers' of their children may be far from accurate in many contexts, women's education may result in significant changes in family relationships such that children (and the women themselves) get a larger share of the family's resources. In addition to the possibility that educated women may marry educated men, often of higher economic status so that more resources are available for child care (as shown in Bangladesh by D'Souza and Bhuiya, 1982), there is also the likelihood that educated women may 'choose' or acquire husbands who share values inherent in taking better care of children or that they may influence their husbands and mothers-in-law more in this regard.

LeVine (1980) has proposed that schooling is a form of 'assertiveness training' which enables women to form their own opinions and act on them, believe in the efficacy of their actions, and not be intimidated by others. An educated woman thus takes greater responsibility for her children's health and is permitted to pursue appropriate strategies by other household members. In support of this, an indepth investigation of the relationship between female education and lower child mortality in Bangladesh (D'Souza and Bhuiya, 1982; Chen, 1984) showed that intra-familial decision-making processes do indeed change with the education of women. Educated women apparently asserted themselves more, ventured beyond traditional confines more often, and used 'external resources', such as, health services, more effectively.

Women's Employment and Household Health

Yet another way in which women's education can influence child health and survival is by increasing female employment. Increased female employment tends to restrict child-bearing and this may, in turn, result in lower mortality, as discussed earlier. However, there is also the suggestion that increased female employment results in better child health because of the mothers' wages. For example, Schultz (1979) analysed data from Colombia and concluded that mothers' education acted through increases in income to decrease child mortality in urban areas. Where women's wages were greater, given age and education, child mortality was lower. However, he found that in rural areas women's wages were less strongly associated with child mortality, than their education *per se* (although this must be qualified because only a small proportion of women were in wage earning occupations). However, an assumption in this mechanism is that women's wages are used to 'purchase health goods and services,' implying that the mother is the decision-maker regarding the disposal of her income. In the Indian context, as we know, both assumptions are questionable.

While no negative effects of higher education on health have been brought to light, there is some cause for concern regarding women's employment. Women who work outside the home or even those engaged in agricultural activities on their own land may sometimes give short shrift to certain of their domestic responsibilities, particularly those related to child care. Feeding and care of children, including breastfeeding, are time-consuming activities, and in poor households where prepared foods and labour-saving devices are unavailable, these tasks may compete with women's economic work. Getting medical attention often means a lengthy trip to a distant health facility where waiting is the order of the day (or, sometimes, days) and may result in a loss of wages. Women who are employed obviously have less time to spend on these health related tasks, and this may have unfortunate negative effects on child health. These negative effects may not be adequately offset by the increased quantity of food or the better standard of living which the woman's income 'purchases' for the household, driving home the need for women's employment strategies to be accompanied by efforts to enhance household knowledge of and access to health care.

Proponents of the 'new household economics' (Schultz, 1974) have dwelt on the effects of women's work on fertility. Based on the presumption that the mother assumes the total time-cost of bearing and rearing children, the 'cost' of having children can be worked out in terms of women's lost labour. However, it is not easy to size up the implications of women's work for child health and survival. One has been witness to women having to shut their infants and young children up in their homes to go to work. In situations where the economic survival of the family or household depends on the woman's work, she is unlikely to leave her work to care for a sick child (depending on which child, perhaps). She is faced with having to 'juggle' both her work and her domestic responsibilities—with potentially severe implications for both the sick child and the mother's own health.

Another caveat. Within the household, child care—in health or sickness—may be delegated to a member other than the mother. This may minimise the 'cost' of health care to the household and thus be beneficial but it may also have severe negative consequences for health. Often, the substitute child-minder is a sibling, barely six or seven years old herself, ignorant and incapable of looking after a well or sick child, or an aged person unable to spend the energy necessary to feed, clean, or comfort a young child.

While women's double burden of domestic and productive work is immensely relevant to health within the household, yet another aspect of the sexual division of labour relates to their access to external health care. By and large, in traditional societies, women rarely deal with agents or agencies outside the household including health care institutions, a responsibility usually assigned to men. This is an extension of the passive and fatalistic nature of health decision making in the household and is the unfortunate corollary of women's restricted role in production. It explains to some extent the paradox between propositions 2 and 3—that while women are the main health care providers within the household, they and their immediate charges (children) suffer the worst health. And it creates a curious dilemma: while women are responsible for primary health care within the household, they are not 'permitted' to carry this responsibility to its logical next step, seeking professional help from external health care providers or institutions (whether government or private). Both the paradox and the 'discontinuity' in women's roles in health care provision have important implications for health policy and planning.

POLICY: FORMS AND EFFECTS

The foregoing three propositions should form the basis of the policy to develop health and nutrition for women and the household. Their salient features can be summarised as follows: Women and children are severely disadvantaged in health related matters for which the household has first level responsibility. Within the household, women are the main health care providers but they have limited access to external health care institutions. Women's educational and employment status affects both the quality of health care provided within the home and the degree to which outside help is sought and utilised, eventually affecting their own health and that of other household members. Given the poor health status of women and children, policies must be oriented for providing them with the necessary health *care* in an accessible manner. And given women's responsibility for health maintenance and sick-treatment, policies must also aim to build women's *competence* in these areas. (My use of the word 'competence' is not at all intended to imply that women are incompetent in matters of health but rather to signal the need for policies to deal with factors predisposing health). While it is clear that policies in many sectors—health, nutrition, family planning, education, employment and others—are relevant, the health sector bears a major responsibility for providing care and building competence, and I shall focus particularly on its policies.

Historical Background

Before examining how India's current health policies address these two requirements, however, it may be well to briefly describe the situation prior to the advent of 'modern' health policy-making. Jeffery *et al.* (1983) have summarised the role of traditional medicine in women's health. The traditional Indian systems of medicine were male-oriented and male-dominated and largely ignored 'women's diseases.' The practitioners were male and had little or no role in treating female illnesses. Shame and seclusion denied women access to them. The only traditional medicine available to women was in the hands of *dais* who dealt mainly with obstetric events. Besides these, women's illnesses were often considered spiritual in origin and so women resorted to spiritual healers and magical treatments.

The spread of modern medicine in the pre-independence period was confined largely to towns, and hence had little impact on women's health at large. The traditional masculine perspective continued into the 'modern' era, as humourously illustrated in the opening scene of *Midnights Children*, where Salman Rushdie (1980) describes how the young, newly qualified Dr. Aadam Aziz comes to attend on the land-owner's daughter (who is 'good news indeed to a doctor with a career to make . . . *because* she is ill')! Aziz is shown into the *zenana* by a woman servant where two more are holding up a bedsheet above their heads, with a hole seven inches in diameter cut in the centre of the sheet. 'My daughter is a decent girl,' explains her father, Ghani the landowner. 'It goes without saying. She does not flaunt her body under the noses of strange men . . . accordingly, I have required her to be positioned behind that sheet.' Although this may be fiction, similar and worse facts describing women's segregation from medical care are ralated in the *Avarodh-basini* of Kokeya Sakhawat Hossain, a Bengali Muslim woman writing in 1931 (Jahan, 1981). Though these descriptions refer largely to the well-to-do class, we have no reason to believe that the poor were any better-off.

The establishment of funds, nurses' training schools and a few *dai* training programmes in connection with the women's movement or missionary work in the early part of this century increased the availability of female personnel practising modern techniques. However, the expansion of women's medical facilities was limited by a paucity of women doctors, and there were only isolated efforts to improve the availability of women's services in rural areas.

Rural health services developed in the post-independence period following the recommendations of the National Planning Committee (1948) and the Bhore Committee (GOI, 1946). Both reports gave high priority to the development of Maternal and Child Health Services. Within the health service network, the development of a cadre of Auxilliary Nurse Midwives (ANMs) was regarded as a key extension effort. MCH services were intended to be 'deprofessionalised' and 'community based' as long ago as the 1950s: ANMs were to be minimally trained health workers catering to rural women and children and supervised by Public Health Nurses or Lady Health Visitors (who had somewhat more training and were based at block-level primary health centres).

While this has been the major effort to overcome the inequality in women's and children's access to health care, the personnel population ratios envisioned by the Bhore Committee in 1946 have never been achieved, making it impossible for ANMs to attain the coverage of women and children that is necessary to have an impact on their health problems. Even their major responsibility, attendance at births, has remained largely unfulfilled. With the inclusion of family planning into the job specification of ANMs, in the early 1960s, and their consequent pursuit of 'targets', MCH services became subordinate to contraceptive motivation and delivery efforts. This has led to the neglect of women's health in general and child health altogether.

Current Policy

More recently, emphasis on maternal and child health has been resumed, largely because the intransigency of the problems of high mortality among women and children, high fertility, and their interlinkages (the 'Child Survival Hypothesis', Taylor *et al.*. 1980) have been recognised. The National Health Policy adopted by the Government of India in 1982 recognised the high rates of mortality affecting women and children, the extent of malnutrition and disease among these groups, and their lack of access to potable water and sanitation. It placed the blame for this situation largely on the 'inappropriate and irrelevant' health service and manpower development policies of the past. In redress, it proposes the adoption of a comprehensive primary health care approach which emphasises preventive health, improves health awareness, and involves the 'community' in all aspects of health care. The policy identifies Maternal and Child Health Services as deserving priority attention, citing the need for special programmes, for a focus on the under-privileged, and for decentralisation.

Of necessity, a primary, preventive and community health approach should focus on women who are the providers of first-level health care within the household and who are, themselves, severely disadvantaged in health. Yet the National Policy statement is silent on the specific issues of *reaching women* in order to improve the health status of the population, and of *employing women* in the health sector to cater to the needs of other women within homes, even though these issues are central to the proposed three-pronged strategy for achieving universal health, namely, the reorientation of medical education and training of health personnel, the reorganisation of health services, and the integration of health and socio-economic development. In the absence of specific suggestions for innovation one is led to believe that the policy will be implemented through the two existing programmes which are intended to provide health care and health information at the household level—the *Dai* Training Scheme, which seeks to modernise traditional maternal care and delivery techniques, and the Village Health Guides (formerly Community Health Workers/Volunteers) Scheme. Yet there is little evidence to date that these schemes have had any positive impact on the health of women and children.

Existing Programmes

Training of Dais

Dais are perceived as an important health asset because they are members of local communities, accepted and experienced in midwifery. There is a rich anthropological literature on their roles and functions, which demonstrates great variations in different cultural settings. Recently, Jeffery *et al.* (1984) have provided a detailed account of the role of *dais* in child bearing in some U.P. villages. In their field study, almost all women gave birth at home attended by an untrained *dai*. There was little or no contact between a pregnant woman and the *dai* before delivery. Instead, a *dai* chosen by the mother-in-law was summoned during a woman's labour. Although women depended on the *dai* to diagnose any life-threatening situation, *dais* were not considered experts and few had had any previous training or apprenticeship. Their decisions were subordinated to the mother-in-law's or other older female relative's wishes, and their roles largely confined to doing the 'dirty work' during and immediately after the delivery. The *dais* themselves did the work out of economic necessity and considered it underpaid, 'polluting' work. The authors refer to the 'ethos of shame which permeates midwifery.'

In this situation, the *dais* had virtually no role as community healers because they lacked specialised knowledge, had only very short contact with the pregnant women, and dealt with very few cases. 'Midwifery provides an income for desperately poor women with few marketable skills.' Five of the 25 *dais* observed by Jeffery deviated from this stereotype: they were intelligent, trained, well reputed, had busy lucrative practices, and practiced some form of 'medicine' (e.g., gave injections). However, they too had limited 'outreach' and did not educate their clients in health matters.

Although the concept of training indigenous midwives·in better techniques goes back more than a century in India, the official programme to train *dais* to provide village-based maternal and child health and family planning services was launched during the Second Five Year Plan (1957–62). During this and the subsequent plan period about 27,000 *dais* were trained. In the Fourth Five Year Plan (1969–74), when family planning was realigned with maternal and child health care, the programme was transferred to the Family Planning Department and another 16,500 *dais* were trained. These numbers have been consistently short of the set targets (by about 40 per cent). In the Draft of the Sixth Plan (1978–83), 100,000 *dais* were to be trained every year! It is believed that there is at least one traditional *dai* in every village in India, so that the total number would be considerably over half a million in the country. Indeed, to reach the currently proposed ratio of one trained *dai* per 500 people by 1985, over 1.5 million *dais* would have to be trained altogether, a most unlikely feat.

Qualitatively as well, the programme has fallen far short of its objectives. Among others, some recent studies of *dai* training in Tamil Nadu (Mani, 1980), Karnataka and Maharashtra (Bhatia, 1982a + b) point out some of the problems with this programme. First, there are grave difficulties in recruiting traditional *dais* into the programme. *Dais* suspect the 'motives' of health system personnel, and are unwilling to act as family planning promoters which is expected of them. Typical of a supply rather than demand-oriented programme no felt need is created either for the training or for the trained midwife. For example, although a demand for certain services such as post-partum care often exists, it is not considered in the programme design. Administrative lapses result in a scarcity of trainers, teaching aids and equipment for the training programmes which, in turn, have led to poor quality training. Midwives frequently find the courses too technical and too long. They drop out of training programmes because training centres are distant and transport to and fro is inadequate, or because they lose income which is not made up either by incentives during the training programme or by increases in income after training. Indeed, villagers often assume that following training the *dais* have become government personnel who should render their services free!

The programme often also fails to provide midwifery kits to trained midwives. Follow-up of trainees is virtually non-existent, largely attributable to a lack of rapport between the *dais* and the ANMs who are responsible for maintaining contact. They perceive each other as competitors. Alternatively, *dais* shy away from a relationship with their local ANM because villagers may distrust them in fear of being recruited for sterilisation. The combination of poor training and inadequate follow-up often leads trained midwives to recede to their traditional approaches and techniques.

At a practical level, therefore, the *Dai* training programme does not meet the needs of women even in the limited matter of childbirth, and an adequate domiciliary midwifery system remains a major lacuna. Furthermore, given their low status and limited role, *dais* can hardly be expected to cater to any other health problems of women or household members or to build health awareness in any substantial way.

Village Health Guides

A common feminist criticism of modern (Western) medicine is that it views women primarily—or solely—as reproducers, ignoring their other health needs (Sathyamala et. al., 1986; Zurbreigg, 1984). This is no less true of health planning and policy-making in India where 'women-specific services'—Maternal and Child Health, Female Contraception, Medical Termination of Pregnancy and the Post-partum Programme—are all concerned with reproduction or its prevention. The general health problems of women have been subsumed into disease categories which are tackled by 'general' health staff at health centres or addressed by the 'vertical' disease programmes. In a previous paper (Chatterjee, 1983) I explored the factors that lead to low use of health facilities by women in contrast with their needs, terming them 'permission', 'ability' and 'availability'. While permission and ability relate to a woman's own social and economic status, availability encompasses the quantity and quality of services directed at women which we know are woefully inadequate.

The extension workers connected with the national programmes against malaria, smallpox, tuberculosis, etc., were formerly unipurpose workers but more recently have been renamed and retrained as Multipurpose Workers (MPWs). This includes the

ANMs who are now female MPWs, expected to cater to women's health needs by dint of being women themselves. (Male MPWs, similarly, address themselves to men). From their subcentre headquarters they liaise with the village *dai* to deliver pregnancy related services and with village health guides to provide non-reproductive health care.

While the induction of village-based health workers is a step in the direction of making health care available at the household level and thereby overcoming some of the constraints in 'permission' and 'ability', this scheme has faced numerous problems which have limited its ability to reach women. Initially, the vast majority of Community Health Workers were men. Restricted from approaching and dealing with women, these workers confined their efforts to treating minor ailments and well chlorination work. Following the recommendations of the Central Councils of Health and Family Welfare in 1981, more emphasis has been placed on the recruitment of female village health workers. However, some allege that the purpose of these efforts is merely to bring about 'surface change designed to improve the relationship' between medical personnel and rural women (Jeffery *et al.*, 1983) so that family planning work can be given a much-needed boost. Whether or not this is intended, it is true that in practice the high priority accorded to contraceptive motivation work and the shortage of female health personnel has severely restricted any effort 'beyond family planning.' It remains to be seen how effectively these workers will provide household level health care and particularly how they educate women in health matters. Besides these workers there are *no* mechanisms within the health sector to build the competence of women and the household, despite repeated acknowledgements of the need to provide health education to the people.

Family Planning

It is nowhere more evident that women are caught between traditional norms and practices and inadequate state policies than in the arena of family planning. For atleast the past two decades, sterilisation has been the most promoted method of contraception in the National Family Welfare Programme. A 'one-time' method, such as, sterilisation is deemed appropriate because of the problems of access to women in rural areas, their illiteracy, their lack of time to travel frequently to health centres, and their lack of privacy within joint or crowded households. However, a story of the repercussions of a woman's tubectomy operation on her family, told to us by Pettigrew (1984), poignantly illustrates the failure of policy to take into account other realities facing rural women.

Women who have undergone tubectomies frequently complain of post-operative pain, but this is not accepted either by society or the medical profession as a legitimate illness. Consequently, women must continue to perform their laborious tasks following tubectomy although they may need and want to rest. Pettigrew has described the nature of these tasks, the amount of bending and stretching and exertion involved in collecting fodder and firewood, making dung cakes, caring for animals, collecting and preparing food, doing agricultural work and so on *ad infinitum*. In the story, a woman labourer who had undergone a tubectomy was in severe pain but was forced to work in the fields at harvest time as well as collect firewood and fodder as usual. There were, it seems, no other members in the household to take over these tasks. Under the circumstances she expected her eldest child, a 13-year old daughter, to help her in these tasks. But the child—already engaged in paid work herself—was apparently 'playful'. This enraged her mother who kicked and beat her, causing her accidental death.

The effect on the household and on its health and nutrition was profound. The mother had lost her main helper. She had one son and other female children who were too small to labour. She could have no more children because of her tubectomy. After the death of her eldest daughter, she began to foster her only male child by giving him the milk which should have gone to one of the female children who was suffering from third degree malnutrition. And so the vicious cycle was repeated.

This story shows in several ways how state policy can overlook the household context. First, it demonstrates that the manner in which policy is interpreted—here, into the promotion of tubectomy—may be inappropriate for rural women given the type of work they must perform. Pettigrew contends that the emphasis on tubectomy has resulted because 'doctors' (health planners and policy-makers) are out of touch with the needs and circumstances of rural women and don't consult them. The priority promotion of sterilisation represents the predilections of state health cadres and medical professionals and not of women.

Second, the story points out how concepts underlying policy may be inadequate. Here, the 'small family norm' was applied to a context in which there was a high risk of child death on the one hand, and a demand for children on the other. The frequent occurrance of child death renders the two child norm a risky proposition for the poor rural household in which women depend on child labour and later on sons for old age support. One can allege that this family planning policy disregards health realities, the economic role children play in the household, and the social demands on women.

Third, the story illustrates the lack of linkage between family planning and health care services—a failure of both policy and implementation. Pettigrew alludes to the poor clinical milieu and hospital conditions in which sterilisations are performed. The poor, in particular, receive abyssmal care because they are given an incentive to undergo the operation. Furthermore, although healing is a long process made more difficult by women's work, which cannot be avoided economically and socially, there is virtually no post-operative follow-up and care. The health system does not, in any way, compensate for the lack of support from family and community while aiming this service at women. Poor ante-natal and post-natal services are further evidence of a generally negligent attitude towards women's health. This attitude on the part of health services can generate intra-household conflicts and the kind of tragedy described here.

Nutrition

While nutrition is another priority problem mentioned in the National Health Policy, there is no comprehensive national policy for the improvement of nutrition at the household level. Although the system of food distribution through fair price shops and the food-for-work and employment guarantee schemes aim to increase the quantities of food available to poor households, their nutritional impact has not been assessed. Besides these, government intervention in the sphere of nutrition consists of supplementary feeding programmes and an integrated health and nutrition scheme.

These are aimed largely at individuals—young children of pre-school age, those in school, or pregnant/lactating women.

A common problem these programmes have faced has been their failure to induce women to attend, once again because of social strictures against their congregating or eating in a public place, or because of their lack of time. Programme designers or workers sometimes attempt to overcome this difficulty by giving the food supplements as 'take-home' rations or delivering them to homes. However, the rations are then often shared among household members—particularly in poor households—and the programme's impact on the target group is thus 'diluted'. Target members are also often faced with 'substitution', that is, they are denied their share of the household pot because they receive the programme's food supplement. As additions to the total house-hold food supply, the rations given (usually around 300 calories per day for a young child and 500 for a pregnant or nursing mother) are insufficient. Thus one could well conclude that the mechanics of supplementary feeding schemes largely ignore the total household context, failing to see a mother or a child as a member of a larger unit or group of kin.

The Integrated Child Development Services (ICDS) Scheme has perhaps been more 'household health-oriented' in conception than most other programmes. It combines supplementary feeding of children and mothers with a health check-up and referral, immunisation, pre-school education, and health education of mothers. A village-based *anganwadi* worker is responsible for enrolling every pre-school child in her village in the feeding programme based at an *anganwadi* (day care centre), monitoring their health, and referring them to the ANM in case of need. Pregnant and nursing women are also offered these facilities and are provided health education along with mothers of young children. This programme has met with success particularly where the workers are motivated to visit homes to 'follow-up' their clients. In the household, the workers are able to demonstrate basic health techniques, such as, the use of oral rehydration during diarrhoea, educating women about and motivating them to seek health care as well as linking them to a health service provider when neces-sary. Though not without its shortcomings, the ICDS scheme holds out some hope in terms of reaching women and the household.

A SUGGESTED DIRECTION FOR POLICY

Anthropologists and those studying Asian societies in particular have long used the household as their basic unit of analysis because it is, indeed, the unit of most economic and social actions in almost all societies. However, despite the clear linkages between 'household' and 'health,' this approach has usually eluded health planners and practitioners. One can ascribe this largely to the fact that there have been medical professionals who, following the classic western model of health care, have looked upon the individual—the patient—as the basic analytical piece. I do not need to dwell here on the reasons why in the Indian society—particularly among the rural or the poor—this is an inadequate approach. It becomes even more so when our concern is women, because women are socially restricted from the 'individual' behaviour required of the typical allopathic patient. The exceptions to individual patient oriented health practitioners have been epidemiologists and community health professionals. These have generally taken a 'population' or 'geographic' view of health, in which forces external to the individual are recognised as requiring attention in order to prevent or treat diseases but only rarely are these forces seen as lying within the confines of a household as opposed to some larger environment. In accordance with this wider perspective, the focus of health planning has recently turned to 'communities'. Although numerous examples of community-based health care are available worldwide, the ultimate role model is the Chinese 'commune', that has performed enviable health, nutrition and demographic miracles. I need hardly point out that this model is as inappropriate for India as is the 'individual approach'. With our social and economic stratification, villages—the population and geographical units—are rarely 'communities', and our political framework does not, as yet, make it easy to turn them into homogenised, healthy groups.

Given the inadequacy of these two widely different approaches, I would propose that health planners would do well to follow anthropological practice and adopt the household as the primary unit of health analysis and care.

Such an approach would focus on the factors that determine household health—the health environment (hygiene) of the household, the availability of food, knowledge about health and child care, access to external health services—and seek to improve these. As a key health resource, women's role in health care provision would then be acknowledged and emphasis placed on aiding women to fulfill this role for the betterment of the health of the household. A 'task-oriented' view of women (implicit in the household orientation) would have significantly different implications for health and health care than the prevalent 'link-oriented' approach. The latter view has focused on the mother-child and husband-wife links and led to the pursuit of Maternal and Child Health and family planning objectives. It has ignored women's role as health care providers and therefore not sought to build up their access either to health knowledge or health services. Such a view of women should also lead to *all* women in the household being included in health development efforts—young female children, adolescents, 'reproductive-age' women and the elderly— who are all important members of their current or future households.

A household-oriented approach would also be concerned with the intra-household distribution of health and health resources and thereby focus automatically on the members who are most disadvantaged. It would also focus on specific health problems (diseases, illnesses) that impair the functioning of the household as a unit, or its economic viability.

An operational view of the household as the main point of delivery for health care and health education is considerably different from the concept of target groups for health programmes or of the community as the entry point for health. It would thus require a reorientation of health personnel. The *modus operandi* of field workers must be the home visit on which they can examine household health in its totality and influence its dynamics through dealings with the 'decision-makers' and main actors. The ICDS scheme has made a beginning in this regard and some private sector health programmes in different parts of the country have had success with this approach and developed techniques which are worthy of emulation.

While health education by personnel in contact with women and households is important, many health problems are rooted in beliefs, attitudes and practices which may not be influenced by health knowledge alone. From the evidence available we can accept without hesitation that the education of women generally produces attitudes and behaviour which positively affect their own health (and that of their household). Women's participation in health services can be enhanced through education which brings about change in social and cultural attitudes. Thus, policies to expand women's formal and non-formal education are of immediate relevance and concern.

REFERENCES

ANKER, R., 1978: 'Demographic Change and the Role of Women: A Research Programme in Developing Countries' (Geneva, International Labour Organisation Population and Employment Working Paper No. 69).

BATLIWALA, SRILATHA, 1982: 'Rural Energy Scarcity and Nutrition: A New Perspective,' in *Economic and Political Weekly*. Vol. XVII, No. 9, pp. 328–34.

BHATIA, J.C., 1982a: 'Evaluation of Traditional Birth Attendents (*Dais*) Training Scheme in the State of Karnataka' (Bangalore, Centre for Population and Health Management, Indian Institute of Management).

———, 1982b: 'Evaluation of Traditional Birth Attendants (*Dais*) Training Scheme in the State of Maharashtra' (Bangalore, Centre for Population and Health Management, Indian Institute of Management).

CALDWELL, J.C., ed., 1975: *Population Growth and Socio-economic Change in West Africa* (New York, Columbia University Press).

———, 1979: 'Education as a Factor in Mortality Decline: An Examination of Nigerian Data,' in *Population Studies*, Vol. 33, pp. 395–413.

CHATTERJEE, MEERA, 1983: 'Women's Access to Health Care: A Critical Issue for Child Health,' Paper presented at the ICMR Conference on Child Health, Nutrition and Family Planning, Bangalore, November.

CHEN, L.C., 1984: 'Micro-Approaches to the Study of Childhood Mortality in Rural Bangladesn,' Paper presented at the IUSSP Symposium of Micro-Demographic Studies, Canberra, June.

COCHRANE, SUSAN H., 1979: 'Education and Fertility: What Do We Really Know? (Washington, D.C., World Bank Staff Occasional Paper No. 26).

D'SOUZA, S. and A. BHUIYA, 1982: 'Socio-economic Mortality Differentials in a Rural Area of Bangladesh,' *Population and Development Review*, Vol. 8, pp. 753–9.

GOPALAN, C., 1983: 'Measurement of Undernutrition: Biological Considerations,' *NFI Bulletin*, Vol. 4, No. 3, pp. 1–3.

Government of India, 1946: *Report of the Health Survey and Development Committee (Bhore Committee)* (Delhi, Manager of Publications).

Government of India, 1982: *Statement on National Health Policy* (New Delhi, Ministry of Health and Family Welfare).

Government of India, 1983: 'Health Statistics of India,' (New Delhi, Ministry of Health and Family Welfare, Directorate General of Health Services, Central Bureau of Health Intelligence).

JAHAN, ROUSHAN, 1981: *Inside Seclusion: The Avarodh-basini of Rokeva Sakhawat Hossain* (Dacca, Women for Women).

JAYA RAO, KAMALA, 1984: 'Undernutrition among Adult Indian Males,' *NFI Bulletin*, Vol. 5, No. 3, July, pp. 3–4.

JEFFERY, R, P.H. JEFFERY and A. LYON, 1983: 'The Medicalisation of Female Illness in North India,' Paper presented to the IXth European Conference on Modern South Asian Studies, Sweden, July.

JEFFERY, R., P. JEFFERY and A. LYON, 1984: 'Only Cord-Cutters? Midwifery and Childbirth in Rural North India,' in *Social Action*, Vol. 27, pp. 1–37.

JESUDASEN, V. and MEERA CHATTERJEE, eds., 1979: 'Health Status and Behaviour of Two Rural Communities—Report of a Sample Survey in Madhya Pradesh' (New Delhi, Council for Social Development).

KAMATH, K.R., R.A. FELDMAN, P.S.S. SUNDAR RAO and JKG WEBB, 1969: 'Infection and Disease in a Group of South Indian Families II General Morbidity Patterns on Families and Family Members,' in *American Journal of Epidemiology*, Vol. 80, pp. 375–383.

KYNCH, JOSALYN and A. SEN, 1983: 'Indian Women: Well-being and Survival,' in *Cambridge Journal of Economics*, Vol. 7, pp. 363–360.

LEVINE, R.A., 1980: 'Influences of Women's Schooling on Maternal Behaviour in the Third World,' in *Comparative Education Review*, Vol. 24 (Supplement), pp. 78–105.

MANI, S.B., 1980: 'A Review of Midwife Training Programs in Tamil Nadu,' in *Studies in Family Planning*, Vol. 11, pp. 395–400.

National Planning Committee, 1948: *National Health* (Bombay, Vora & Co.).

PETTIGREW, JOYCE, 1984: 'Problems Concerning Tubectomy Operations in Rural Areas of Punjab,' in *Economic and Political Weekly* Vol. XIX, pp. 995–1002.

RUSHDIE, SALMAN, 1980: *Midnight's Children* (New York, Alfred A. Knopf).

SATHYAMALA, C., N. SUNDRAM and N. BHANOT, 1986: *Taking Sides: The Choices Before the Health Worker*, (Madras, Asian Network for Innovative Training Trust).

SCHULTZ, T.W., ed., 1974: *Economics of the Family Marriage, Children and Human Capital* (Chicago, University of Chicago Press).

SCHULTZ, T. PAUL, 1979: 'Interpretation of Relations Among Mortality, Economics of the Household and the Health Environment,' in Proceedings of the Meeting on Socio-economic Determinants and Consequences of Mortality, Mexico City, June.

TAYLOR, C.E., R.S.S. SARMA, R.L. PARKER, W.A. REINKE and R. FARUQES, 1980: 'Integration of Family Planning and Health Services: The Narangwal Experience,' (Washington D.C., World Bank mimeo).

United Nations, 1983: 'Findings of the World Fertility Survey on Trends, Differentials and Discriminants of Mortality in Developing Countries,' (Rome, UN Department of Economic and Social Affairs Expert Group on Mortality and Health Policy, Paper for International Conference on Population).

ZURBRIEGG, S., 1984: *Rakku's Story: Structures of Ill-Health and the Source of Change* (Bangalore, Centre for Social Action).

Son Preference, the Household and a Public Health Programme in India

BARBARA D. MILLER

'*Health for all* by the year 2000' was the call of the governments of 134 countries that met at Alma Ata in 1978. A major thrust of many developing nations towards achieving broad-based health improvements was through the use of decentralised community health care programs. Community health care practitioners, policy-makers, scholars interested in health care, and average people guided by common sense are well aware that health, like so many other valuable things in the world, is often distributed unevenly within a society. It is generally known that particular socio-economic classes, various ethnic groups and regions within a

Note: Research for this paper was conducted with the support of a grant from the Wenner-Gren Foundation for Anthropological Research, Inc., no. 4454. Funding allowed me to visit Ludhiana Christian Medical College, Punjab, India in November 1983. I gratefully acknowledge the generous assistance I received in Ludhiana from Dr. Betty Cowan, Principal of CMC Ludhiana, Dr. Jasbir Dhanoa, Dr. H.N.S. Grewal, and Dr. R.K. Sachar. I thank Dr. David Rush of Albert Einstein College of Medicine for putting me in contact with Dr. Betty Cowan of Ludhiana CMC. A briefer visit to Vellore Christian Medical College in Tamil Nadu provided important insights on the very different context of South India. My time in Vellore was made useful by the help from Dr. P.S. Sundar Rao, Chief of the Biostatistics Department and Dr. K.V. Srilatha of the Rural Unit for Health and Social Assistance. I am also grateful for the continuing support of my work provided by the Metropolitan Studies Program, The Maxwell School, Syracuse University, and for the skill and care of Esther Gray in typing numerous revisions of this chapter. Sections of this chapter are included in 'Prenatal and Postnatal Sex Selection in India: The Patriarchal Context, Ethical Questions and Public Policy,' Working Papers on Women in International Development (East Lansing, MI: Office of Women in International Development, Michigan State University, forthcoming). This chapter has greatly benefited from comments received at the Conference on Women and the Household, New Delhi, 1985.

country fare better than others in terms of bare survival as well as the quality of life. It is less known and less accepted that, in some parts of the world, gender is a key factor differentiating the health status of the population. In this chapter I argue that in North India, health care programs for children must take gender into account as well as the household which is the key institution where day-to-day decisions are made, more or less consciously, about resource allocations that will affect the health of boys versus girls.[1] In the absence of radical and widespread social change in North India concerning the worth of daughters compared to sons, operating community health measures must seek to equalise the life chances of boys and girls by penetrating household care patterns. One might argue that such efforts will be futile if there is no wider social change in which to embed equalisation of intra-household allocations, but evidence from one effort in Punjab shows that some progress may be made.

This chapter proceeds from a review of the context of Punjab to a discussion of how resource allocation patterns in the household differentially create risk factors affecting the health and survival of boys and girls. Societies where son preference is not present are compared to societies where son preference is strong. The conclusion discusses the modest but encouraging success of one health care program in altering household dynamics and improving the survival rates of daughters.

BACKGROUND: THE PUNJAB

The preference for sons and disfavour towards daughters is a complex phenomenon that has tenaciously survived through the centuries in North India.[2] Sons, especially in the rural North Indian context are economic, political and ritual assets; daughters in most respects are liabilities. Sons are needed for farming the land, or, if they emigrate, are valuable sources of remitted income. Sons play

[1] Increasingly, public health physicians are realising that programs operating in isolation from, or ignorance of, household dynamics will be less successful than those that take into account the household (see Rush, 1984).

[2] An expanded discussion of the cultural and demographic dynamics of son preference in India can be found in Miller (1981). Throughout this chapter, 'North India' refers roughly to the region of the Gangetic plains stretching from the Pakistan border to Bihar in the east and to the Maharashtra state line in the south.

important roles in local power struggles over land boundaries and rights to irrigation water. Sons often stay with the family after marriage and thus provide security for the parents in their old age; North Indian daughters marry out of their natal villages and can provide no support for their families of birth. Sons bring in dowries which often contain large amounts of cash and which can be used by the parents of the groom; daughters drain family wealth by requiring dowries upon marriage and a constant flow of gifts to their family of marriage for years thereafter. Among Hindus, sons are also needed to perform rituals which protect the family after the death of the father; daughters cannot perform such rituals.[3]

There is good evidence that in British India, during the eighteenth and nineteenth centuries, female infanticide was practised by a large proportion of the North Indian population.[4] According to a modeled estimate that I have developed, one-fourth of the population in the northwestern plains region allowed no daughters to survive while the remaining three-fourths of the population did nothing to alter the sex ratio of their offspring (Miller, 1981 p. 61–65; Miller, 1984b). Under pressure of colonial rule from the late nineteenth century to the present time, the practice of direct female infanticide abated, only to be supplanted by the practice of indirect female infanticide through the fatal neglect of female children. In rural North India there is today still a marked imbalance in the number of boys to girls, with district sex ratios for the under ten-year-olds as high as 117 males per 100 females (Miller, 1981). An increasing number of studies, both household surveys (Simmons et al., 1982) and hospital-based demographic surveillances (Cowan and Dhanoa, 1983) document that mortality rates for girls greatly exceed those for boys in North India.

The wealthiest state in India is Punjab, home of the Green Revolution in wheat which has brought increased prosperity to the area. Punjab also possesses a well-developed, decentralised health care system and one of the finest medical colleges and hospitals in the country, the Ludhiana Christian Medical College and Brown Memorial Hospital, located in Ludhiana city. But Punjab continues to lag behind much of India in lowering its infant and child

[3] Among Hindus, one daughter is highly desired because *kanyadan*, or the gift of a virgin daughter in marriage, is a route to salvation for the girl's father.

[4] For a fuller discussion of the practice of outright female infanticide in India, see Miller (1981 p. 49–67).

mortality rates. The IMR (Infant Mortality Rate, or deaths per thousand live births to children under the age of one year) in Punjab in 1975–1977 was 104, much higher than poorer states, such as, Kerala with an IMR of fifty-two and Jammu and Kashmir with an IMR of sixty-six (Dyson and Moore, 1982; Mundle, 1984; Miller, 1985). Punjab is located in the northwestern plains of India, in the heart of the region where the scarcity of girls is the most marked in the country.

It is already known that infant and child deaths in the area are to a large extent non-random by sex. Analysis by two public health physicians of data for a subpopulation in the Ludhiana surveillance area revealed that, among deaths to children aged seven months to thirty-six months, 85 per cent were female (Cowan and Dhanoa, 1983). There are such clear patterns in the deaths that village level health workers can spot with reasonable accuracy 'high risk' children—usually high parity daughters or any child born into a family that already has several sons and daughters.[5] There are, however, many unknowns regarding risk factors related to these death patterns. There are also many unknowns concerning the specific age patterns of deaths. A particularly difficult period is that of the first month of child's life, a time shrouded in privacy and very difficult for medical care personnel to penetrate, and a time when many of the mortalities occur.

For nearly a decade, high quality demographic and social data have been gathered as a routine part of the community health care program initiated by the Ludhiana Christian Medical College, now run in collaboration with the Government of India. The CMC program first started putting data into individual Household Folders on pregnancies, births and deaths, family characteristics, and events surrounding children's death and illnesses in 1975 in three rural locations: Narangwal, Lalton Kalan, and Jamalpur. At that time there was no intervention program. In 1978 the community health care program began an intensive outreach project involving home visiting, and Household Folders were continued for all households in the three locations. In 1981 CMC was asked by the Government of India to assume community health responsibilities for the entire surrounding block of Sahnewal with a population of

---

[5] Parity refers to birth order; high parity in India implies third, fourth, etc., births.

about 85,000.[6] By June 1981, data on pregnancies, births and deaths, and all other data for the Household Folders were being collected for the entire block. The basic data are gathered daily as village level health workers visit homes and update each House-hold Folder. Every month the health workers enter certain information into master registers kept at forty-nine village centres throughout Sahnewal block.

Two physicians, Dr. Betty Cowan and Dr. Jasbir Dhanoa, and I developed a plan to abstract relevant data from the master registers on all births and deaths up to the age of three years, and then to obtain details on the children who died from the individual Household Folders (also kept at the forty-nine centres). We began preliminary data abstraction early in 1984 but our efforts were interrupted by the violence in Punjab and the unsettled situation continues to impede our efforts. This paper presents some data from the Ludhiana area analysed earlier by Cowan and Dhanoa and some analysed by myself in a pilot exercise I undertook in November 1983. It also presents perspectives and insights I gained through interviews and discussions with medical personnel and site visits to local health centres near Ludhiana city.

RISK FACTORS WITHIN THE HOUSEHOLD

Separating various 'risk factors' is a difficult task, as is any attempt to measure their separate effects.[7] Some are closely inter-related such as mother's age at marriage and mother's age at first birth. An important factor such as mother's health and nutritional status may affect other factors such as birthweight of the infant, though birthweight may be a function also of other factors.

Risk factors must be separated from the immediate cause of death or illness. This separation is often difficult to achieve on the basis of available data.[8] An autopsy may reveal that a child died of measles, but the severity of measles may well be related to impaired nutritional status of the child caused, in turn, by neglectful feeding

---

[6] A block is an administrative division comprising of an average population of 100,000.

[7] For a fuller discussion of these important interactions, see *Population Reports* (1984 p. J-676).

[8] A similar difficulty is mentioned in Fortney et al. (1983) in their analysis of causes of death to women in Egypt.

because the child was female. Where a clinical condition such as measles interacts closely with a social factor such as systematic neglect, the difficulty of separation is extreme.[9]

I have assembled a list of the most important risk factors associated in the literature with infant and child health, ignoring for the present any interdependencies that exist since weights will not be assigned to them. The guiding question is: which factors could alter 'normal' sex patterns of mortality and morbidity among children under the age of three years? Table 1 lists the risk factors and my assessment of their potential sex-differential effects in societies with weak or no son preference compared to societies with strong son preference. I made the assessments on the basis of informed logic, discussions about children's health patterns in rural Punjab, and an examination of some of the raw data from Ludhiana.

Where Son Preference is Weak or Non-existent

Much research on infant mortality has documented increased risks for infants born to very young and very old mothers, born to mothers who have already had several children (which interacts with age), and born within a short time after a previous birth. Along with these factors, the first birth is reported to incur greater

[9] I had a very interesting conversation with Dr. Betty Cowan of Ludhiana CMC concerning how we would address the question of cause of death. She insists that only clinically trained persons can make a diagnosis concerning the cause of death and without an autopsy, or at least a 'verbal autopsy' from someone who was present when the individual died, cause of death can only be inferred, never known. This, if the neonatal mortality data were to reveal a significantly high number of female deaths at or near the time of birth, she would be reluctant to assume that such deaths were 'infanticides.' We are working on categories that will differentiate immediate cause of death (such as, suffocation) from underlying factors (such as, unwanted daughter smothered at birth), from broader culturally determined risk factors. The records note, for example, a 'cause of death' such as 'gross neglect—infant fell in a pond and drowned.' In fact, the child died from drowning, with the underlying cause probably being sex-selective neglect. In the case of many mortalities we have 'verbal autopsies' recorded by a health centre physician who was called in after the death and who interviewed the mother about the death. In all cases, the Household Folders contain a separate card for each child with information on the child's age, weight, arm circumference, illness history, etc. In the case of neonatal deaths, and particularly of neonatal deaths that occurred outside the block, very little is recorded beyond the reported sex of the child and date of birth and death.

Table 1

Risk Factors and Their Estimated Potential for Affecting Sex-Differential Mortality and Morbidity

Risk Factor	Societies with Weak or No Son Preference			Societies with Strong Son Preference		
	Potential			Potential		
	Strong	Weak	None	Strong	Weak	None
Pregnancy before mother age 18 years			x	x		
Pregnancy after mother age 33 years			x	x		
Pregnancy after four births			x	x		
Pregnancy less than two years apart			x	x		
First birth			x	x		
Last birth			x	x		
Antenatal health care			x	x		
Maternal desire for child			x	x		
Lack of birth attendant			x			x
Hemorrhage, other birth complications			x			x
Low birthweight baby			x	x		
Congenital birth defects	x				x	
Twins			x	x		
Puerperal depression			x	x		
Breastfeeding problems			x	x		
Maternal education			x		x	
Sanitation facilities			x			x
Health care provisions			x		x	
Episodes of infectious disease			x	x		
Household socioeconomic status			x	x		
Number of cows and buffaloes (tetanus hazard)			x		x	

SOURCE: The list of risk factors was gleaned from **Morley** (1973), **Lilienfeld** (1976), **DaVanzo** et al. (1983), *Population Reports* (1984), **Phillips** and **Mozumdar** (1984), **De Sweemer** (1984), **Omran** and **Standley** (1976), **Puffer** and **Serrano** (1973), and **Serour** et al. (1981).

risks, as is the last. In a society where daughters are desired as much as sons, these factors should have no effect on the survival of boys compared to girls.

Antenatal health care which improves the health status of the mother likewise should benefit both sons and daughters, and maternal desire would not vary by sex. At birth, if there is no birth attendant or there are other circumstances which make the delivery difficult, the consequences should not differ depending on the sex of the baby. Low birthweight babies are at relatively high risk, regardless of their sex, in societies with little or no son preference. If twins are born and one is a girl and one a boy, all other things being equal, each child has an equal chance to thrive. Congenital birth defects are one area where slight sex differences may arise, since certain birth defects are sex-linked. Muscular dystrophy is one inherited disease that strikes male offspring and thus has sex-selective risks.

Depression in the mother, which has been documented as sometimes impairing attachment to the baby (Morley, 1973 p. 81), would not be related to the sex of the child nor would breast-feeding problems. It is true that smaller babies may be weaker and thus less able to suck properly; it is also true that generally male neonates tend to weigh a bit more than female neonates and thus there may be a male suckling advantage.[10] However, I have not seen any documentation of any survival function inherent in the size differential. According to current knowledge, as the infant grows into childhood, feeding and child care produce no differences by sex in the child's ability to thrive, and all other factors in the wider social environment including sanitation, health care infrastructure, maternal education level, and the socio-economic status of the household has no sex-differential effects.

Where Son Preference is Strong

Table 1 also displays the assessments for the potential of the risk factors affecting the survival of boys compared to girls in highly son-preferential societies. The assessments differ greatly from those discussed above where just a single factor was shown to have a weak sex-differential effect. In son-preferential societies, only three factors lack potential for creating sex differences, while four have weak effects. All the other risk factors have strong effects.

[10] In developed countries male infants (under one year of age) have a slight survival disadvantage compared to female infants. The sex ratio at birth is about 105 males per 100 females; by the end of year one, the sex ratio is generally balanced.

The factors with no potential are: lack of a birth attendant, hemorrhage or other birth complications, and sanitation facilities. The lack of a birth attendant would not, in itself, differentially affect the survival of boys compared to girls; compensation for that lack, however, may be greater if the child is a male. For instance, if the child is male, greater effort may be made to get help from a knowledgeable older woman but I lack documentation for this hypothesis. It is possible also that with birth complications such as hemorrhage, greater investments will be made to improve the health of the mother if she has borne a son. I can foresee no potential sex-differential impact that sanitation facilities in themselves would have.

Now we come to the risk factors which I assessed as having a weak potential effect on sex-differentials in survival: congenital birth defects, maternal education, health care provisions, and the number of cows and buffaloes (which create a tetanus risk). The first factor, congenital birth defects, has the same effects in a son-preferential society as in a society where there is little or no son preference, but may be exacerbated by a son-preferential culture in cases where the birth defect is slight—greater efforts might be made to preserve males than females since a female with a visible defect will have very impaired marriage chances, whereas a male with a slight birth defect will have only slightly more difficult marriage chances than a normal male. In rural India, very few children, either male or female, with visible birth defects reach maturity, but those that do in North India are most likely to be males.

I rated maternal education and health care provisions as having a weak effect in that they may actually help reduce what would otherwise be significant sex differentials. The evidence on the effect of maternal education and the reduction of son preference/daughter disfavour is by no means established, but on the basis of some tentative indications from Ludhiana, I have given it a 'weak' rating. The same is true for health care provisions which have been shown in certain cases to reduce sex differences in health and survival in Ludhiana (Cowan and Dhanoa, 1983). The evidence again is tentative, and other reports show that increased availability of health care may be primarily utilised for boys, thus, creating greater differentials than existed previously (Srilatha, personal communication, 1984).

A similar line of thinking prompted me to give the tetanus

hazard, created through the presence of cows and buffaloes, a 'weak' rating. Tetanus injections are available at local health centres throughout most of India. Parents, however, do not always obtain free injections for their children, but if parents realize the value of the tetanus immunisation it is likely that they will make a greater effort to take sons than daughters to a health centre for an injection. This statement is conjectural at the present time, for I have no data on sex ratios of children who receive various inoculations, but the sex ratio of children brought to health care centres for treatment in Punjab is very high, i.e., preponderantly masculine.

I have rated all the other risk factors as having a strong potential effect on sex-differential health of children in son preferential societies. There are important details for each factor that should be reviewed.

In the case of pregnancies to very young mothers, or first births in general, a son is most desired as a first child and will be most invested with care and resources. Nevertheless, a first daughter is not such a great disappointment as are second, third or fourth daughters. The Ludhiana data, when analysed, will reveal what differences may exist in health and survival between first-born sons and first-born daughters; surely the differences will be less dramatic than between third-born sons and third-born daughters. Thus, I believe that the risk to first daughters is strong relative to that of first-born sons, but certainly not as strong as to higher birth order daughters, daughters likely to be born after the mother is aged 33 years.

The risks to children born to mothers above the age of 33 years are varied, depending on whether the mother has a married son in the house as well as her own reproductive history. There is a strong cultural rule in North India that grandmothers should not bear children (Mandelbaum, 1974). By the time a woman is 33 years old in many parts of rural India, her oldest son may be married and cohabiting with his wife, putting the 33-year-old woman in the position of potential grandmother. Medical personnel at Ludhiana CMC state very clearly that 'grandmother's babies' never survive, no matter what their sex. Many women aged 33 in North India, however, will not be at the end of their childbearing period. Reports from Ludhiana indicate a very high risk for daughters born into large families, and a relatively high risk even to sons in families that already have large number of sons and daughters. Here the age of the mother interacts strongly with the family formation at the time of the child's birth. It is likely that a first daughter born to a mother over 33 years old who has only sons will be quite welcome and thus at less risk than would be a sixth son.

Short pregnancy intervals may exacerbate sex differentials in survival in complicated ways. If the index child is a low priority female and the previous child a high priority son, then the mother may continue to feed the son to the detriment of the daughter. A short birth interval may reduce the daughter's chance for survival, combined with discrimination in care, because the child at birth tends to be smaller and weaker and the mother may have less breast milk. In another case, if a high priority son is born following a low priority daughter, the daughter may be abruptly weaned at an early age. Again, the short birth interval exacerbates the situation because if the daughter had been three or four years old the risk at weaning time would not have existed (she would have been weaned earlier) or would have been less severe. Short birth interval in isolation from cultural factors is not a powerful sex selective factor, but in combination with son preference it can create a male survival advantage.

I rated antenatal health care as having a strong potential influence. I reasoned that if the mother is given health care, better nutrition, and relief from onerous work loads, and if her child is of higher priority then the interaction between her health status and cultural preferences will largely be to the advantage of male survival. Of course, even if her child is an unwanted daughter the status of the infant at birth would benefit as well so that antenatal health care can be seen as having some mitigating effects on sex differentials.

The maternal desire for a child is an important psychological component which may affect the survival status of the child. In societies where son preference is not strong, maternal desire for the child does not vary depending on the sex of the child. In most of North India, however, maternal desire for a son is extreme and is reinforced by the entire household. As a risk factor, maternal desire in North India should be translated into *household* desire since the health status of the child is intricately interwoven into household preferences sometimes perhaps overriding maternal preferences.

A low birthweight baby is always at greater risk than a larger baby, and if the baby is a low priority female then the risk is compounded. We do not yet have answers about the differential survival rates between low birthweight boys and girls, but one can imagine the extra lengths to which a family would go in order to protect the life of a low birthweight but high priority male child. Ironically, such extra lengths in villages in Ludhiana sometimes result in dangerous 'overprotection', such as, a resort to bottle feeding for a weakly suckling infant. Inevitably, as reported by medical personnel at Ludhiana, bottle feeding results in the death of the child through improper sterilisation.

Twinship can create sex-differential risk for a child. In rural North India, surviving twins are rare, and especially surviving twin females. Breast milk is allocated to preferred infants, and in the case of fraternal twins it is highly probable that the boy will fare better than the girl. Twinship in many cultures creates risk (Morley, 1973; Gransberg, 1973) for any twins born, regardless of sex, via, infanticide. In son preferential cultures, the risk of twinship is compounded by gender to the detriment of female twins.

Puerperal (post-partum depression in a son preferential culture would tend to occur more frequently upon the birth of a daughter. I know of no data on the incidence of maternal depression after the birth of a daughter compared to a son, but it seems a logical consequence in rural North India. After the birth of a son in North India there is loud fanfare and celebration with feasts and music.[11] The word is sent out that a son has been born and auspicious leaves are hung over the doorway to proclaim the good news. On the birth of a daughter there is only silent disappointment. A woman who bears a son gains status in her husband's family while a woman who bears only daughters is regarded as little better than a sterile woman and her husband may consider taking a second wife. When one realizes that a woman's household status and her future security, which comes from her sons, depend on the sex of her child it is not difficult to infer serious disappointment and 'depression' at the birth of a daughter.[12]

Such depression ties in closely with the ability to breastfeed successfully (Morley, 1973). Contrary to uninformed opinion,

[11] See the review of this topic in Miller (1981 p. 85).
[12] For an insightful discussion of how the desire for sons affects relationships among women in joint families in rural North India, see Hyde (1984).

successful breastfeeding does not occur automatically. It requires psychological ease on the part of the mother, and it is often dependent on support and advice from more knowledgeable women (Raphael, 1973). Such assistance will not be given as readily to a mother who has just borne a low priority daughter as to a new mother of a precious son. If breastfeeding is not established early on, the difficulties increase as the child becomes weak and fretful, the mother's breasts become engorged, and the mother is less and less interested in trying to feed a non-responding child. In the words of Western child developmentalists, 'synchrony' in feeding is lost and will be difficult to reestablish.

If the infant survives its early weeks of life, the next critical period is around the age of six months when supplementation to breast milk is needed because its quality and quantity diminishes in respect to the growing child's needs. Medical personnel at Ludhiana report great difficulty in getting mothers to supplement the diets of low priority children, generally females. They have found that the best solution is to ask mothers to break up a bit of *chapatti* (wheat flour bread) and mix it with tea brewed with milk. This procedure requires the mother to do little extra; she need not purchase anything that would not be in the house already nor prepare anything special. To ask that something special be done for a low priority child is futile. A hypothesis worth investigating concerns work patterns of mothers after they have borne high priority sons compared to low priority daughters. It may be that mothers of daughters are more willing to go back to work in the fields than mothers of sons, and such work might reduce their capacity to breastfeed satisfactorily.

I have documented elsewhere (Miller, 1981) the care and feeding differentials for boys and girls in North India. It is clear that in North India most sons receive more and better food in the household than most daughters. In Ludhiana, boys are rarely left uncared-for in the house if the mother goes to the fields to work. It is also clear that boys receive more and better medical care. The hospital in Ludhiana cannot fill its girls' ward but the boys' ward is well-attended. This pattern does not result from more boys than girls being ill, but because more parents are willing to take their boys to the hospital for treatment.

In the Ludhiana area, among a population of 911 children in their second and third years, it was found that second and third degree malnutrition was distributed very unequally between boys and girls (Cowan and Dhanoa, 1983). The overall percentage of malnourished children was lower among the privileged (landed) castes, but the sex *disparity* was greater among the same privileged castes (Table 2). Further research on the larger population monitored in the Sahnewal block will show whether this pattern holds true.

Table 2

Prevalence of 2nd/3rd Degree Malnutrition in 911 Children in Second and Third Year of Life, Ludhiana, the Punjab

	Number	Sex Ratio[a]	With 2nd/3rd Degree Malnutrition[b]	Ratio of Male to Female Malnourished
Privileged Males	231		2	
		111.0		1:6
Privileged Females	208		13	
Under-Privileged Males	244		11	
		102.5		1:3
Under-Privileged Females	238		29	
Total	911	106.5	55	1:4

[a] Sex ratio refers to the number of males per hundred females.
[b] The numbers in this column were read from a graph and may be off by a small margin.
SOURCE: Figure 5 in Cowan and Dhanoa (1983, 352).

One might think that even in son preferential cultures the incidence of infectious diseases would be random by sex, that no matter what the parents' preferences, measles and colds will strike boys and girls randomly. It is true that measles and colds will randomly strike children of either sex, but the seriousness of the infection, as with most childhood diseases, is affected by the nutritional status of the child (Morley, 1973). This truth is especially meaningful in the case of childhood diarrhea from which most childhood mortalities in developing countries result (Behar, 1974; Jelliffe, 1968; Scrimshaw et al., 1968). The interaction between nutritional status and infection is proven. We have seen that son preference seriously raises the nutritional status of boys compared to girls, thus infectious diseases generally will be less dangerous to the health status of boys than girls.

The effect of the household socio-economic status on sex differences in mortality and morbidity of children is not completely clear. In my earlier work (Miller,1981) I stated that differentials would be greater in North Indian propertied castes and classes since it is in such groups that the son preference/daughter disfavour complex makes most economic sense: daughters are a burden to families because of the large dowries required for their marriage and they are a burden to the rural economy which relies much more on male labour than female labour power. In lower castes and classes, large dowries are not generally required (though the practice of giving dowry is spreading among these groups) and women are more often economic assets to the household because they work for wages.[13]

Recent data on caste/class differences in children's health and survival are not conclusive. For Punjab, Cowan and Dhanoa's research (1983) on the Ludhiana data implies significant sex differentials in the nutritional status of boys and girls in both 'privileged' and 'under-privileged' castes, but the mortality patterns have yet to be examined. Preliminary reports from a study in Chandigarh, also in the Punjab, reveal that higher castes have a greater sex differential in infant mortality than the lower castes (Rush, personal communication of interview with Nina Datta, 1983). I have rated the effect of household socio-economic status as strong, meaning that in upper, propertied castes and classes the survival disadvantage to girls will be more significant than in lower castes and classes, but we badly need more data on this question from all over India. In terms of nutritional status of the survivors, the sex differential may be less in propertied than unpropertied groups because parents tend to take better care of the girls who are high priority children, and they may have more resources (but see ratios of male to female malnourished in Table 2).

CONCLUSION

Intense preference for sons can alter dramatically the entire

---

[13] A good study of a low caste community of sweepers in Banaras, Uttar Pradesh, which documents the economic importance of women's wages in the family is Searle Chatterjee (1981). Houska (1982) reports on the nearly equal treatment of sons and daughters among a community of sweepers in Allahabad, Uttar Pradesh.

pattern of allocation of household resources to sons compared to daughters. The exercise described above shows how children's health and survival can be skewed depending on the sex of the child, with some variance affected by birth order.

Working within such a cultural system, can a health care program, which seeks to provide equal health care for all, be successful? There is a controversy on the impact of the health care programs in alleviating sex differences in child survival in patriarchal cultures, particularly of North India. Some say that a simple increase in health care services will improve the situation for girls (Minturn, 1984); others have found that increased services will be diverted to priority children, i.e., boys, and that girls will benefit only secondarily.[14]

Cowan and Dhanoa note that one important result of their intensive home-based visiting approach is the reduction in percentage of deaths to female children (1983 p. 354). There is no doubt that their approach can be effective, though it requires much effort. Two questions arise from this finding: a related result of increased survival for girls in an increase in the percentage of malnourished girls. That is, girls' lives have been saved but the quality of those lives may not at all be equal to that of the males. How much more intensive must home visiting be to overcome this problem? Furthermore, some would argue that the death of unwanted children is preferable to their extended mistreatment and suffering.[15]

Second, the cost of saving the life of a low priority female child must far outweigh the cost of saving and improving the lives of priority males. We have not figured the unit health care costs by sex and priority; such an analysis would be very revealing. The time is not far off when, with fiscal stringency the watchword of the day, the cost of extending intensive health care for girls becomes a strong objection to programs, such as, the one at CMC Ludhiana. Two arguments can be developed to counter policies which would truncate special efforts to equalise life chances between boys and girls. First, one might look to the broader social costs of a society in which the sex ratio is seriously unbalanced. It

[14] Srilatha (1983) reports, that in a large study area in Tamil Nadu the infant and child mortality rates have declined significantly in the last ten years, but dramatically for boys and only slightly for girls. The implication is that improved health services may be being differentially allocated to boys and girls.

[15] The ethics of this situation are discussed in Kumar (1983).

cannot be proved beyond a shadow of a doubt that unbalanced sex ratios lead to social disturbances, but there is much cross-cultural evidence to that end (Divale and Harris, 1976). Of course, a balanced sex ratio does not guarantee social tranquility, but it seems to be one step in the right direction of smoothing out at least one of society's possible rupture lines. Second, in a strongly son preferential culture, women bear many children in the attempt to produce many sons. The pattern of selective care which promotes son survival to the detriment of daughter survival is built on 'over-reproduction' and much child wastage. Mothers bear a physical burden in this system. The Ludhiana program seeks to keep children alive and wanted, and to promote family planning after a certain number and sex composition of children have been born in a household. This goal should reduce the physical burden on mothers created by extended childbearing. The three goals of equal health for all, possible reduced social tension due to more balanced sex ratios, and reduced childbearing for mothers, clearly constitute ends worth attaining.

REFERENCES

BÉHAR, MOISES, 1975: 'The Role of Feeding and Nutrition in the Pathogeny and Prevention of Diarrheic Processes,' *Bulletin of the Pan American Health Organization*, Vol. 9, No. 1, pp. 1–9.

COWAN, BETTY and JASBIR DHANOA, 1983: 'The Prevention of Toddler Malnutrition by Home-based Nutrition Education,' in D.S. McLaren, ed., *Nutrition in the Community: A Critical Look at Nutrition Policy, Planning, and Programmes* (New York/London, John Wiley and Sons) pp. 339–56.

DIVALE, WILLIAM T. and MARVIN HARRIS, 1976: 'Population, Warfare, and the Male Supremacist Complex,' in *American Anthropologist*, Vol. 78, pp. 521–38.

DYSON, TIM and MICK MOORE, 1982: 'Gender Relations, Female Autonomy and Demographic Behavior: Regional Contrasts Within India,' (Unpublished manuscript, Population Studies, London School of Economics).

HOUSKA, WILLIAM, 1981: 'The Characteristics of Son Preference in an Urban Scheduled Caste Community,' in *Eastern Anthropologist*, Vol. 34, No. 1, pp. 27–35.

HYDE, JANICE, 1984: 'The Ties That Do Not Bind: Women Against Women in India,' Paper presented at the New York Asian Conference, Cortland, NY.

JELLIFFE, DERRICK B., 1968: Infant Nutrition in the Subtropics and Tropics (Geneva, World Health Organization, Monograph 29).

KUMAR, DHARMA, 1983: 'Male Utopias or Nightmares?' in *Economic and Political Weekly*, January 15, pp. 61–4.

MANDELBAUM, DAVID G., 1974: *Human Fertility in India: Social Components and Policy Perspectives* (Berkeley, University of California Press).

MILLER, BARBARA D., 1981: *The Endangered Sex: Neglect of Female Children in Rural North India* (Ithaca, NY, Cornell University Press).

——, 1984: 'Daughter Neglect, Women's Work and Marriage: Pakistan and Bangladesh Compared,' in *Medical Anthropology*, Vol. 8, No. 2, pp. 109–126.

——, 1985: 'Economic Development and Health in India: The Missing Link of Gender Discrimination,' in *Manushi*, July–August.

MINTURN, LEIGH, 1984: 'Changes in the Differential Treatment of Rajput Girls in Khalapur: 1955–1975,' in *Medical Anthropology*, Vol. 8, No. 2, pp. 127–32.

MORLEY, DAVID, 1973: Paediatric Priorities in the Developing World (London/Toronto, Butterworth).

MUNDLE, SUDIPTO, 1984: 'Recent Trends in the Condition of Children in India: A Statistical Profile,' in *World Development*, Vol. 12, No. 3, pp. 297–307.

Population Reports, 1984: 'Healthier Mothers and Children Through Family Planning,' Series J, No. 27, May–June.

RAPHAEL, DANA, 1973: *The Tender Gift: Breastfeeding* (Englewood Cliffs, NJ, Prentice-Hall).

RUSH, DAVID, 1983: Personal Communication concerning interview with Nina Datta of the Department of Community Medicine, Postgraduate Institute, Chandigarh, Punjab, India. (Dr. David Rush is an epidemiologist at Albert Einstein College of Medicine, New York.)

——, 1984: 'The Behavioral Consequences of Protein-Energy Deprivation and Supplementation in Early Life: An Epidemiological Perspective,' in J.R. Galler, ed., *Nutrition and Behavior*, Vol. 5 of *Human Nutrition: A Comprehensive Treatise* (New York, Plenum Publishing), pp. 119–158.

SCRIMSHAW, NEVIN S., CARL E. TAYLOR, and JOHN E. GORDON, 1958: *Interactions of Nutrition and Infection* (Geneva, World Health Organization, Monograph 57).

SEARLE CHATTERJEE, MARY, 1981: *Reversible Sex Roles: The Special Case of Banaras Sweepers* (New York, Pergamon Press).

SIMMONS, GEORGE B., CELESTE SMUCKER, STAN BERNSTEIN, and ERIC JENSEN, 1982: 'Post Neo-Natal Mortality in Rural India: Implications of an Economic Model,' in *Demography*, Vol. 19, No. 3, pp. 371–89.

SRILATHA, K.V., 1983: Personal Communication. (Dr. Srilatha is an epidemiologist, Senior Training and Research Officer, Rural Unit for Health and Social Assistance, Vellore Christian Medical College, Tamil Nadu, India.)

Health Education and Nutrition of Rural Women in Bangladesh: The Household Interface

NAZMUNNESSA MAHTAB

The year 1985 is significant for the people of Bangladesh, especially for the women. We are standing at the tail end of two momentous periods—the enunciation of the Women's Decade (1976–1985) and the completion of the country's Second Five Year Plan (1980–1985).

In 1975, the UN General Assembly proclaimed 1976–85 as the UN Decade for Women to establish equality between the sexes, and to integrate women in the development process. As a member of the United Nations, Bangladesh expressed her solidarity with the UN resolutions to 'guarantee women their basic human rights and fundamental freedom,' and to adopt requisite policies to accelerate their integration in the development process (UN, 1967).

More than a decade has passed since the country has achieved independence and during this period we have completed two plans for national development (1973–1978; 1978–1980), and are approaching the end of the Second Five Year Plan (1980–1985). This period has been sufficiently long to reduce the disparities between the sexes and attain the goal of 'equal participation of women with men in all fields.' However, Bangladesh is still far from attaining its objective.

This paper, however, limits the discussion to three important and basic aspects of development with respect to rural women in Bangladesh—health, nutrition, and education. These are the three indicators of rural poverty. The development of the individual life is basically determined by these three key aspects. All three variables are inter-related, inter-twined and inter-dependent. Their total impact is the prime determinant of an individual's life. It is in this perspective that this paper reviews the progress of women in development efforts. Based mainly on secondary sources, this paper evaluates the policies adopted by the government to achieve the objectives set out in the Second Five Year Plan, and aims at revealing the extent to which the pronounced goals of the government have been met. The major factors which cause inappropriate policies are the cultural and structural aspects of the household wherein women live. Whether it is health, nutrition or education, development efforts are negated since all three aspects are influenced by the position of women in the household and the values that determine their roles, their responsibilities, and their entitlements to family and social resources. These factors are often ignored when devising policies which could redress the gender imbalances. State policy often tends to reinforce the gender biases already existing at family and social levels.

WOMEN IN BANGLADESH: SITUATION ANALYSIS

Bangladesh, one of the least developed countries in the world is riddled with overwhelming problems of poverty, poor health, malnutrition, unemployment, illiteracy, high fertility and mortality rates, and a high population growth rate. According to the Census of 1983, the population of Bangladesh is estimated to be 94.7 million. The vast majority of the population (78.40 per cent) live in rural areas in a 'below poverty level equilibrium trap' (Alamgir, 1978), where the rural women have borne the brunt of poverty even more than the men. Women constitute 48 per cent of the country's total population but *they form the single largest neglected group*. About ninety per cent of our women live in rural areas. They are mostly illiterate, tradition bound, and a vast majority of them are victims of severe poverty, hunger, destitution, and malnutrition as are their menfolks but women are more deprived than men. There is excessive disparity between men and women in access to health care, nutrition and medical services. There is a large gap between men and women in education and literacy (P. Ahmed, 1979). If we look at the total dimension of the problem we can visualise the extremely poor conditions in which the vast majority of rural women live.

As regards the health situation, it has been observed that women in Bangladesh suffer more from continuous malnutrition and diseases than men, and the mortality rate is also higher among women than men. Lack of proper health care and medical facilities, absence of basic nutrition from childhood, continuous sacrifice in the service of the family due to prevailing socio-cultural values take a heavy toll on the lives of the rural women in Bangladesh (FREPD, 1983).

Although, equal access to educational opportunities for both sexes has been guaranteed by the constitution, the actual educational situation of women presents a gloomy picture. The female literacy rate is 16.0 per cent as against 31.0 per cent for males. The situation is worse in rural areas where only 10.9 per cent women are literate while the corresponding rate for men is 25.7 per cent (S. Islam, 1977). Thus, despite the pronounced intentions of the government over the decades, women in general and rural women in particular, have not been getting a proportionate share in the socio-economic development of the country nor are they receiving equal benefits with men.

GOVERNMENT POLICIES AND THEIR IMPLICATIONS FOR WOMEN

An assessment of the situation of Bangladeshi women does indicate that the issues affecting the rural women must be dealt with in the context of their lives as it might have tremendous implications for programme planning. The efforts during the last two plan periods (FFYP, TYP, 1970–75, 1978–80) have failed to touch even the fringe of the female population, let alone change their situation in the existing social structure of lower status and socio-economic roles limited to household activities. However, the spelled out strategies of the Second Five Year Plan (1980–85) (SFYP) point to the government's renewed commitment to improve the status of women in the country. 'The objectives of the Second Five Year Plan have been formulated in the context of overwhelming problems of poverty, poor health, malnutrition, illiteracy and unemployment of the mass, mostly living in the rural areas.'

Health

While minimum medical care to all is the immediate goal, health for all by 2000 A.D. is the broad national objective, and primary health care (PHC) as the major component of health services has been accepted as the key to attain the objective of the SFYP. The main target group of PHC are women and children. Following are the tentative targets of the country's Second Five Year Plan (SFYP, 1983). The salient points are:

1. Maternal mortality from 10/1,000 births to 5/1,000;
2. The birth rate from 43/1,000 population to 32/1,000;
3. The Infant Mortality Rate (IMR) from 150/1,000 live births to 75/1,000;
4. Child Mortality from 250/1,000 live births to 125/1,000;
5. The Morbidity Rate;
6. The prevalence of malnutrition in children;
7. The prevalence of waterborne diseases from 80 per cent to 60 per cent;
8. The incidence of night-blindness.

The next section reanalyses the female health situation against these proclaimed targets.

FEMALE HEALTH STATUS: THE SOCIETAL CONTEXT

Any attempt to review the health situation of women in Bangladesh must first address itself to the general conditions under which most women live. The status of women's health is inextricably tied to their socio-cultural and economic conditions. The particular socio-cultural conditions of the society have a direct impact on the health of women. Women cannot be thought of as abstractions from these realities. Traditionally, women in Bangladesh have an inferior social status and this inferiority is reflected in their health status. Women are subordinate to the men in all phases of their lives. A female is used to bowing to her father in childhood, to the husband in adulthood, and to the son in old age. Due to the tradition of male domination women have become dependent and conditioned to bear all sufferings silently. An independent existence apart from the man to whom she is subordinate is not recognised. The bulk of the economically dependent rural women are subjected to many disadvantages in life—lack of educational facilities, poverty, early marriage and large numbers of children.

As a result, women face far more intense health hazards than other sections of the social population. Thus the health problems are closely related to and arise out of the social situation and cultural traditions that define the subordinate position of women in the society (Chowdhury, 1980).

HEALTH INDICATORS

The level of female health in the country is much below the health conditions of the total population (Mahtab & Ahmed, 1979). The female health situation may be characterised by the following indicators:

1. Maternal mortality resulting from illness in connection with pregnancies, deliveries and their consequences;
2. Effects of fertility on maternal health status;
3. Infant mortality;
4. Disease pattern of women;
5. Health facilities and women's access to health care.

Maternal Mortality

Maternal mortality in Bangladesh is highest among the developing countries. It is about seven per 1000 live births as against 0.14 per 1000 births in the developed countries.

For rural women in Bangladesh, maternity poses a special problem. In addition to the transition which a woman must undergo from being young and carefree to suddenly becoming a mother and becoming responsible for bringing up her baby, she is faced with real health problems during this period. And each time she becomes pregnant, her health hazards increase. A major contributing factor to women's hardship in rural Bangladesh is indeed repeated pregnancies. Between the ages of 15 and 45, a rural woman will have an average of eight pregnancies at least one of which will end in abortion or stillbirth. She will breastfeed each of her children for 2 to 3 years. A woman can expect to spend more than half of her adult life either in pregnancy or lactation. The mortality rate is specifically higher among women of child bearing age, that is, between 10–40 years.

Effects of Fertility on Maternal Health Status

It has been observed that the rural women in Bangladesh produce many children. Sixty per cent of women aged 40 and above have seven or more children. Time gap between a mother's first marriage and the first pregnancy is an important factor from the point of view of female health and population control in Bangladesh. It is found that 28.32 per cent become mothers within one year; 42.23 per cent in two years and 29.45 per cent in three years' time (Mahtab & Ahmed, 1979). Soon after a girl is married she has to demonstrate her ability to perform the role of the mother by begetting children as soon as possible. If she does not have a male child in the first few pregnancies, she has to undergo the process frequently until a male child is born (Chowdhury, 1980). This illustrates the very high fertility levels of rural women in Bangladesh. High fertility is also a basic cause of high female mortality because the child bearing periods or uninterrupted fertility makes rural females vulnerable to death at every pregnancy.

Infant Mortality

The child population of Bangladesh belonging to the age group of 0–14 years accounts for about 47.5 per cent of the total population in rural areas (FREPD, 1981). Child mortality is a sensitive index of the health status of a country. In Bangladesh, the infant mortality rate is as high as 117 per 1,000 live births for both sexes (GOB, 1983). The mortality of children aged 1–4 years has been estimated to be 22.9 per 1,000 children. High infant and child mortality is one of the reasons for high birth rate in Bangladesh because parents want to ensure the survival of as many children as possible in order to have caretakers for themselves in their illness and old age.

Multiple pregnancies play a vital role in the lives of rural women in Bangladesh. Infant mortality leads to quick subsequent pregnancies in women. High infant mortality is mainly due to Tetanus in the new born boby. Tetanus is probably due to bad sanitation, unhygienic maternity practices, and use of an unclean sharpened bamboo piece for cutting the umbilical cord by traditional *dais* or older women relatives. Absence of adequate maternal/child care, and lack of control over her reproductive capacities render a woman totally subordinate to the desires of the family.

Morbidity

Children are vulnerable to many diseases, communicable or non-communicable, which are aggravated by poor living and unhealthy environmental conditions. Children of this country are plagued with various types of diseases. Infectious diseases like measles, cholera, T.B., Tetanus and Diphtheria are widely prevalent in Bangladesh affecting a large number of rural children. The incidence and mortality rates for measles, diphtheria, diarrhoeal diseases, TB and Tetanus are very high (FREPD, 1983). These are the major and most important causes of deaths amongst infants and children resulting in high infant and child mortality rates. Immunisation is considered to be an inexpensive and practical means of controlling these diseases and it is a way to reduce childhood mortality from these diseases, but it is a sad fact that these measures hardly reach the rural children (Shahidullah, et. al., 1981).

The major cause of morbidity in rural areas are diarrhoeal diseases. This is due to less availability of pure drinking water and sanitary latrines, and the habit of open defaecation (Chen, *et. al.*, 1980). This practice also explains the incidence of more infectious diseases in the rural areas. A country wide health survey in rural areas in 1977 (GOB, 1977), revealed that diarrhoeal diseases were the number one killer for the age groups of 1–4, 5–9, and 14–44. Diarrhoea itself further reduces the intake of food and causes loss of body fluids, resulting in further malnutrition.

Disease Pattern of Women

In Bangladesh, females are liable to die from general diseases. Females are most vulnerable to infectious diseases, such as, diarrhoea and tuberculosis; communicable diseases, such as, intestinal worms and diseases caused by malnutrition; and under nourishment, such as, dropsy. (Dropsy may be literally defined as anemia—meaning greater portion of water in the body causing the limbs to swell to unnatural proportions.) Anemia is a widespread deficiency disease that affects women more than men. Apart from these, white discharge, post-natal diarrhoea, prolapse of the uterus, menstrual complications and infection in the breast are major common ailments that rural women suffer from (Mahmuda Islam, 1984). Hypertension, however, is also found to be more frequent among rural women; this might be due to frequent pregnancies and recurrent urinary tract infection (Chowdhury, et. al., 1981).

Health Facilities and Women's Access to Health Care

Health facilities in Bangladesh are inadequate in proportion to the total population. The inadequacy of medical facilities is revealed by the poor distribution of doctors on the basis of population. A large part of the medical infrastructure is concentrated in urban areas and in the hospital sector.

Nevertheless, efforts are being made to extend facilities to rural areas, and during the last few years rural medical facilities have considerably increased. There are nearly 2,500 rural medical centres besides district hospitals (excluding private facilities). Of the family planning and MCH facilities, 85 per cent are located in rural areas, and out of the total 28,000 hospital beds in the country, nearly 37 per cent are available for women (GOB, 1977). In reality, however, a much smaller number of rural women actually utilise the facilities. According to a WHO survey, among the outpatients who come for medical treatment to various medical centres, 32.32 per cent are female and 20.5 per cent are children, compared to 47.09 per cent males (Mahtab & Ahmed, 1979). Socio-cultural practices, cost of modern medical care, inadequate communication system, concentration of facilities at certain places limit the actual health coverage of rural women.

On the other hand, women are the major users of family planning services in Bangladesh. A survey conducted by the Planning Cell of the Population Control and Family Planning Division in 1982 shows that the percentage of female attendance at the Family Planning Clinic is 65.44 per cent as against 28.33 per cent of males (S. Khan, 1984). The implication of this fact indicates that for effective population control women still constitute the main target group. The health and family planning divisions have been merged together with the implicit assumption that in such a merger both the MCH and Family Planning together will be more effective. The sad fact is that in such MCH-FP programmes, MCH exists more in name and the focus of activity lies more with the family planning component (Rizvi, 1984).

Thus, relative neglect by society and men, and the oppressed condition of women affects the total female health situation.

Excessive childbearing—too early and too often—takes its toll. Social compulsions like universal marriage, marriage at early age, high fertility and the value attached to fertility (especially the bearing of sons) have the effect of pushing up the number of pregnancies and births per annum. childbearing and rearing is considered a woman's prime function. High infant mortality reinforces the desire for more children as insurance against death and the vicious circle goes on (Chowdhury, 1980). That a high percentage of women do not get even the minimum MCH care during childbirth is reflected in the high percentage of deaths during childbirth. The health care system does not reach these women. Family planning is important but the family planning programme by itself cannot provide an answer to the health problems faced by women once they are pregnant, and family planning can be effective only when health care is ensured for the living child. In the development of public health, even preventive measures like sanitation and general health education have been neglected, let alone the knowledge of curative aspects. This has a particularly adverse effect on women who bear a triple load; house work, child rearing and economic activity. Health care is grossly underdeveloped and antenatal services are deplorably inadequate or absent.

NUTRITION

Any discussion of women's health problems must start with the fact of malnutrition for this compounds all other problems. Women are particularly vulnerable to malnutrition. A woman's health and nutrition in particular must be seen as a processual event occurring throughout her whole life. The nutritional and health status of rural women in Bangladesh shows a consistent pattern throughout their lives with cycles of malnutrition and infection. The importance of nutrition has been mentioned in the strategy of programme formulation in the SFYP which expects MCH and nutrition to be part of the package of health services extended to the community through its primary health care services (Rahman, 1983). To correct existing levels of malnutrition, the SFYP provided a package of services directed at the vulnerable groups in the community, that is, women and children. The plan stated:

Pre-natal, natal and post-natal care of mothers at domicillary and institutional levels, training of traditional *dais* on hygienic delivery, detention of malnutrition cases and supply of nutritional drugs and foods, immunisation and education would be provided.

The agency for delivering this package would be the primary health care unit.

Despite such well-meaning efforts by the government, the state of maternal and child nutrition is precarious. In Bangladesh, malnutrition is usually caused most directly by inadequate food intake and presence of infectious diseases. Infectious disease is a function of poverty and poor sanitation, whereas inadequate food intake is determined by shortage of food, low income, and social attitudes, traditions and beliefs. To this complex of causes, rural women are particularly vulnerable (M.R. Khan, 1979).

The three national nutrition surveys carried out in 1962–64, 1975–76, and 1980–81 provided information on the food intake and nutritional status of women in different age groups, and concluded that malnutrition is still a great problem and a manifestation of the socio-economic deprivation of rural women ('Nutrition Survey,' 1983).

According to recent survey reports (1980–81), the intake of food in the rural households, according to age and sex, was higher for males than for females. The intake of the members were tabulated under the following heads: (1) food groups; (2) nutrients; (3) calories; (4) proteins. The study confirms that the intake of food was markedly higher for males than for females in all age groups. The highest intake of 1236 gm was recorded for adult males of 20–39 years of age. Among females, the maximum intake was found to be 898 gm for lactating mothers. This intake was, however, well below the average intake for even boys of 13–15 years of age! Except for cereals, the dominance of the males in all food intake was noted (K. Ahmed, 1983).

As regards the intra-family allocation of nutrients, calories, proteins and calcium the survey report indicated that females as well as mothers (both pregnant and lactating) were the worst sufferers as they could not even meet the prescibed norms. Children, pregnant and lactating women were found to be deficient in calories, proteins, calcium, Vitamin A, riboflavin and Vitamin C.

In absolute terms, amongst the children in the age group of 5–11 years, who number 17.4 million as many as 13.6 million suffered from various degrees of malnutrition. Protein-energy malnutrition (PEM) is an acute problem among children. In addition, low intake of Vitamin A by mothers contributes to Vitamin A deficiency and blindness among children. An estimated 50,000 children go blind every year. About 73 per cent of children below five do not have the minimum acceptable level of hemoglobin in their blood. The prevalence of anemia is found to be the highest among the females. All these are attributed to sex discrimination against females in intra-family allocation of food in the rural households (K. Ahmed, 1983).

Cultural inhibitions and discriminatory food distribution practices within the family which allow the adult males to receive the greater and most nutritious part of the diet, leaving the residual for the mother to share with her children, lies at the root of the health and nutritional problems of rural women in Bangladesh.

EDUCATION

The Second Five Year Plan reflects special concern for women's education in the country. The plan devoted a special section on 'Women's Education,' and even went to the extent of mentioning that 'in the process of implementation of the programmes priority [would] be given to cater to the needs of women in the rural areas,' and measures would be taken to recruit more women teachers to ensure retention of girls in schools. The plan clearly indicated the relation between status of women and education, and envisaged adequate steps to be taken to provide increased educational facilities for women so as to remove the imbalances between the sexes in enrolment, and in drop-out rates in both urban and rural areas (Khan, 1984).

The main features of the educational plan assumed that the provision of Universal Primary Education (UPE) by 1985 would remove disparity at the first level. The plan had given immense importance to the issue of mass literacy as complementary to primary education where the needs of women are expected to be automatically taken care of. One of the gigantic efforts of the government in the SFYP was the massive expansion of non-formal education by introducing the Mass Education Programme.

However, at the implementation level, the success has been rather meagre compared to the policies adopted for expansion of female education. Women constitute the majority of school drop-outs, and the number of female illiterates is ever increasing, thus rendering women in Bangladesh to be one of the most deprived groups in terms of education. In order to reveal a clear picture on the review of rural women's education, emphasis has been given to the areas of literacy, primary and secondary education because very few rural girls go beyond that.

Literacy

The concept of literacy used in various censuses conducted in Bangladesh has not been uniform. The 1961 census defined a person as literate if he/she could read any language, with understanding; the 1974 census defined literacy as the ability of both reading and writing in any language, while in the 1981 census a person was considered literate if he could write a letter in any language.

As regards literacy the percentage of females is disconcertingly low, that is only 16.0 per cent against the 31.0 per cent for males (BBS, 1981). In rural areas also, only 10.9 per cent of the rural women were found to be literate as against the much higher literacy rate (25.7 per cent) for rural men. There is also a marked imbalance in the rural/urban literacy rates among females.

The urban literacy rates among women during 1974 in the age group of 5–14, 15–24 and 25 and above were 31.03 per cent, 43.25 per cent and 23.52 per cent respectively, compared to 14.76, 18.20 and 7.56 per cent respectively amongst women in rural areas. These findings signify that rural women belonging to the age group of 25 and above are the most disadvantaged. The literacy rate for this group is at the bottom of the scale (7.56 per cent). Literacy rate of this age group among the urban women is found to be 23.52 per cent while the literacy rate for rural men in the same is 28.09 per cent (S. Islam, 1977).

It is clear that rural women constitute the majority of illiterates in the country. The number has now reached approximately 23.9 million or 93.53 per cent and their number is still increasing.

EDUCATION LEVELS

The main stream of the national system of education broadly comprises of three stages—primary, secondary and higher.

Primary Education

This is the base of the country's educational pyramid and has a duration of five years (I-V) and is meant for children in the 6–10 years age group. Primary education has been made free; but despite significant improvement in the provision of schooling facilities from 39,279 in 1974 to 43,323 in 1983 there are still imbalances in the schooling facilities in the different districts of Bangladesh implying that children do not have equal access to schooling in the different regions of the country. As for the enrolment situation, although there is an improvement in the overall enrolment, female enrolment constitutes only 36.74 per cent of the total enrolment and there is a wide variation between the sexes in the primary age group participation. There are also significant area differentials in terms of female enrolment. The proportion of out-of-school girls is alarmingly high compared to out-of-school boys (S. Islam, 1977). There is no denying the fact that there still exists a large gap between male and female drop-out rates at the primary stage and the gap between male and female drop-out rates, instead of closing over the years, has widened from 3 to 12 per cent during 1974–83. In rural areas female drop-outs tend to be much higher (only 41 per cent of rural girls reach class V compared to 60 per cent of urban girls).

Regarding Universal Primary Education (UPE), the schools have failed to make much headway in attracting children to schools and achieve UPE for all children (S. Islam, 1984).

Secondary Education

After five years of primary education there are two types of secondary schools open to students: Junior High School offering Classes VI-VIII, and Senior High Schools offering Classes IX-X. In Bangladesh, secondary education for women is full of inequalities that reflect both conservatism and unrealistic policies. The number of secondary schools for girls between 10–14 years of age lags far behind those of boys. Regarding the rural areas, it is estimated that the distribution pattern of rural schools is not based on the need in different areas. It is, therefore, clear that both in the urban and rural areas, in the absence of adequate facilities for girls, girls will have to attend boys' schools which are, in effect, 'mixed' in nature.

Inspite of the inadequacy of girls' secondary schools, girls' enrolment has increased significantly. However, girls' enrolment constitutes only one-third of the total and is far behind the age group population. There is quite a big discrepancy between sexes in age-group enrolment ratios. The drop-out rate is also more pronounced for females than males (S. Islam, 1981).

The wide disparity between males and females in respect to education may be attributed to the socio-cultural environment of the rural areas. However, the main reasons for non-enrolment and drop-out of females from both primary and secondary education levels may be summarised as follows: (1) poverty; (2) education level of head of the family; (3) distance from school; (4) indispensable household assets; (5) family cycle of child rearing; (6) discrimination; and *purdah* (segregation).

Female Teachers

Next to students, teachers are the most crucial inputs in the educational system. Although the need for female teachers at the primary stage is duly recognised, their number constitutes only a marginal segment (5.17 per cent) in the overall structure. The inadequacy of female teachers becomes more prominent when considered against the situation of female teachers in rural primary schools. Out of 33,931 rural government primary schools, only 3,417 schools (10.06 per cent) have female teachers (FREPD, 1977). The number of trained female teachers in urban rural schools is also inadequate.

Although the number of female teachers in secondary schools has increased significantly from 1106 in 1974 to 8044 in 1983, they still constitute only 2 per cent of the total teaching force (S. Islam, 1984).

Thus, a review of the progress of development of women in the three key aspects—health, nutrition and education in the light of the policies of the government adopted in the SFYP does indicate that women instead of being equal partners with men, are lagging far behind.

POLICY GAPS

The government of Bangladesh occupies a distinctive position among other nations in so far as from its very inception Bangladesh was committed to the cause of women. Starting from the special constitutional provision empowering the state for '. . . making special provisions in favour of women and children . . . ' (GOB, 1979) to promulgation of different laws and ordinances to preserve the woman's right, to ensure her representation and to encourage her participation, was initiated by the government. The Constitution of Bangladesh grants equal rights to women with men, and so it is a declared policy of the government of Bangladesh to take special measures to bring women at par with men (S. Khan, 1984).

To promote equality of sexes, full participation of women is a declared policy of the government of Bangladesh and it has the distinct credit of creating the first full fledged Ministry of Women's Affairs (MWA) in the Asia Pacific Region. The establishment of a separate ministry in December 1978, to deal with women's interests is a milestone on the road for female integration in the national scene. The basic objective of the ministry is 'attending to the problems and affairs of women,' involving a wide range of activities starting from specific policy formulations to creating a more congenial atmosphere for women to participate in socio-economic activities (S. Khan, 1984).

The functions assigned to the MWA are of a general nature. Like all other ministries it is to work within the tradition of department oriented policies and programmes. This makes it apparent that the major role of the ministry is to oversee and co-ordinate specific activities undertaken by other ministries/agencies for the betterment of women—viz, health, education and employment which are under the jurisdiction of other ministries. Herein lies the contradiction. The establishment of a separate ministry sometimes creates the false impression that the ministry will take care of all women's problems—that other ministries need do nothing about women. There is a danger that since there is a separate women's ministry all other ministries and agencies wash their hands off from any concern about women. The absence of inter-departmental coordination and cooperation is particularly dysfunctional in so far as formulation of policies towards women is concerned. The MWA is functioning more as an implementing agency rather than a policy-making body 'attending to the problems and affairs of women.'

Side by side with the MWA, the government of Bangladesh has

also set up various women's organisations to cater to the needs of women. Among these, the Mahila Parishad (1970), the Bangladesh Women's Rehabilitation and Welfare Foundation (1971), the Mahila Samity (1972), the Bangladesh Jatiya Mahila Sangstha (1976) and the Bangladesh Shishu Academy (1977) are important in the cause of integrating women and children in national development planning. However, their activities are generally limited to urban middle class women who form these associations to promote the 'welfare' of the 'less fortunate' and 'needy' sisters residing in the rural areas. They generally emphasise two types of policies for women—policies for legal reforms and welfare-oriented policies and programmes (Jahan, 1977). The programmes for women do not follow any uniform policy or pattern. Whenever needs arise any programme is undertaken. For example, the MCH and the Family Planning Programme is devoted to the task of population control; nutrition programmes undertaken to eradicate malnutrition among pregnant women and children; universal primary education is emphasised to maintain retention of girls in schools; income generating schemes are introduced to provide income and develop skills. Thus, the policies relating to women's development are often formulated without conceptualising the problem of integration in the right perspective. The attitude of policy formulation reminds me of a quotation by Jawaharlal Nehru. Nehru while talking to Mountbatten, about Gandhi, said:

> going around with ointment trying to heal one sore spot after another on the body of India instead of diagnosing the cause of the eruption of the sores and participating in the treatment of the body as a whole (Collins & Lapierre, 1982).

This is rightly applicable to the formulation of policies and programmes for women in Bangladesh. Instead of identifying the *main* cause for women lagging behind men in all spheres the government is announcing one policy after another to make women equal to men. Another characteristic of the women's programme is the welfare orientation. Anything dealing with women has to be welfare as if the 'rich are giving alms to the poor'. As the saying goes:

'Prayers go up and blessings come down.'

Anything recognised as women's needs has to go up as prayers and then the blessings would be bestowed.

The nature of policies being welfare oriented, having a reformist approach and indicating remedial measures, many programmes that have been set up with the aim of improving women's condition are not linked with the broader movement of reaching beyond women's problems to touching the oppression of the majority of women. They fail to bring about a radical improvement in the condition of women (Anens & Beurden, 1977).

Thus, the major constraints in achieving desired responses to women's need lie at the root cause of our *religious and cultural ideologies leading to the negative attitudes towards women*. It is necessary to illustrate how women are thought about and how men behave towards them.

From her very birth a girl is treated as an inferior in relation to a boy. The birth of a son is rejoiced in the family and indicated by a (+) sign meaning that sons will *add* to the family. When the son grows up he will earn an income and through marriage will bring in wealth by the system of dowry. On the other hand, the birth of a girl is unwelcome, indicating a loss (−) to the family. A girl has to be reared then sent to another family through marriage with a huge amount of dowry. Again if the girl is ill fated she returns to her father's house after divorce or widowhood. From birth the female child suffers from 'psychological' deprivation in the family.

One particular factor for women's oppression in Bangladesh is the Islamic religion. Islam has reinforced and consolidated women's inferior status. It has provided men with an ideological instrument for dominating women. The Quran proclaims:

'Men are superior to women on account of the qualities in which God has given them pre-eminence and also because they furnish dowry for women (*Koran*, 1972).

Women have to observe *purdah* and have to behave in a modest way. *Purdah* is one of the strongest means of oppression of women in rural Bangladesh as it restricts them in many ways. The veiled and sequestered Muslim woman is today still a kind of a slave in rural Bangladesh (de Beauvoir, 1983). This implies 'religious' inferiority of women in relation to men.

The inferior status of women is also reflected in social institutions, such as, marriage, education and religion. A marriage is first of all an economic burden. A man needs his wife to take care of him in order to maintain himself as a labourer. She also has to bear him children, preferably sons, who will produce and contribute to the family income. A man regards his wife as his possession and uses her freely for his own maintenance and pleasures. So cultural traditions confer on women an inferior status.

Socio-economic and cultural practices limit the participation of village girls. Compared to boys, girls have to cross many more hurdles in addition to poverty, attitudinal barriers and role conflict. They have to assist their mothers in the drudgery of domestic work and meet their educational needs through whatever informal learning is available at home. Opportunity for formal schooling is hard in this environment. Women are relatively less socialised than men in Islamic values and doctrine. After all they do not participate in the Islamic community that prays together. Being secluded they are less exposed and are less literate than men (Blanchet, 1984).

Further, beliefs and attitudes that discriminate against women control the secluded world of rural women. In health and nutrition preference is given to boys and adult males. Sexual segregation and ideas regarding female modesty have caused many women to die rather than allow their treatment by male doctors. In intra-family food distribution, food is always made available to adult men and is least available to mothers and children. It is a known fact that pregnant and lactating women need more food nutrients but it is not available for these women. They are always the last to eat in their homes and often, particularly for the poor village women this means scraps or foregoing a meal for some days.

The prejudice that women are inferior is reflected in the way women's work is regarded as non-productive. Women in Bangladesh have two major functions, neither of which is recognised as having any value, either by women themselves or anyone else. One is food production, the other child bearing and child rearing. Rural women in Bangladesh are responsible for 70 per cent of the food production, 50 per cent of the animal husbandry, and 100 per cent of the food processing and child rearing. Since women are not paid for these jobs, the productive character of some of their work is overlooked. They work on family enterprises as 'family labour'. The development process in practice displaces or bypasses women and leaves them worse-off than they were before. Development activities in a great many cases have had an adverse impact on them. Training in agriculture, food production, dairy, industry and marketing has been given to the better educated men. Men and machines have replaced women (Chowdhury, 1980). Since women usually do not earn money they are economically dependent on men.

All these facts go to show the dependence of rural women upon men in all aspects—religious, psychological, cultural, economic, educational, and political—giving them an inferior status throughout their lives. Rural Bangladeshi women are caught between the pincers of poverty and prejudice. These two are the basic causes for their discrimination, leading to the deplorable condition among the majority of rural women. These factors are particularly detrimental to the rural women who suffer from the hardships resulting from their dependence on male dominated power structures in their families, households, communities and country.

From time immemorial it has been ingrained in the minds of the society at large and the women themselves that they are subservient to the male society. Their presence and goal of life is to give comfort and peace to others. Rural women are kept within a 'cocoon' composed of all the prejudices and beliefs and they have accommodated themselves to stay inside the cocoon, to accept the oppression and exploitation by adapting to it. They have internalised the ideas that they are inferior creatures who are dependent on their husbands and not able to do much themselves. For the rural women it will be very difficult to break the hard shell of the 'cocoon' and come out of the existing male dominated structures. It is the men who have made the laws and who have used religion, culture and tradition as tools to instill in women a feeling of inferiority, dependence, subjugation and seclusion in relation to men.

The inferior status of women is not confined to the rural sector. In the urban society many women though highly educated have an inferior status in the family. This is mainly attributed to the conservative outlook of our men. Working women or mothers, although adding enough wealth to the family, are usually looked down upon in society. Inspite of the government's policy for 10 per cent employment to be filled up by women, the posts remain vacant not because of lack of opportunities for women but due to the outlook of men who do not consider them suitable, or would not allow their women to work outside the family. According to these men, marriage for a woman is the most honourable career, freeing her from the need of any other participation in the collective and public life.

It is quite evident that only slogans for emancipation and projects would not bring about emancipation. Women must help themselves by changing their attitudes towards themselves. No amount of legislative compulsion can bring about any effect or sustained result if the attitudes towards women are not changed. The words 'equality' would be distorted to connote 'disparity' and 'development' would only bring about 'degeneration' unless the government identifies and eradicates the root cause: the attitudes of men and society towards women. Mere welfare measures are not sufficient to bring about development or equality; the role of women should be identified and defined clearly so that the whole society and the women themselves understand the roles they have to play in society and realise their status. Not only should men change their attitudes to women, but women too must change their attitudes towards themselves.

POLICY ISSUES

The discussions make it clear that the inequality between the sexes in Bangladesh is due to two main causes: (1) the formulation of policies by male dominated machinery and (2) the negative view about the attitudes towards females in the society that condition women's role in the household and outside. Women's problems should no longer be men's problems. Problems and issues relating to women should be identified by women themselves.

It is essential to reform the education system of the country. Only through education can the masses change their attitudes. However, this education should not be the education followed and prescribed through the formal or non-formal schemes as at present. It is education for *change*. Change that would break the distorted views of religion, psychology, economics, politics, education, cultural traditions and prejudices which lead to internalisation of the inferior and subordinate status of women in Bangladesh. Such an education should also change the outlook of men towards women. Women should come forward to break the age-old medieval and colonial prejudices of being inferior, subordinate and dependent on men. For development and equality of women in all spheres it is essential that the change is initiated by the women themselves rather than being imposed on them as at present. The misguided and distorted view that a female child is inferior from birth should be withdrawn from the minds of mothers, and both male and female children should be treated alike, given equal education so that marriage no longer remains an economic burden for the girl's father. The abolition of the practice of dowry should be accepted by the society at large to help women maintain an equal status with their husbands in marital life instead of being threatened all the time. The laws of Muslim inheritence should also be changed to allow women an equal share in the property of the family. The work of women should be recognised as productive by attaching value to their work the way men's work is valued. Thus, by breaking through the barriers of all the tools of inferiority, women may be able to come out of the hard shelled cocoon. It is needless to say that the roles of both men and women are equally important in this regard and both have to work simultaneously to bring about the change.

Although it would take a generation to make this dream a reality, the policy strategy should be initiated with immediate effect. Only then would the cause of emancipation of women be fulfilled, and only then could the women have some hope of a decent life in the not too distant future. Nevertheless, in the light of present circumstances and in view of the country's imminent Third Plan, the following measures may be adopted by the government to lessen the disparity and discrimination against women.

1. All government policies have important implications for women's needs. It is therefore imperative that women's interests be represented in the planning, implementation and evaluation of women's projects.
2. Women representatives of every socio-economic group should be systematically included in all decision-making bodies both at the local and national levels. Without women's input, projects risk being irrelevant, inappropriate and even counter-productive.
3. The Women Affairs Ministry is allied to the Ministry of

Social Welfare. Due to this, most of the activities are welfare oriented. Ideally, a separate women's ministry should be housed in the Planning Commission (Jahan, 1977). The function of the women's cell in the Planning Commission should be to devise strategies so that women are given equal participation in all spheres of planned social development. Women must be represented at the highest levels of decision-making in the Planning Commission so that the question of integrating women gets top policy priority.

4. Public policies relating to women should have continuity encompassing all related aspects rather than aiming at particular issues (S. Khan, 1984). There should be intersectoral linkages between programmes. Programmes to improve the status of women should be linked with literacy and income distribution programmes. Health and nutrition programmes should not only be directed at mothers and children. Health programmes should not restrict their attention to the child-bearing aspects of women but rather view mothers in the total context of womanhood.

5. Women's organisation should be extended to the grassroot level to ensure proper integration of rural women in the development process.

6. Women Affairs Ministry should be assigned specific functions and provide inter-departmental coordination of programmes.

CONCLUSION

The status of a woman is reflected in the authority and power she holds within the family and the prestige she commands from the members of the family and the community. Power and authority are bound to follow if the women are given proper status and provided with an atmosphere, where they get education and make themselves equally competent as their male counterparts in all spheres of life. Unless women are treated as 'persons' and not as 'dependent' and 'inferior' like at present, they cannot expect much from development efforts. Self-awareness and self-respect on the part of women is fundamental to any real progress. It is only then that the policies of the government to improve health, nutrition, education, employment of women would have any value and bring about accepted results.

Last, but the most important point regarding the formulation of governmental policies relating to women is that whatever policy is formulated should be backed by a strong political commitment. Till now, the basic inadequacy of the governmental policy is that it is rarely supported by any political programme. Examples may be cited from the fact that the government has proclaimed that dowry should be banned and any acts of cruelty and violence to women should be strictly penalised. To make these effective the Prohibition of Dowry Act, 1980, and the Deterrent Punishment Ordinance of 1983 have been passed but we are yet to see them implemented. For this, I reiterate that political commitment is a must. Mere lip service will not help in the implementation of any policy concerning women, if there is to be real upliftment of women in society.

REFERENCES

AHMED, KAMAL, eds., 1983: *Nutrition Survey of Bangladesh (1981–82)* (University of Dhaka, Institute of Nutrition and Food Science) December.

AHMED, PARVEEN, 1979: 'Issues for Women in Bangladesh,' in *Situation of Women in Bangladesh* (Dhaka, Women for Women, UNICEF).

ALAMGIR, MOHIUDDIN, 1978: *Bangladesh—A Case Study of Below Poverty Level Equilibrium Trap* (Dhaka, Bangladesh Institute of Development Studies).

ANENS, JENNEKE, JOS VAN BEURDEN, 1977: *Jhagrapur—Poor Peasants and Women in a Village in Bangladesh* (New Delhi, Orient Longman).

DE BEAUVOIR, SIMONE, 1983: *The Second Sex* (Middlesex, Penguin).

BLANCHET, THERESE, 1984: *Women, Pollution and Marginality—Meanings and Rituals of Birth in Rural Bangladesh* (Dhaka, University Press Limited).

CHEN, ET AL., 1980: 'Epidemiology and Causes of Death Among Children in a Rural Area of Bangladesh,' in *International Journal of Epidemiology*, Vol. 9, No. 25.

CHOWDHURY, ET AL., 1981: 'Demography, Morbidity, and Mortality in a Rural Community of Bangladesh,' in *Bangladesh Medical Research Council Bulletin*, Vol. VII, No. 1, June, pp. 22–39.

CHOWDHURY, ZAFRULLAH, 1980: 'A Double Oppression in Bangladesh,' in Patricia W. Blair ed., *Health Needs of the World's Poor Women* (Washington D.C., Equity Policy Centre), pp. 4–6.

COLLINS, LARRY and DOMINIQUE LAPIERRE, 1982: *Freedom at Midnight* (Delhi, Vikas Publishing), 11th edition, p. 86.

FREPD, 1983: *Assessment of Female Education in Bangladesh* (Dhaka), July.

———, 1977: *Situation of Children in Bangladesh*, (UNICEF).

Foundation for Research and Educational Planning and Development (FREPD), 1981: *Situation of Children in Bangladesh*, (Dhaka).

Government of Bangladesh, 1977: Country Health Programme, Ministry of Health and Family Planning, May.

Government of Bangladesh, 1979: 'Article 29,' in *Constitution*, modified up to February.

Government of Bangladesh, 1983: Health Section, Planning Commission, May.

ISLAM, MAHMUD, 1984: *Female Health Status in Bangladesh—A Case of Female Subordination*, (Dhaka, Mimeo).

ISLAM, SHAMIMA, 1977: *Women's Education in Bangladesh: Needs and Issues*, (Dhaka, FREPD).

————, 1984: 'Women's Education in Bangladesh and the Women's Decade: Dream and the Reality,' paper presented at the two-day Seminar on *Integration of Women in Development*, organised jointly by Women for Women and UNIS, Dhaka, November 8–9.

JAHAN, RAUNAQ, 1977: 'Public Policies, Women and Development: Reflections on a Few Conceptual and Structural Problems,' paper presented at the Regional South and Southeast Asian Seminar on *Women and Development*, Dhaka, March 28–April 1.

KHAN, M.R., 1979: 'Socio-Economic Determinant of Nutrition,' First National Seminar on *The Role of Health in Nutrition*, sponsored by Ministry of Health and Population Control, organised by Institute of Public Health Nutrition, Dhaka, November.

KHAN, SALMA, 1984: 'Women's Development and Public Policy in Bangladesh,' paper presented at the National Seminar on *Integration of Women in Development*, (Dhaka, Women for Women and the United Nations Information Service), November.

Koran, 1972: (Middlesex, Penguin), pp. 360–441.

MAHTAB, N., and P. AHMED, 1979: 'Health Nutrition and Implications for Women and Children,' in *Situation of Women in Bangladesh* (Dhaka, Women for Women, UNICEF).

NUTRITION SURVEY OF RURAL BANGLADESH, 1962–64: 1975–76: 1981–82, Dhaka, Institute of Nutrition and Food Science, University of Dhaka, 1965, 1977, 1983.

RAHMAN, HABIBUR M., 1983: 'Nutrition Improvement Programme in Bangladesh,' paper presented at FAO Workshop, Chenghmai, Thailand, 1983.

RIZVI, NAXMA, 1984: 'Nutrition and Health of Women in Bangladesh,' paper presented at the National Seminar on *Integration of Women in Development* (Dhaka, Women for Women and UNIS), November.

The Second Five Year Plan, 1983: Chapter VII, May.

SHAHIDULLAH, ET AL., 1981: 'Under Five's Morbidity and Mortality in Dhaka,' in *Bangladesh Medical Research Council Bulletin*, Vol. VII, No. 2, December, pp. 59–68.

Statistical Pocket Book of Bangladesh, 1983: Bangladesh Bureau of Statistics, Statistics Division, Ministry of Planning, Government of the People's Republic of Bangladesh.

United Nations, 1967: Convention on the Elimination of all Forms of Discrimination Against Women, Article 3, November 7, New York.

Rural Women and Childbirth in Bangladesh: The Social Cultural Context

SHAMIMA ISLAM

In a rich man's house, a woman was going to give birth to her first child. The woman came to her mother's house for her first delivery. As soon as the pain symptom could be felt, a man was sent to call the known *dai* (birth attendant) of the house. Her first task was to help the woman wear a torn *shari*. The *dai* then examined her. The *dai* felt that it would be a delayed delivery. So, she made the woman lie down and started pressing of woman's abdomen frequently which was soaked with oil. As a result, the pain increased. The *dai* started the process of delivering the baby. But nothing worked. On her advice and on the mother's consent, the local homeopathic doctor was called. His medicine also failed. Then the other known neighbouring doctors were called to the house who pushed a few injections in her body. The water bag broke, but the baby did not appear. Two days [went by]. The local village doctors kept on trying and finally the *kaviraj* (herbal practitioner) came. The next day, a leg of the baby came out. The woman was completely senseless. The leg was pushed in with great effort but after an hour or so, it came out again. By then, everybody decided to take her to the urban hospital. But it was the mother of the woman who successfully resisted all such attempts to save the family's *ijjat* (prestige). Then another doctor appeared and claimed that he could bring out the baby if the *dai* worked with him. He clearly pointed out that in this process, the baby would be dead because he would cut out the body of the baby. The other members of the house agreed because this was still better than taking the woman to the urban hospital where violation of the *purdah* (seclusion) was inevitable. The doctor first cut out the leg of the baby that came out first. Next, with the help of the *dai* the other leg was brought out. That too was cut in the same manner. In this process, the whole baby was cut to pieces and was released out of mother's womb. The *dai* felt that she never saw such a difficult case in her whole practising career. It took four complete day's work on that woman to save her life as well as the family's *ijjat*. (Islam, 1979)

The above incidence is merely an example reflecting the notion that issues of education, health and nutrition are phenomena which are intricately inter-woven in the social, cultural and economic fabric of a given society. The incidence of poor literacy rates among women with accompanying high rates of birth, mortality and preventable diseases among infants and children are indirect indices of inadequate knowledge and services among poor rural women of Bangladesh. While the malaise of illiteracy (84 per cent) amongst poor women is readily identified and immediately taken into consideration, health needs of rural women are the most neglected issues in the policy making state. Micro-studies can provide crucial links to our knowledge-base. The fact that approximately 20,000 women in the age group of 15–49 die due to the child bearing act alone, or that 80 per cent of maternal deaths are due to direct obstetrical causes and 44 per cent die during delivery in which 39 per cent are due to complicated labour alone (Chen et al. 1974), is amply indicative of the health status of rural women and sufficient enough to draw our attention to the gravity of the problem. The other findings which are equally disturbing— 91 per cent of the fifty-eight women whose deaths were readily identified, occurred outside the health facilities of which 37 per cent were due to septic abortions, 28 per cent due to complicated labour and 21 per cent in eclampsia—call for serious attention to the health and education policies of this country. The situation is further aggravated by the fact that thousands of women take recourse to indigenous systems and a significant proportion end their lives in abortion complications (Islam, 1981).

The curative oriented ill-conceived MCH facilities are under utilised to a great extent. The National Dai Training Programme aims to train one traditional birth attendant (TBA) from each of the villages, serving a population of nearly 1500, by the Family

Welfare Visitors (FWVs) within her union catering for approximately fifteen villages. This is woefully inadequate (UNICEF, 1984). In reality, the health planning process stays away from any integration with the education system. The task of educating the illiterate millions who stay away from the formal school system in the concept of safe delivery is yet to be integrated with the non-formal education programmes of the country. The magnitude of this task of education and prevention which is expected to be carried out by a single TBA from each village thus suffers from serious deficiencies.

In reality, the project of taking the TBA services down to the *thana* level to serve the underserved is misguided, given the geographic conditions of the rural areas where, in order to reach the *thana* center, one may need to walk ten-twelve long miles through muddy roads and marshy areas without much transport facilities. Rural women are thus automatically left out of the modern services. They are then compelled to be the biggest consumers of the indigenous health care practices which they can avail of easily and which operate within the given socio-cultural constraints that are imposed on them.

In contrast to the popular notion that the midwifery function is performed by a category of people known as *dais*, varied groups of women are discovered to be engaged in performing this role (Blanchet, 1984). In my experience, I have found that there are women who perform this function mostly at *para* (section of a neighbourhood) level and their function is concentrated within a specific class in the village. Their mobility is not merely restricted to within their village but extends beyond, however, only to their relatives' circle. They are distinctly recognised as deliverers of a baby within their village but not as *dais* who, according to popular perception, happen to be women with the specific function of being attached to the government family planning programmes which necessitate women's mobility beyond the village.

In identifying the village midwife, the term *dai* is inadequate. It has an urban flavour. A village may be identified by the complete lack of any *dai* where the function is performed by a group of women known as *dhoruni* (catcher of the new born, or the person who relieves the woman's womb). This latter meaning implied by the term *Khalash Kora* may imply not only delivery but also induced abortion. These are all women's words, often expressed along with gesture in a group discussion. It is usually the literate households in the village who refer to practitioners of this function as *dais*. The term *dhatri* is attached to better-off women who have some education and perform this function only in very select houses, usually in the well-to-do educated sections of the community. These *dhatri* are found in sub-divisional headquarters or prosperous *thana* headquarters or in areas adjoining urban areas. In these areas, the term nurse is also used by the educated community to identify this group of women.

The other group of birth attendants consist of women who are not recognised as formal practitioners but consist of middle aged or elderly women relatives, usually mothers of a few children who perform this function only at the family level. Village women are not used to identifying this group by any specific name because when the time for delivery approaches or labour pain starts, the elderly lady of the house usually instructs others to call somebody's mother/aunt/grandmother who usually happens to possess some experience in such cases. At best, they call her *dhoruni* but rarely *dai* which is used by a little literate section of the population. In complicated cases, the tendency to call in a trained *dai* is visible.

This paper, to some extent, is a follow-up of the author's previous study on indigenous abortion practitioners in rural Bangladesh. Although accessibility and availability were key criteria in the selection of cases, effort was made to choose one case from each division of the country based on selected case studies using open-ended schedules. It aims at highlighting the nature and functions of those who attend village birth. Though recent studies in Bangladesh focus on birth practices and rituals to a significant extent, many gaps still exist regarding our knowledge about the motivation, perceptions and practices of birth attendants, which can serve as a crucial link for education and health related policies in similar situations. Because of the limitations imposed by the given method, the findings have limited applicability and do not extend beyond the selected cases or in similar situations.

BAREFOOT OBSTETRICIANS: A LOOK AT THE REALITIES

Case-I *Gulabjan: who, after her death, hopes to enter heaven by performing hundred and one deliveries on this earth.*

Gulabjan, who proudly proclaims herself a mother of twenty-two children comes from a big village. According to her own estimate, it is almost half a mile long. *It is a mixed village.* Currently, she has nine living children. About her age she mentions, 'How do I know? I don't have any idea about it.' Her husband sells vegetables but mostly stays in the house. The house where they reside now is occupied by her nephew-in-law, who is the current chairman in the locality.

Her first baby was born when she was about twelve years old. She was married to her step brother. When Gulabjan's father died, her mother re-married and it was her step-father's son who was ultimately married to Gulabjan. Their family *Pir* (religious leader) was the chief negotiator in this marriage, so no objection was raised. At the time of her marriage she was only a minor as she started wearing the *shari* only when the negotiations for her marriage started. She began menstruating at least four years after her marriage.

Gulabjan is a trained *dai* working as a family planning motivator for her village and in nearby villages. In her mode of bringing clients to the Dhaka city, she has to cross the river twice by boat and walk a long way from her home to avail of the nearest bus service. She has been a trained *dai* for family planning motivation programmes for 'at least the last thirty years.'

When she first menstruated, Gulabjan was completely ignorant about it. Many rituals were followed. An assortment of foods were cooked along with the fish which was kept in the room for seven days, but she was neither allowed to cut any fish nor was she allowed to go out of the room for fear of *dosh* (evil influence). She still believes in *dosh* but is not sure why it appears only on women.

Gulabjan's first son was delivered by her own grandmother, who was an expert *dhoruni*. She said 'I was almost going to die that time.' She is still not sure what caused such a problem except that she feels it was due to 'too much slimness of her body.' Her pain lasted for three full days. Her grandmother being an expert *dhoruni* could save her life even though she said, 'the head of the baby was too big.' This boy died when he was four years old due to the *ghate-jaoa* (cholera) disease.

Gulabjan's next two sons were also delivered by her grandmother who resided in the same household. Since then, Gulabjan started becoming pregnant every year. On one such occasion, she gave birth to triplets. All of her sons died one after another due to cholera, losing thirteen children in this way, some of whom were born dead. Five of her pregnancies were lost due to the influence of the evil wind. 'None of my *doa-kalam* (prayers and religious verses) could save any of my pregnancies.' She feels all of her later pregnancies could only be saved by the influence of one *pir* who provided some herbal medicine chanted with power of *doa* and proclaimed that all of her pregnancies ended due to her *narer dosh* (the whole cord being spoiled). She believes that all of her thirteen pregnancies which ended in abortion, still birth, in the post-natal period, and even these who died later were caused by this *dosh*, although the symptoms varied greatly in each case.

Although all the thirteen pregnancies, according to Gulabjan, were handled with great caution and capability by her grandmother and some by her other relatives, she decided to deliver herself from then on. She visited the *pir's* doctor brother who resided with his more religious brother and advised her to cut her nails, clean her clothes, wash her hands, feet, blades, clothes with soap and dettol, and asked her to keep two new cooking pots cleaned with hot water everytime she delivered in the house. She immediately realised that none of the relatives who had helped her in her previous deliveries, maintained any such thing. In later years, she performed for herself the role of *dhoruni* in all her later deliveries.

Gulabjan learnt the skill of 'catching the new-comer' primarily by watching her own grandmother who helped women all over her village. When she first accompanied her grandmother for a delivery, she was the mother of one child. Initially, she was motivated by nothing but curiosity but she also had an urge to learn the skill. Gradually, Gulabjan began to accompany her grandmother on many more such occasions. The day she handled her first delivery all by herself, her grandmother was out of the village. She had left Gulabjan with the injunction to keep an eye on her own aunt who was approaching delivery time. Gulabjan was by then a mother of five children. While the grandmother was away, her aunt began to experience labour pain and so a *dhoruni* was fetched from a neighbouring village to help in the delivery. A child was born to Gulabjan's aunt but the placenta was not expelled. The *dhoruni* tried her best to pull it out but nothing worked. It took almost the entire day, from *Fazar* to *Asar* (prayer times), before the placenta could finally be expelled from her womb. Many women tried to get it out but to no avail. Towards the end of the day Gulabjan volunteered. She examined the cause of its non-expulsion. She broke open her glass bangle to free her own hand and took a piece of the bangle, and slowly pushed her hand all the way almost upto the placenta. She worked for quite some time rotating her hand in order to get hold of the placenta with the help of that broken piece of glass bangle. After rotating for a long time, she felt proud that she could get hold of the placenta within her fist and successfully pulled it out of her aunt's womb. Her aunt was in a fainting state but Gulabjan's fame spread all over the village. After this other households started calling her for help in delivery. In the case of her own aunt, she could not think of receiving any remuneration.

This incidence gave Gulabjan courage and confidence to come forward and assume the role of a birth attendant. But, in the initial days, she never went alone or without taking permission from her grandmother who always encouraged her. Gulabjan's style of delivery was to perform many tasks in sequential order—massaging with oil, making the woman eat, forcing her to walk, making her drink the *pora pani* (water chanted with verses) which she herself prepared for the client. She had learnt the skill of preparing the *pora pani* from both her grandmother, who also knew the skill of a *fakir* (religious leader), and her own mother. Gulabjan mentions:

I always tried to learn. I tried to watch and swallow all the skills of the people whichever I thought 'worthy of learning'. I always spoke to myself why can't I do that myself? I have great courage to know and show people that I am capable. This way I learnt the full skill of delivering the baby and started being mobile.

Her husband, recognising her potential never said 'no' to her. Another factor which motivated her to practice the skill was her belief in the saying, 'the road to heaven is a straight way to a person who helps delivering 101 babies without taking any remunerations.' She thus refrains from accepting any remuneration while she performs this task.

Gulabjan serves all over her village. According to her, at least twenty other women know the skills of a *dhoruni* in her village. But, not all of them are as capable. Thus, some women are automatically driven out of this role. But there are five more women who regularly perform this task, of whom two are trained by the government. Gulabjan is not only a trained *dai*, she also considers herself as a consultant to others and makes herself available in difficult cases. She claims that her expertise is known in the relevant government quarters all over her *thana*. Fifteen women were selected for government training from the whole *thana*, of whom Gulabjan was one. She received 500 taka for three months' training but the money lasted her for only twenty-five days.

Gulabjan restricts her role of a *dhoruni* solely to her village because she is performing many other roles and she needs some monetary benefit for her own family. Now she prefers to play the role of *dai* for family planning programmes which ensure some monetary gain, beyond her abortionist's role (Islam, 1981). Currently, she takes 10–15 women every month for sterilisation. But she tries not to leave the village during *amabosha* (the day of the new moon) and *purnima* (full moon) when 'proneness to labour pain intensifies' and can cause much harm to women. She forgoes potential earnings through the *dai's* role during this time even if motivated clients are ready for sterilisation. She arranges for them to be taken by another person to the service centre but she herself tries her best not to leave the village. She tries to maintain the confidence of her clients in her by staying in the village and by giving them a helping hand in times of need.

In narrating her experiences of complicated delivery cases she mentions one such experience when she had helped in the delivery of a woman in a neighbouring household. This was the woman's sixth pregnancy. Immediately after the onset of her labour pain, the family sent for Gulabjan. In the absence of Gulabjan, who was outside the village for that day, the family called for another *dai* from the same village. By the time this *dai* reached their home, the labour had started and the baby's head was slightly visible. The *dai* realised that the baby was already dead. As the *dai* failed to bring the baby out of the mother's womb, another *dai* was called in to help but she too failed in the task. The woman with the slightly visible foetus's head, remained thus for two full days. But she could not push the baby out. The whole village thronged in the yard of that household for two days. Almost everybody stopped by that house to inquire about the progress of the woman's labour.

On her way back home, Gulabjan came to hear of the woman's plight and instead of reaching her own home, she made straight for that woman's house. She immediately examined her by pressing o her abdomen. Gulabjan found the baby dead and the mother's delivery route in a wounded and sore condition because of excessive handling by the two previous *dais*. She said to herself, 'there is no way that I can help the baby, but the tree must be saved.' Gulabjan ordered everybody to leave the yard and helped the woman, who could barely stand, on to her feet. She gave her a bath. Then the woman was made to drink a cup of hot milk. The woman who could barely stand was made to walk for almost an hour. When Gulabjan let her lie down again, she asked the family to provide her with long fishing hooks made of iron pieces, the tops of which were crooked. Each of these *kochs* (fishing hooks) carried lots of small crooked hooks. Gulabjan pulled one crooked hook out of the wheel and pushed that inside the baby's head and kept on turning incessantly. Thus, she could pull the entire brain out of the dead baby's head. Thus, as the entire brain was out, the size of the baby's head became small. Then three or four hooks were pushed in at a time and she could successfully pull out the baby as in a fishing operation. It was a big infant. Then, when everything was cleaned and the baby buried in a hole, Gulabjan asked the family to fetch a doctor for an antibiotic injection which she believed could cure the woman soon. As to the cause of the baby's death, she said, 'it is only the parents who can tell you why the baby was not alive.' The family was well off. The head of the household offered her one hundred taka.

Gulabjan uses dettol in most cases because that gives her prestige even though it costs her money. This, she now believes, makes the wounds heal and dry soon. She never uses ashes. Instead, she uses *sindur* for quick healing and it is not difficult to procure in any village home.

In another recent instance, Gulabjan handled a complicated case of an inserted coil problem. Since the woman was pregnant, the couple took for granted that the coil was already out of the body. When the labour pain started, it was erratic. The husband of the woman was a *fakir* type. He fetched *moulavis* (religious leaders) to pray in the house and asked the *Imam* (mosque leader) to start *milad* (special prayer). Ritually, he released cows from his stable. Some person was sent to get Gulabjan from her house and the man begged Gulabjan to save his wife. Gulabjan immediately asked for some water to transform it through chanting verses to quicken the labour contractions.

In the process of making it into *pora pani*, she identified red curly things inside the water. She wanted to be sure whether the woman ever used coils. Her queries led to many discussions on 'how can a woman be pregnant with the coil inside?' In order to be sure, she probed the vagina and found her guess to be correct.

She prepared the woman with regular rituals, and made her a special drink with almost one seer of milk to keep her strength and made her sit with another woman behind her. Going out of the room she said to the woman's husband, 'if you want the tree, you can't get the leaf and vice-versa. But if you want the tree you have to give up the slightest hope for the leaf.' Gulabjan said, 'I knew very well that the baby would be dead. In this way, I prepared the would-be-father mentally for the loss.' When her husband agreed to her saving his wife's life she worked with a set of fishing hooks. In the first pull, a hand appeared. She managed to get the baby in position and a boy was born. The baby was alive and Gulabjan left the mother to be taken care of by other female relatives and she herself took care of the baby. Of course, her guess was correct; the coil was also out along with the newborn. In order to save time, the placenta was pulled out by Gulabjan.

The woman's husband wanted to please her with anything she wanted but Gulabjan remained silent. They offered her a good amount of money. On the *choti* (end of confinement) occasion, they specially invited Gulabjan and made her wear a new *shari*. At the end of the year, two boats full of people came with one maund of rice, one goat, and one pair of *shari*, near their ferry ghat, beating drums and flutes. All the young people touched Gulabjan's feet. She felt great pride and was pleased to cook for all the people that day because of the honour she had received from them for her expertise and skill.

Case-II *Shahar Banu: who greatly believes in the evil wind*

Forty year old Shahar Banu only knows how to read Arabic. Married at twelve, she is now the mother of nine living children. Two of her children died. One of her daughters is now married. The family belongs to the landless class. Her husband, a day-labourer, earns approximately 150/- taka per month. Her daughters work in the next-door chairman's house. The family lives on, according to her, in a 'half-starving condition'.

Shahar Banu regards herself as a brave woman. For the delivery of her own babies she accepted help only twice—in the first case by her mother-in-law, and in the second delivery by her own mother. But for these two instances, in all her nine successive deliveries, Shahar Banu successfully managed to deliver herself.

Shahar Banu did not formally learn the skill of delivering from anybody else except that she was present in approximately a dozen cases exactly at delivery time. All these occurred after her own marriage. Banu claims to have learnt the skill all by herself. Thus, she started her career as a birth attendant when she was sixteen or seventeen years old. By now she has gathered about twenty-two years of experience. Currently she is the only one in her village who works in all the neighbouring houses helping women in their deliveries. Beyond these three villages where she serves regularly, Shahar Banu does not mind visiting other villages if such calls ever come her way. She declares that it is only 'the urge to serve human beings in their real needs' which motivates her to perform this role. Otherwise, she does not receive any cash benefits out of this service.

The very first case that Shahar Banu handled independently was at a time when her aunt-in-law was going to give birth and nobody else was available near at hand. Her grandmother-in-law became very upset. At that point, she volunteered to help to 'catch the new-comer.' Other women in the house were skeptical of her. She calmly took her seat next to her aunt-in-law and continuously checked the position of the baby's head inside and successfully pulled the baby out. This first experience gave her confidence and motivated her to work in successive cases. By then, her expertise became known in the village and many households started calling her for help in delivery.

Shahar Banu cannot remember the number of all the cases she has handled in the last three months; she could however, only recall upto sixteen such cases. She does not receive any remuneration for such services except that she is invited to have a meal in the *bari* (household) on the day of the celebration. Even then Banu helps because 'it is a time when people like her need to help the helpless women in the household.' Thus in her role, she never discriminates between the poor and rich households. Rather, she attends to all the households, whoever chooses to call her. But Shahar Banu feels that there are many families who can afford to repay her services but intentionally try not to give her anything. For example, in her neighbour, the chairman's house, she was called upon to help when his sister-in-law was going to give birth. Considering that it was a rich man's house, on arrival at their house, she wanted a *shari* from them to change from her half-dirty one. They refused saying, 'our clothes are no better than yours.' She had no other alternative but to perform the task wearing her own half-dirty, half-torn *shari*, This household also provided her with a meal once a day. On such occasions she feels cheated as she says, 'people take advantage of my poverty.'

Shahar Banu neither took any formal lesson from anybody, nor received any training from government programmes. She acquired her expertise merely from watching delivery cases in different households. Thus, she tries to perform those necessary rituals she has seen her relatives do. Shahar Banu has, thus, not acquired any new knowledge in this field.

She prepares her clients ahead of time by informing them about the differences in the symptoms of real and false labour pain. Shahar Banu invariably cautions the 'first timers' about occasional *upri* pain which should not be confused with real labour which will follow with the rupture of the water bag. She warns them to keep everything ready like water, oil, thread, ash, etc. She even advises those who can afford it to procure and keep ready at home some medicines, in case there is an absence of the pain symptoms, or the woman fails to push. But Shahar Banu does not know any names for such medicines; she relies on chemists in the market. She also advises the client to inform her as soon as the symptoms of the pain appear.

Shahar Banu believes that those women who work less, invariably suffer from swollen bodies during their pregnancies. She believes in herbal treatment as a perfect remedy for this. Under no circumstances, is she ready to tell others the name of her special herbal root. This knowledge she has gathered from her mother-in-law who was not a professional *dhoruni*. Shahar Banu believes that in case the pregnant woman suffers from too much fluid accumulation in her body, she needs the help of a doctor. Besides, she believes in 'fire and water as inseparable inputs' in the room where a woman gives birth.

In preparing for a delivery, she hurriedly gets ready to reach the delivery place when she is informed that the client is facing a problem or the woman is facing excessive labour pain. Nearby houses, she attends by herself, but for far-off places she takes her aunt-in-law with her. In the delivery room, she prefers the presence of elderly relatives like a grandmother. For deliveries in distant places, she does not know in advance which house she has to visit but she knows about her required services in the neighbour's houses. Shahar Banu comes back home at the end of her job after taking a bath in the client's house. She changes her *shari* after she reaches home because she has to clean herself after the unclean job.

In handling a delivery, after she reaches the said household, she immediately examines the woman. In order to be convinced about the real pain, she makes the woman walk, sit and lie down so that she can feel about the nature of the pain and the different positions of the foetus. In cases where the head of the baby is visible properly, she is confident about a problem-free delivery. But in all other positions, the woman is expected to suffer. Also, if the pain fails to appear in proper duration and intensity, Shahar Banu believes that it would be a delayed delivery which will cause suffering to the woman. She herself tries not to take recourse to any method to intensify the labour pain. Usually, except in complicated cases, the baby is born, within one to four hours. But she confirms that in some instances it can be a matter of 2–3 days.

Shahar Banu usually makes the woman deliver in a squatting position if she is found to possess good health and strength. In complicated cases and in cases where the woman is found to have extremely poor health, she makes her lie down for the delivery. She invariably stays behind the woman because she feels 'performing the job of catching is easy in this process.' In cases where the placenta is not expelled soon, she helps in extricating it out by physical pulling. This has happened in many cases. The umbilical cord is usually severed by a blade but in cases where that is not readily available, scissors used to cut paddy in the fields are used instead. Then it is tied with jute strips and the jute threads are subsequently pulled out of it. The baby is given a bath with hot water. Shahar Banu cleans the place where the delivery takes place but not the woman's soiled clothes.

Where the client feels really ill Shahar Banu prefers to stay with her for a few days but otherwise normally she returns home in a few hours. Shahar Banu believes in the evil wind. Recently, a woman suffered from swollen breasts. When she came to know that the newborn baby suffered from diarrhoea due to this, Shahar Banu advised the mother not only to pump all the milk out of her breast but also to consume some *pora pani* (water chanted with religious verses). She herself does not dispense any such water or provide any treatment for the evil wind to her clients. In other severe cases where the mother is the target of the evil wind, the baby suffers and Shahar Banu advises the family to seek help from the *vaidya* (indigenous medical practitioner).

In order to help the new mother recover quickly from the delivery, Shahar Banu firmly believes in food restrictions. According to her, a new mother can consume milk, *sagu* (Sagu), *Chira* (parched rice), *muri* (puffed rice) and some other fried items. She believes in the new born's diet to consist of *misriwater*, breast milk and at best goat's milk.

According to her own guess, Shahar Banu has helped deliver 400–500 cases in her life. In narrating about difficult cases that took her more than a day to handle, she mentions about her distant niece's case, a mother of four children, who recently gave birth to another. It was winter time. Shahar Banu tried hard to get the baby out, but it was of no use. Her niece was screaming desperately. Shahar Banu became totally upset. After repeated probing about the sources of trouble, her niece reported of a band of bees which had flown over her head in the recent past. Shahar Banu immediately ordered the inmates of the house to procure honey and *sacha pitha* (sort of flour cake) for the woman. She felt that the baby could be safely released out of its mother's womb in that late hour only if the mother could be fed with *pitha* mixed with honey at that point.

In another recent instance she helped a woman deliver a still born instantly. Within an hour, the woman called her again and she discovered the head of another baby as she approached the woman. This one was alive. After a short while, Shahar Banu really became irritated when the woman started screaming again. Shahar Banu never saw a woman giving birth to so many babies. She murmured, 'like dogs or foxes. How can a woman conceive so many at a time?' At last, she helped her niece to deliver her second live baby. But in a few day's time, both the babies died. Although the total time taken by this woman to deliver did not exceed two or three hours, this was a very tricky situation.

Shahar Banu does not feel that the family planning programme has resulted in any loss to the demand for her services. She usually walks to her client's house except in situations where she has to commute by boat.

During *choti* (end of confinement) rituals she does not see much difference in the celebrations of the rich and poor households. It uniformly ends on the fifth day for the girl and on sixth day in the case of a boy. In poor households, the baby's first hair is cleaned by the members of the household; in the well-to-do class, they engage a barber to do it. The blade which is usually used by the poor household is sharpened by rubbing against a broken glass and if it is *khur* (indigenous razor), on grinding stones. The ritual is followed by cleaning and mud plastering the floor. The *dhoruni* is invited that day along with other close relatives for a feast. The new mother eats with other women after her special bath. The nails of the baby are buried under a plantain tree.

Shahar Banu believes that a pregnant woman and the new mother must obey certain rules, viz., she should refrain from exposing herself during the day of the new moon or full moon, at mid-day, at sun set, at night and especially during the lunar and solar eclipse, in order to avoid influences of the 'evil wind' which may cause abortion during pregnancy. If violation occurs, the baby is expected to have a defective nose, lips and leg. If the pregnant woman works with scissors or kitchen *bothi* (indigenous kitchen knife) or falls in a hole, the baby will be born defective. Shahar Banu cites innumerable cases to prove her statements. She is especially concerned about outside exposure during pregnancy. During eclipses, if exposed the pregnant women invariably runs the risk of experiencing either abortion or a complicated delivery.

She cannot remember any of her clients dying during child birth when she attended on them. But there were a few still born babies and about a dozen babies died within three months of delivery. She has never bothered to find out why. Shahar Banu believes that while the new mother is affected by the evil wind, her breasts swell and the baby suffers from diarrhoea and in acute cases, the baby also suffers a change of complexion. In such cases, 'chanted oil-water therapy' serves best.

Case-III *Sahera Khatun: a great believer in herbal medicine*

Thirty two years old Sahera Khatun knows that her village is very big but she is not sure about its size. She could only say, 'people from outside say it takes three days to make a full round of this village.'

Muslim by religion, Sahera Khatun is married and is a mother of eight children. Neither she nor her husband know how to read or write. The family is near landless and possess only about one *pakhi* of land.

Sahera Khatun is the recognised 'catcher' of babies not only in her own village but in the neighbouring villages as well. She has been acting in this capacity in her own village for the last three years. There is one other recognised midwife in her village but Sahera feels that because of her old age people tend to call on her services more often. Her mobility is not restricted to any one *para* rather it spreads all over the village. She even goes to neighbouring villages if people need her services. According to her perception, 'it is a humanitarian cause. So, I cannot but go even if I have to accommodate to lots of inconvenience for this going.'

In Sahera Khatun's father's family nobody was performing this function. She learnt this skill from her aunt-in-law. Initially, out of sheer curiosity, she would accompany her aunt-in-law only to watch her act. Slowly, she started helping her aunt-in-law in small affairs like quickening labour pain by pressing the woman's stomach; tying the baby's cord , etc. Gradually, seeing her knack, her aunt-in-law taught her all the skills needed for delivering a baby. In remembering her experience when she first accompanied her aunt-in-law, Sahera said that she could not feel much reaction because by then she was already a mother of four children. She could only recall her own experience as a mother.

Before she started performing this service all by herself, she had already observed twenty-five to thirty cases attended to by her aunt-in-law in her native village. The very first day when she could independently deliver a baby, she felt satisfied thinking that, 'a life could be saved with her hands.' At that time, she was a mother of six children. Her main motivation behind this career as far as she would see was due to her aunt-in-law's interest in teaching her the skill. Since then, she has been following all the procedures in exactly the way her aunt-in-law had taught her. Recently, she attended a special training course on midwifery in the last *Ashar* month. She feels she has not learnt anything new from this training which she could adopt in her practice.

Sahera Khatun is not sure about how many babies she has

helped deliver in her career but she guesses that it must be some-where near a thousand. But on persistent probing about how many she *actually* helped deliver in the last three months, she replied, 'approximately ten to twelve babies and this is the estimated number I usually handle throughout the year.'

Sahera Khatun relies on people's satisfaction for remuneration. She has no fixed fees. 'People's satisfaction,' she thinks, 'is the main asset in this work.' So, she accepts whatever people offer her for her services. But, eating a meal is more or less fixed in the house where she serves. Sometimes, in the well-off houses she receives a *sari* or 10–15 taka but in poor houses, she does not even want to eat a meal. Instead, she prefers to ask the woman to offer that food to her children.

In the last case that she handled, the family booked Sahera in advance so that she could be available at the time of need. She also advised them to call her at the first symptom of the appearance of pain. Accordingly, as soon as the pain appeared just immediately after the *maghrib* prayer, the family sent a person to call her whom she immediately accompanied. The family lived at a distance of fifteen or sixteen houses from her own.

In this case, the woman's mother-in-law was near at hand to help Sahera. According to Sahera Khatun's prior advice, the mother-in-law had all the necessary items ready—blade, a clean, soft, washed thin piece of cloth, thread from washed cloth and hot water. Sahera Khatun usually washes her hands with warm water as soon as she reaches the client's home because she has to examine the woman. She feels that if her hands are not properly washed, it may lead to a variety of problems. She even washes the blades in hot water but she never changes her clothes because she feels dirty or clean clothes do not have anything to do with the delivery. The most important thing in this work, as she says, is 'clean hands.'

The mother-in-law's role as usual is to hold the woman and give her courage by giving consolation. All other work Sahera Khatun performs by herself. On reaching the place, her first job is to examine the woman. According to the position of the foetus, Sahera judges the time for delivery. If the process is to be a long one, she makes the woman stand up. With hands soaked in warm mustard oil, Sahera applies pressure to the upper portion of the lower abdomen frequently. After some time labour commences. Sahera Khatun then makes the woman sit in a squatting position.

She mentioned that if pressure does not help in stimulating labour, she procures three white tablets from the village doctor by sending a man from the client's house and that invariably helps in quickening the pain.

In all the cases, as in this one, the delivery is done in a sitting position. Sahera has no fixed rule about her own position of staying either in front or at the back of the delivering woman. In her last case, Sahera helped the woman from the front position. The baby was born after two or three hours of her arrival on the spot.

Sahera's last case was the woman's second pregnancy. With increased pain, the baby's head came out. With a clean cloth in hand, Sahera Khatun pulled the head out. She tied the umbilical cord with the clean thread. Sahera Khatun said, 'if the placenta does not come out easily, I pull it out with my hands.' In this case, it came out automatically.

She then performed all the things that are traditionally done in all stages of post-delivery, like, cutting the cord; washing the baby with soap and warm water; cleaning the navel of the baby and tying it with a thin material; wrapping the baby in *kantha* and making it sleep; washing the mother from her feet upto the waist with warm water; cleaning the delivery place; plastering the whole room with cow-dung mixed with water and finally washing herself with soap water. She then had her meal and slept there until the morning because it was quite late at night to go back home.

Sahera Khatun advises the new mother to give a bath to the baby on alternate days if it is a hot day until *choti* time when special things are done to end the delivery process but the mother under no circumstances should have her own bath for three days. She, at best, can wash herself upto her waist.

Sahera Khatun does not have any special role in the *choti* function which is dominated by the barber. But the usual practice is to invite her for that function when the barber cuts her nails too along with those of the other members. At the end of the rituals where she is an invited guest she eats a meal there with the rest of the members.

Sahera Khatun strongly feels that a pregnant woman is susceptible to evil wind which causes *khichani* (distort the face), *upri* (symptom of tetanus), bodyache, thinning of the body, etc. She strongly believes that the evil wind can touch the new born baby through the mother. As a result, babies easily fall prey to the above diseases, especially *Lal-Nil* which causes a *red-blue* colour in the baby's body. The only effective treatment, as she sees it, in such cases is done through *fakirs* (indigenous healers) who treat the patient with amulets and through other magic charms like . exorcising.

Sahera Khatun strongly recommends mother's milk for the baby in the absence of which cow's milk may be given. But she feels that the mother's diet in the post delivery stage should be strictly restricted to milk, chili paste, mashed potato and the like, along with rice. But in all circumstances the mother should be prevented from imbibing any sort of juicy and liquid items in her diet except for milk. Milk helps in healing, especially the umbilical cord.

According to Sahera Khatun, 'God's blessing is most important in this job.' Neither a mother nor a child ever died or faced any serious complications in her hands. She can remember only two memorable instances. Once in her career, a baby's hand came out first. She became extremely nervous but her aunt-in-law who was also present, advised her to push the hand back in. She acted following her advice and from then it was a normal delivery. On another occasion, a woman gave birth to a *rishkinda* baby. This baby did not have any head. The head seemed to be fixed on the baby's back with only two eyes. Everybody in the house was nervous. The mother, on looking at her new born lost consciousness. Sahera Khatun poured water on the mother's head for a long time to bring her around. The baby was already dead.

Sahera Khatun cannot remember any year when her work might have suffered. She does not feel that she was ever refrained from doing her job due to any natural calamity. She herself became pregnant four times during these years when she started accompanying her aunt-in-law. 'I delivered myself in my last two pregnancies. Even then I have not suffered any loss.' Sahera Khatun strongly feels that the current family planning programme is not affecting her work in any way.

Sahera Khatun is known for her herbal medicinal practice in the area. She gives this medicine to those women who cannot conceive. She learnt this skill from her father who was a renowned practitioner in his village. 'I can even tell the sex of the unborn child of that woman to whom I give that medicine. If the woman gives birth to a son, the plant will come up intact with all its roots in one pull. But if she is going to get a daughter, the plant instead of its full size will be torn in the middle.' She never claims any money even for herbal medical treatment. If any well-to-do family offers her cash or kind, she, however, does not refuse.

Sahera Khatun does not know how to stop a woman's pregnancy but she knows how to help a woman to abort a foetus. This skill was also taught to her by her father. She does not even accept any remuneration for this service. She claims that she helps in aborting upto four months of the foetus. But she does not do it if the pregnancy goes beyond that period because 'it then equals the killing of a life.' She recounts this experience: once a woman from a well-off family came to her to seek abortion. The woman claimed that she was three months pregnant but when Sahera examined her she found her to be 5–6 months pregnant, and so she declined to abort. The woman was then taken to a hospital where too her case was rejected because it was too late. According to Sahera Khatun, women from all economic strata terminate their pregnancies—some do more frequently than others. The basic causes, she feels, are a woman's ill-health or the earlier baby being too young. But it is poverty-stricken women who show more tendency to abort.

In recounting her experience of being chosen as the *dai* for the government family planning programme, she mentioned this incident. It occurred nearly a year and a half ago. A man of her village was suffering from *bagi-tan* (sort of a carbuncle). The family sought many types of treatments but nothing worked for him. In the end, the doctor from the *thana* hospital was brought to the man's home. The doctor advised the family to take him to the *thana* hospital for surgery. But neither the family members nor the patient wanted to go to the hospital. They told the doctor to perform his operation right there in the village, but the doctor declined saying it was inconvenient to bring the necessary surgical instruments to the village. Hearing all this, the family asked for Sahera Khatun's help in the operation. She declined to operate the carbuncle right on the spot. According to her, 'it was really not that serious.' Moreover, she felt that in any case when there was no other way but taking him to the hospital, why not give a last try? The patient was by then groaning in pain. She asked the family members to bring a clean thin cloth, thread, needle, blade, soap, and hot water immediately. She then washed not only her hands with soap and hot water but the rest of the items as well.

Then she opened the *bagi* with the blade, cleaned all the pus and blood from inside it with the pieces of material; she then put some cloth inside and sewed it on top. In this way she changed the dressing for two-three days. The man was relieved of his pain and he did not have to go to the hospital. Seeing her expertise, the doctor was pleased and offered her the government job of bringing clients for sterilisation. She is the only one to bring clients from one of the wards in her union. Although her pay has not been fixed yet for this job as it is a new involvement for her, she gets free food and lodging facilities for three days plus the transport charges to and from her village for the three-day period when she has to stay with the client. Besides, the client too pays her approximately 10 to 15 taka for these three days because she has to look after the client's babies for the three days the client has to stay on the clinic premises.

CONCLUSION

It is evident that *thana*-based health care facilities have little impact on the nature of utilisation of services by rural women who try to meet their own needs within the given socio-economic constraints. In matters of maternal health, the barefoot obstetricians in rural areas, all of whom are women, play as crucial liaisons between the health care system and the rural household. There is uniformity in the nature of perceptions and practices of the barefoot obstetricians and diversity in their roles.

Some aspects of birth practices are readily recognised by planners and policy makers, but gaps exist in policies because of our weakness in the knowledge-base regarding the practices prevailing in the households in matters of maternal health and the varied roles played by village-based barefoot practitioners.

Contrary to popular notion, the village-based barefoot obstetricians do not stand in a vaccum. They themselves are large reservoirs of knowledge, skill and belief which are not commonly appreciated in the context of health care planning. To the extent that given practices and perceptions of village level practitioners are ignored, the goal of improving maternal and child health in rural areas will run the risk of attaining limited impact.

Although the vast majority of rural women stay away from the formal system, this does not indicate that they stay without education. Elaborate informal education encompasses their lives.

Barefoot obstetricians learn, practice and transmit their knowledge and skill informally which women in *bari* utilise in their day-to-day health care needs. This informal learning at home provides strength to women to resist intervention.

The contextual issue is extremely important. Any non-formal education programme that fails to appreciate these realities is expected to end up with limited achievements. Also crucial is the fact that non-formal education will be successful to the extent this informal home-based learning is successfully integrated to the vast scope of non-formal learning which carry potentials for meaningful change.

Identification of needs, issues and practices is crucial to the building of our knowledge-base for policy planning purposes. It carries an immense potential. This suggests a need for undertaking some qualitative rural studies (Islam, 1982) in order to identify different dimensions related to women's health in rural households. The study suggests that it is not enough to consider the issue of survival or mortality alone. There is need for focusing on the morbidity pattern also in matters of women's health.

This study, though limited in scope, voices a concern for the policy of training *dais* which merely segments rural women because it bypasses the vast majority of women in the households who should be integrated in the non-formal health education programmes. Gaps exist today as messages of safe delivery are not reaching these women in the *bari* in a systematic way through a good information mechanism except for the one trained *dai* for an entire village.

REFERENCES

BLANCHET, THERESE, 1984: *Women, Pollution and Marginality: Meanings and Rituals of Birth in Rural Bangladesh*. (Dhaka, UFL).

CHEN, ET.AL., 1974: *Maternal Mortality in Rural Bangladesh* (Dacca, The Ford Foundation).

ISLAM, SHAMIMA, 1981: *Indigenous Abortion Practitioners in Rural Bangladesh* (Dacca, Women for Women).

——, 1979: *Nonformal Education for Rural Women in Bangladesh: A Few Reflections* (UNESCO-UNDP sponsored Seminar).

——, 1982: *Exploring the Other Half: Field Research with Rural Women in Bangladesh* (Dhaka, Women for Women).

JAHAN, F.A., 1984: *Report on Maternal Mortality* (Dhaka, Preliminary Findings).

UNICEF, 1984: *Maternal and Child Health in Bangladesh*, A Review of the National TBA Training Programme, Dhaka, May.

About the Contributors

Khwaja Muhammad Ashraful Aziz is an Associate Scientist at the International Centre for Diarrhoeal Disease Research, Bangladesh. An anthropologist by education, he is also on the international editorial board of the *South Asian Journal of Anthropology*. He has published over twenty-two articles on issues of health, family planning and development.

Meera Chatterjee has been a Senior Fellow at the Centre for Policy Research, New Delhi. Since 1978 she has worked on various health planning projects in India, incorporating her interest in social anthropology and gender dimension in the context of development and social change. Her publications include a book entitled *Implementing Health Policy*.

Kamala Ganesh is a Reader in Sociology at the Centre for Post-Graduate Studies and Research, SNDT Women's University, Bombay. She is also the recipient of the Kulapati Gold Medal as well as the Chandrakant Vohra Memorial Gold Medal. Her interests lie in researching the issues of caste, kinship and family, ethnicity and gender. Dr. Ganesh is currently involved in editing a volume of papers drawn from cross-cultural research on anthropological perspectives on teaching, concerning women.

Shamima Islam is a sociologist and an educationist by training and a researcher by profession. She is the author of a number of books and a participant in varied team research on issues related to women and development in Bangladesh. She is the Founder President of the Centre for Women and Development, Dhaka. Dr. Islam's publications include *Indigenous Abortion Practitioners in Rural Bangladesh; Women's Education in Bangladesh: Needs and Issues; Invisible Labour Force and Women: Victims of Violence; Exploring the Other Half: Field Research with Rural Women in Bangladesh* (edited).

Usha Kanhere is a Reader in Sociology at the School of Social Sciences, Gujarat University, Ahmedabad. She is the recipient of the M.C.C. Desai Gold Medal. Her research interests lie in white-collar trade unions, the urban society and related women's issues. She has published extensively on urban and industrial sociology, caste structure and women's issues. Included in her publications is a book entitled *Women and Socialisation: A Study of their Status and Role Among the Lower Caste Communities in the Metropolis of Ahmedabad.*

Nazmunnessa Mahtab is an Associate Professor at the Department of Public Administration, University of Dhaka, Bangladesh. She is associated with various women's organisations both at home and abroad. She has published extensively on issues related to rural development, and the life of women in Bangladesh.

Joan P. Mencher is Professor of Cultural Anthropology at Lehman College of CUNY and the City University of New York Graduate Centre. She has been working in India since 1958 and has spent many years in the rural areas of Tamil Nadu, Kerala and West Bengal. Her publications include numerous papers on agricultural development, family relations and on women (especially female agricultural labourers) in these regions, as well as a book on *Agriculture and Social Structure in Tamil Nadu*, and an edited book on the *Social Anthropology of Peasantry*.

Barbara D. Miller is a Visiting Fellow and Lecturer with the Department of Rural Sociology, the Population Development Programme, and the South Asia Programme at Cornell University, New York, USA. A social anthropologist, she has studied gender differences in child health and survival in India for over a decade and has written several scholarly articles on the subject as well as a book entitled *The Endangered Sex: Neglect of Female Children in Rural North India*. Her current research is concerned with class-specific patterns of son preference and daughter neglect in India.

Hanna Papanek is a Senior Research Associate at the Centre for Asian Development Studies, Boston University, USA. She has been a member of the editorial board of *Signs: Journal of Women in Culture and Society*. Her major fields of specialisation are women's studies, women's work and education, and development issues.

Index